Race, Colour and the Processes of Racialization

D0162144

So many conflicts appear to be caused by racial and ethnic difference; for example the cities of Britain and America are regularly affected by race riots. It is argued by sociobiologists and some schools of psychoanalysis that our instincts are programmed to hate those different to us by evolutionary and developmental mechanisms. This book argues against this line, proposing an alternative drawing on insights from diverse disciplines including psychoanalysis, sociology, social psychology and linguistics, to give power relations a critical explanatory role in the generation of hatreds.

Farhad Dalal follows Norbert Elias to argue that the primary function of race is to make a distinction between the 'haves' and 'must-not-haves', and that this process is cognitive, emotional and political. Examining aspects of the subject over the past thousand years, *Race, Colour and the Processes of Racialization* describes how the world and mind were made black and white, covering:

- Psychoanalytic and other theories of racism
- A new theorization of racism based on group analytic theory
- A general theory of difference based on the works of Fanon, Elias, Matte-Blanco, Winnicott and Foulkes
- Application of this theory to race and racism.

Farhad Dalal concludes that the structures of society are reflected in the structures of the psyche, and both of these are colour coded. This book will be invaluable to students, academics and practitioners in the areas of psychoanalysis, group analysis, sociology, psychotherapy and counselling.

Farhad Dalal is a supervisor and training group analyst at the Institute of Group Analysis, London. He is also a psychotherapist and group analyst in private practice.

Race, Colour and the Processes of Racialization

New Perspectives from Group
Analysis, Psychoanalysis and Sociology

Farhad Dalal

Brunner-Routledge
Taylor & Francis Group

HOVE AND NEW YORK

First published 2002 by Brunner-Routledge
27 Church Road, Hove, East Sussex BN3 2FA

Simultaneously published in the USA and Canada
by Brunner-Routledge
29 West 35th Street, New York, NY 10001

Brunner-Routledge is an imprint of the Taylor & Francis Group

© 2002 Farhad Dalal

Typeset in 10/12pt Sabon by Graphicraft Limited, Hong Kong
Printed and bound in Great Britain by
TJ International, Padstow, Cornwall, UK
Cover design by Sandra Heath

British Library Cataloguing in Publication Data
A catalogue record for this book is available from the British
Library

Library of Congress Cataloging in Publication Data
Dalal, Farhad.
    Race, colour and the process of racialization : new
  perspectives from group analysis, psychoanalysis, and
  sociology / Farhad Dalal.
      p. cm.
    Includes bibliographical references and index.
    ISBN 1-58391-291-6 – ISBN 1-58391-292-4 (pbk.)
    1. Psychoanalysis and racism. 2. Race – Psychological
  aspects. 3. Race awareness. 4. Racism. I. Title.

BF175.4.R34 D35 2002
155.8'2–dc21   2002025441

ISBN 1-58391-291-6 (hbk)
ISBN 1-58391-292-4 (pbk)

For Pauline

Contents

Figures

Acknowledgements

I owe profound debts of appreciation to many people: in particular my friend Parizad Bathai without whose encouragement and unswerving support this project might never have been sustained. Heartfelt gratitude to Phil Cohen and Barry Richards who have guided me with sensitivity through this lengthy process in true Winnicottian fashion, without impingement or neglect, but precisely so. Also, Amal Treacher who helped with the initial ideas. And finally Stephen Frosh who stepped in at the last minute to help consolidate the entire enterprise.

Thanks also to Paul and Margaret Granowski Wilkins for their help with the Bible, and to Stanley Schneider for taking the time to comment on that material. I have also been helped, sustained and challenged by innumerable conversations with friends and colleagues, many of which I found invaluable; of these I would particularly like to thank Ralph Stacey. Also to be included here are Phil Schulte, Regine Scholz, as well as fellow members from two settings. First, the Group Analytic Network Psychotherapy Service which include Gill Barratt, Sue Einhorn, Sandra Evans, Sheila Ernst, Michael Kelly and Anne Morgan. Second, the faculty (headed up by Ralph Stacey) of the University of Hertfordshire's Business School's Complexity and Management Centre which include Eliat Aram, Douglas Griffin, Wil Pennycook-Greaves, Christopher Rance and Patricia Shaw; the conversations begun more latterly within this faculty have been enormously gratifying.

I would like also to acknowledge my indebtedness to Liesel Hearst for her role as exemplar and for her tutelage over the years – intellectual as well as emotional.

There is one other who believed in this project and without whose presence none of this would have been possible, my wife Pauline Henderson Dalal.

Introduction

A vintner from New Zealand described his first impressions of Britain and France on a recent visit. He said of the people he met on either side of the English Channel 'I don't know why they fought so much with each other, because to me, they look so similar; to me they are the same people'.

It struck me that the vintner was voicing prevalent beliefs not only about the causes of hatreds between groups of people, but also their solution: hatred is caused by difference, and if one gets rid of, or attends to the difference in some way then harmony is more likely to follow. But if we note two obvious things: that people who are 'the same' are not free of hatreds and violences to each other, and that people who are 'the same' in some respect are also 'different' in others, we can see straightaway that things are more complicated than first impressions suggest.

This work then, is about one such difference and its consequences: race and racism. Even more specifically, it is about the racism that is organized via another difference: the notions of black and white. Although I will primarily use the British context to build my arguments, the ideas are of relevance to other territories.

In my experience, the mere articulation of the intention to look at the racism between white and black is likely to set off a series of protests, and so I am obliged to attend to these immediately, but briefly, as more substantive discussions on these subjects are developed as the book proceeds. There are several types of protest that tend to come up, all of which do have a validity. The first is a claim of 'unfair'; if racism is indeed ubiquitous, then all people are prone to it, and so why focus on the racism of the white to the black? I agree that the capacity for racism is not the sole privilege of the white or 'the West', however, at this moment in historical time not only do the notions of black and white dominate contemporary dynamics of racism in Britain, the structure of power relations are such that blacks have the larger burden to bear in regard to racism and tend to be the primary recipients of the negative consequences of racism.

The second challenge to the validity of this project comes in the form of reminding us that hatred and violence are not just organized around this particular difference – of black and white – but around many others, religion, class, gender, and so on. In response I would say that the focus on colour racism is not to imply that it is more basic than, or has any particular privilege over and above other racisms (say anti-Semitism) or other discriminations (e.g. gender or class); but having said that, it is bound to have its own particularities and peculiarities. However, the attempt to broaden the field of view does not just serve the manifest purpose of making the investigation more universal, it also serves at times the more disguised function of avoiding looking in sharp focus at a particular aspect of the larger picture. In part this occurs because of the difficult emotions stirred up by the subject, and so one is prone to diluting the specifics of the situation by dissolving it in a larger generalized sea. But having said that the central focus of the book is racism, the work does in fact proceed by building a general theory of difference which is then applied to the territory of 'race'.

But why the focus on colour racism at all? There are two answers here, one subjective and personal and the other a little more objective. The personal reason comes out of the experience of me, a self-evidently 'coloured' person, living in London where I have been one of the dark people. But my first 12 years were spent in India where, as a Parsee, I was perceived as one of the lighter complexioned people. As a lighter person I was definitely someone to be looked up to and privileged in various ways. In contrast, *aspects* of the experience of being a 'darky' in Britain were at times *feelings* of being fearful and anxious, but not for reasons that could always be clearly seen and stated. This then gives rise to questions of where these feelings came from – what was the cause? There are two crude answers: either inside me – my psychopathology, or outside me – the ills and evils of society. This work offers a more complex answer, one that does not simplistically reduce things to either the *purely* psychological, or *purely* sociological. But in order to do this I will be forced to engage at a deeper level with the relationship of psychology to sociology. The sociologist of knowledge, Norbert Elias, has already begun this task, and so I will make much use of him.

The more objective reason is born out of noticing just how powerful, pervasive and apparently universal were the notions of black and white. It was not just the well-known fact that white was attached to positive things and black to negative, but also the sheer variety and range of things that these terms were attached to: peoples, emotions, behaviours, thoughts, cultural artefacts and so on. We might surmise (although I will dispute this shortly) that objects and people get called black and white because this is their actual colour; but how is it that things that have can have no colour – the emotions for example – get to be called and *experienced* as black and white? How and why has this come about? The common-sense answers are suggestions of the ilk that it is natural to feel frightened of the dark, and it is unfortunately the case that this fear slips over and gets attached to black people and black things. This kind of answer runs several things together. It takes for granted 'black' as a naturally occurring name of a type of people, and it uses this to 'explain' the presence of negative feelings in some other person. But now, if we make the rather obvious observation that people are not literally in any chromatic sense black or white, then clearly whatever is going on, it is not at all straightforward and natural.

Having said something about colour let me now say something about the other term: racism. Racism can be thought of in several ways – overt *acts* of violence perpetrated on those of another group; *feelings* of fear, hatred or aversion felt towards members of another group; and finally, the invisible workings of society that somehow manage to make it difficult for members of particular groups to participate in the centre and partake of the resources generally available.

These descriptions of the manifestations of racism have skipped over two difficulties. First, as descriptions they are so general they say nothing directly about racism. The second connected difficulty is that these descriptions take for granted the existence of the very idea of race. Thus, it is supposed that race is an objective description of groups of people, and racism consists of the nasty things perpetrated by one group onto the other.

If, for the moment, we assume that this is right, then we have a preliminary descriptive frame. First, there is the idea of race; this is a *cognitive* category – a way of dividing and classifying the world. Second, there are the oppressive ways that people of one race treat those of another; this is a description at the level of the *political*. The third element occurs in the domain of the *affects* – the emotions and feelings that are experienced about one's own race as well as towards those of other races. The first of these is taken up by psychologists and is grounded in mental functioning, the second by social theorists who emphasize the external world, and the third by the psychoanalysts who emphasize the internal world. Of these three territories, my primary emphasis will be on the last of these, the analytic, but the work will inevitably draw in the other two as each will be found to interpenetrate the other.

Chapter 1 consists of a critical exploration of the notion of race. I do this in several ways: first, by tracing the history of the notion of race and contrasting it with notions of culture and ethnicity; and second, by detailing its appearance in religious, scientific and political discourses, and delineating the anomalies thrown up by this engagement. What becomes clear very quickly, is that race has little meaning outside the arena of racism and so the two cannot be differentiated. In other words, the preliminary descriptive frame was found wanting. This preparatory work is used to formulate working definitions of racism. This is followed by a discussion on racism, but not in any great depth, because in a sense the whole book *is* this discussion.

I should now explain why I primarily use psychoanalysis and group analysis to examine racism. In the main this is because my interests and preoccupations are stirred by my occupation – a psychotherapist and group analyst practising analytic psychotherapy in a metropolitan British context: a black therapist working with black and white patients.[1]

Having said this, clearly it is not possible to use psychoanalysis *per se* as the investigative tool, as psychoanalysis is not a single body but a variety of disparate theories with conflicting world views, metapsychologies and clinical techniques. I simplified the territory by limiting myself to a study of the British schools of psychoanalysis. I took these to be Freud, Klein, Fairbairn and Winnicott. The reasoning behind limiting myself to this list was that these are the main psychoanalytic schools that are currently of clinical import in Britain. An exception to this is the work of Bowlby and attachment theory; I left this out partly in order to circumscribe the study, but also because many of the relevant points that occur there are already found in Fairbairn. I have also left out the ego psychology schools that flourish in the United States of America, as well as the theories of Lacan that prosper in the Latin countries. Although one reason for leaving out the continentals and the Latins is in order to circumscribe the study, the other is that these schools have not made much impact to date on *clinical* discourse – the work and thinking of the practitioners of psychoanalysis and psychotherapy in Britain.[2] This last point is also true of other analytic contributors, for example Adler (1933), Fromm (1982) and Reich (1970); to my knowledge none of them appear on syllabuses of the main analytic training schools in Britain, and neither do they engage *directly* with the subject of racism.

The work of Chapter 2 consists of a critical summary of the four psychoanalytic theories with a view to see

1   whether they have the conceptual space in which to address the phenomena of colour racism, and if they do then
2   what theoretical structures from within the theory may be brought to bear on the phenomena? and
3   what if anything may be done (according to the theory) to alleviate the situation?

I limited myself to the written words of these theoreticians and avoided alluding to developments of, and commentaries on their work. I proceeded in this way for three reasons. First I wanted to try and get as sympathetic a view as I could of each theory to try to understand each within its own terms, from inside it as it were. Second, I wanted to try to evolve my own interpretation and reading of the theories, informed by the preoccupations of this subject. Third, in as sympathetic a way as possible, I wanted to test the theories against themselves for internal consistency and coherency. I surmised that the points of internal contradiction would be useful as they could be places from which one could begin a process of deconstruction.

I speculated that this process would throw up information about the attitude of the theories to race, aggression and so forth. This gave a strong recursive impulse to this chapter, in that the psychoanalytic understandings of racism were used to critically reflect light back on the body of psychoanalysis to expose the implicit metapsychologies and ideologies contained therein.

A valid criticism that might be made of the choice of subject matter in the previous chapter, is that the four 'vertical-depth' samples of the psychoanalytic frame constitute a sort of archaeology of theory, and so do not necessarily have a bearing on *contemporary* psychoanalytic thinking on the subject of racism. Chapter 3 addresses this criticism by taking a series of horizontal slices through the 'culture of psychoanalysis', to see how it deals with race in the treatment setting of the clinic, and the sorts of explanations it offers for the existence of prejudice and racism. This was done by trawling through the main national and international psychoanalytic journals read by clinicians in the UK (and the USA) for articles relevant to these themes. These articles provide a window onto the 'conversations' taking place in the psychoanalytic community, and in particular the clinical community. This strategy served the supplementary purpose of 'catching' additional ways of understanding racism, ways that might otherwise have slipped the net. Chapter 4 contains brief overviews of the small number of *direct* psychoanalytic theorizations of racism. These are Adorno, Dollard, Kovel, Wolfenstein, Rustin and de Zulueta. It is argued that the psychoanalytic theories considered provide explanations of why *particular individuals* might behave in racialized ways because of their individual stories. The chapter concludes with the argument that the individualistic and internalist metapsychology inherent in these theories prevent them from engaging with the *social* phenomenon of racism.

Whilst the work of Fanon might more properly be grouped with the authors above, I have given over the whole of Chapter 5 to him. I have done this for three reasons. The first and foremost reason is that in many respects Fanon is the progenitor of this work. When I first read him some 20 years ago, he shattered my complacent naïve world view at that time. This book represents my responses to the questions and dilemmas that were raised in me by his work so many years ago. Second, Fanon focuses on the objects of racism in contrast to the previous psychoanalytic theorizations which focused primarily on the subjects of racism (the white, the anti-Semite, etc.). The third reason is to do with the paucity of knowledge amongst practitioners of psychoanalysis and psychotherapy regarding his work; thus this chapter also serves as an introduction to his ideas.

The developing critique of the internalism in psychoanalysis leads into the subject of Chapter 6, the group analytic theory of S.H. Foulkes, as it was supposed that his perspective on the group would overcome some of the previous difficulties. Foulkes began life as a Freudian psychoanalyst, but spent his latter years modifying the psychoanalytic theory of individuals, to develop a specific theory and clinical practice of group analysis. The chapter begins by critically detailing some of his theoretical work and then draws out Foulkesian readings of race and racism. Although Foulkes goes some way to resolve many of the contradictions found in the previous chapters, particularly with his notion of the social unconscious, he does not quite manage to free himself of his Freudian antecedents, and so generates his own set of contradictions which echo those listed at the end of the previous chapter. (It was decided not to include the work of the other main group theoretician, Bion, because many of the relevant parts of Bion's thinking on hatred and difference are sufficiently found in Klein, and so already attended to earlier in this work.)

An overstated criticism can be made of the analytic work previously expounded on, which is that because the theories have prioritized the individual over the social, they have read the manifestations of racism as externalizations of asocial internal psychological difficulties. To counterbalance this tendency, in Chapter 7 I turned to the work of the sociologist Norbert Elias for several reasons. First, Elias and Foulkes were informal collaborators, and many of the ideas of Elias are already found in Foulkes. So the inclusion of Elias is not really a sea change, more an extension of Foulkesian group-analytic theory. Second, Elias is unusual for a sociologist in that he is concerned to evolve a true psycho-social theory which promotes the idea of a deep connection between evolving social structures and evolving psychological structures. His work is central to this book, as it helps show how and why it is that the signifiers black and white, utilized in the organization of society, are bound to be found and similarly used in the organization of the psyche, and how this results in the colour coding of affects, thoughts and actions. His work not only convincingly dissolves the nature–nurture divide, he also renders meaningless the dispute between psychoanalytic (internal) explanations versus sociological (external) ones; in effect he brings power and social relations into the heart of the psychological developmental process.

Chapter 8 gives full attention to notions of black and white. In common usage, there is often a slippage from white to light, and from black to dark. It is argued that this slippage is one of the routes through which notions of good and bad have migrated across and attached themselves to white and black. The linkages are initially examined from the vantage point of physics, and Barthesian semiotics. This is followed by a critical collation of these words in the Authorised Version of the Holy Bible. It was surmised that as the Bible was used as *the* moral handbook for the majority of the last millennium, its colour-coded language would have infiltrated what we might call the superego, to organize the psyche along colour-coded lines. This in turn is followed by a detailed semantic history of the evolving meanings of black and white in the English language. This 'data' was subjected to an Eliasian analysis to further argue for the linkages between the structures of a colour-coded society and a colour-coded psyche.

Chapter 9 draws on some of the themes first presented in *Taking the Group Seriously* (Dalal 1998) and develops them further. Initially, Matte-Blanco's theory of thinking is introduced as it concerns itself with the formation of categories through an interplay between similarities and differences. Following this, the putative radical theory of mind found in Foulkes is made more substantial by giving it a foothold in three interlinked territories – cognition (Matte-Blanco's bi-logic), power (Elias' theory of psychogenesis and sociogenesis), and the emotions (the varieties of psychoanalysis). In effect, the chapter starts building a general theory of difference, which in turn is used to say things about the vicissitudes of identity formation. In particular the chapter describes how it is that the affects and colours of existing 'we's necessarily come to be a part of forming 'I's from the start of the developmental process. This leads to a problematizing of the notion of the 'we' as well as the notion of the 'I'. These theoretical elements are harnessed to formulate a description of how black–white racializations traverse the bridge from the outside to the inside and so order and structure a colour-coded psyche, and how internal racializations migrate from the inside to the outside and so structure the world also in colour-coded ways. The chapter concludes by detailing some of the mechanisms utilized in the maintenance of previously manufactured divides between the 'us' and the 'them'.

Chapter 10 consists of the application of this 'general theory' of difference to the domain of race and racism, and particularly to colour racism. It engages with the enigma of the *presence* of a thing called racism despite the *absence* of a thing called race. The chapter details how and why the three interlinked territories of cognition, power and affect, come to work together to manufacture and sustain racialized differences as well as institutional racism. The chapter ends with a brief excursion into the clinical setting where thought is given to some of the modifications required of the practice of psychoanalytic psychotherapy in the light of the preceding arguments. It is argued that the notion of the transference needs to be extended so that the presence of socio-historical relationships between peoples may be registered in the consulting room.

This whole work is about understanding why the vintner is wrong. The conclusions of the book may be summarized as follows: difference is not the cause of hatred, rather, particular differences are called forth by the vicissitudes of power relations in order to organize hatreds (and other emotions) in order to achieve particular ends. These mechanisms work by lending the differences and the required hatreds an air of naturalness and so legitimates them. One such difference is that of race, which because of its fragility relies on the notion of colour. And finally, it is shown that the structures of society are reflected in the structures of the psyche, and if the first of these is colour coded, then so will be the second.

Notes

1 In this work I use the terms psychoanalyst, group analyst and psychotherapist interchangeably (unless the point applies specifically to one or other territory), as the arguments are of pertinence to those of all three persuasions. They are also of pertinence to those who are described as counsellors.
2 These schools of psychoanalysis have made considerable impact in academia, where the names of Derrida, Kristeva and the like are not at all unfamiliar, but they have yet to penetrate into the syllabuses of the analytic trainings.

Chapter 1

Rethinking race

If one supposes that racism is predicated on the idea of race, then before embarking on the main subject, racism, one is compelled to begin with a prior question '*what is race?*' But as we proceed it will be discovered that it will not be possible to remain with this neat arrangement of race before racism, and this discovery in turn will shed light on the nature of racism itself.

The answers to this question are wide ranging and disagree with each other to an extraordinary degree. However, it is possible to broadly group the types of answer under two headings: those that think race a biological category, an aspect of nature and therefore found by looking, and those that think of it as a reification, a discursive category and an aspect of culture. This way of dividing is not to imply that there is a coherent view within each of the divides.

Norbert Elias says that ideas do not pit themselves one against the other in any pure objective fashion; competing ways of describing the world are *also* aspects of competitions taking place in the socio-political arena at all sorts of levels. Particularly with the notion of race, the various descriptions are not only competing ways of describing the world, they are also ways of appropriating the world by legitimizing certain actions within it. Whether it is real or not, race is certainly used as a descriptor of peoples and as such has enormous impact on the lives of peoples. The different types of descriptions have led, at the formal level, to different types of social policy as enshrined in government legislation on immigration (Gould 1984), at the more informal and casual level to the killing of a young black man at a bus stop in London, and also at a less explicit level, that is harder to grasp, in the everyday relations between people and their attitude to the world.

What is race?

Whatever race is, the term is used to sort varieties of humankinds. Implicit in this possibility is the apparent truism that *there are indeed different kinds of humans to be sorted*. Folk psychology and the popular imagination would balk at the use of the term 'apparent' and say that the varieties of humankinds are clearly self-evident and plainly there for all to see – the African, the Caucasian, the Asian and so on. In contrast to this folk-psychological view, there is an established body of scientific evidence that demonstrates that the notion of race is one with no empirical substance. All attempts at measuring or naming differences by which the races may be differentiated have been found to be wanting. Indeed, as the modern genetic project is showing that 'patterns of genetic variation that appear at the genetic level cut across *visible* racial divides' (Gutin 1994: 73, italics added). These kinds of findings have led Rustin (1991: 57) to say that ' "race" is an empty category' which is filled with different sorts of projection.

It would, however, be a mistake to think that the notion of race has lost all scientific credibility; it retains considerable status not only in psychoanalysis but also in academic psychology. The arguments that the anthropologist M.G. Smith employs to defend the notion of race are not dissimilar to the common-sense arguments of folk psychology. This common-sense account is important because it is representative of the view held by many clinicians (see Chapter 3). Smith says

> Race is an essentially biological concept based on those distinctive sets of hereditary phenotypical features that distinguish varieties of mankind. . . . Those gross hereditary physical differences that all men remark between Negroes, Asiatic Mongols, Whites . . . [are] objective and genetic in their base. . . . When couples of the same race, whatever that be, produce children who are randomly black, white, pygmoid etc. I shall gladly acknowledge my error in disputing current biological ideology on the 'non existence of races'. . . . Jersey cattle do not bring forth Angus or Friesian calves . . . must we nonetheless deny the objective differences between these differing breeds, varieties or races of animals because each contain some genetic variation?
>
> (Smith 1988: 189–190)

This is a good example as it encapsulates many of the tautologies inherent in racialized[1] thinking. The kernel of Smith's argument is that creatures that have similar physical attributes (similar phenotypes) will produce offspring that tend to look similar to them. This indeed is true – my disagreement with him begins with what he proceeds to do with this information. He uses this local *familial* information to infer something general and universal: that these lineages constitute races. One of the first questions to be put here is how different does one have to be before one is classified as being of a different race? And a sub-question: what sorts of differences will be used to classify races?

Let us pursue the logic of his argument to see where it leads.[2] If one were to take a particular species, say dogs, then if one were to look at them with an unprejudiced eye (if such a thing were possible) then we would not see 'types' but creatures with a range of variations that are actually on a spectrum. To be more precise if we use any *one* attribute, say the length of the ear, to line up the dogs, they would be arranged in a particular order. If we were then to chose another attribute, say ratio of height to length, then they would be ordered differently. Creatures that were neighbours in the first line-up will not necessarily be neighbours in the second.

But Smith is saying that Alsatian dogs give forth other Alsatian dogs, therefore they constitute a 'race'. And that if an Alsatian is mated with a Labrador then the outcome would be a 'mixed race' or a 'mixed breed'. But here is the tautology: the notion of mixed breed is predicated on the notion of a pure breed. The fact that Alsatians breeding with Alsatians give forth animals that are also called Alsatians gives Smith the *illusion* that they constitute a 'race'. If we ask how are we to know if an animal is a pure breed, there are two sorts of answers that are given. First, we are referred to history. If the parents of the offspring are deemed to be pure by dint of certificates and so forth, then the offspring is deemed to be pure too. This answer is no answer because all it does is move the problem up one generation. Second, there are institutions that designate and legislate what constitutes the elements of a pure breed – colouring, shape, size and so on. Creatures that do not fit in are *by definition* not pure. This too is a tautology.

For the sake of argument let us name this mixed-breed dog Rover. Now, Rovers who mate with other dogs that look like Rovers will give forth offspring that look like Rovers, and there is nothing remarkable in this. Presumably if this type of dog were deemed to be desirable then eventually over time they too would be deemed to be a breed in their own right. In effect, demand will have manufactured and invented a breed.

We can see then that the notion of a pure race or breed is a reification. The so-called breeds are constructions and not facts of nature. To put it another way, the significance of Alsatians over that of Rovers is only that which is attributed to it.

Before moving on we have to take up one more of Smith's points. When he asserts that *all men remark* upon the gross hereditary physical differences between Negroes, Asiatic Mongols, etc., he is asserting that the 'types' of human beings are self-evidently present. There are several responses to be made here.

First, psychologists conducting experiments have shown how we constantly and inadvertently introduce discontinuities into continuities; and having done so our perceptual tendency is to experience the resulting situation in such a way that the differences *within* groups are diminished, whilst the differences *between* the groups are increased (Tajfel 1981: 150).

Second, as Cohen argues 'Visibility is socially constructed and can ch~ over time' (1988: 14). In other words we are taught to see pa~ ences as meaningful. This is in contrast to Jordan (1977) who the differences between types of people are self-evidently visible because they exist out there as a fact of nature, and so some differences 'naturally' strike one more forcefully than others.

The findings of psychologists concern the mechanism of cognition, and so in a sense where the discontinuities are made are logically arbitrary. But what the socio-political perspective adds is the idea that the place where these ruptures are inserted are not at all arbitrary but socio-politically mean-ingful. After all, it cannot be coincidental that the colour lines drawn to name the races matched so exactly the power relations during the epoch of colonialism. The most impressive of these being the great divide between the colonizer and the colonized, which fell neatly onto those designated as white and the rest, i.e. the coloured, the black.

This then takes us to the third response which takes up the variety of the *kinds* of differences that Smith uses to name the races – Negroes (some kind of racial type), Asiatic Mongols (a mix of geography and type), and white (colour). This lack of consistency is a clue to what is going on. Thomas and Sillen (1979: 26) quote Washburn as saying 'the number of races will depend on the purpose of the classification'. The reasons for the tenacity of the notion of race is something that needs to be explained. It is clear that races *per se*, as biological facts, do not exist. But having said that, I am then faced with the embarrassing difficulty that like M.G. Smith above, I find that I apparently 'naturally' see, experience and name varieties of humankinds, particularly the ones known as black and white. And, worse, despite all my objective belief systems I find myself at times having reac-tions and fantasies that would definitely be described as racist. The point of revealing this personal detail is not a prelude to using the book as a confes-sional. Rather, it is to make the point that something complex is going on, something social, something categorical, something emotional.

In order to help contextualize the *current* debate around the notion of race, there follows a brief history of the emergence of the idea of race in the English-speaking world. This will not be attempted in any detailed way, as it has already been done well by several others, for example Jordan (1977), Gould (1984), Fryer (1984) and Banton (1987).

An overview of the history and use of race

The term race made its first appearance in the English language in 1508 in a poem by William Dunbar (Husband 1982). For the next 300 years or so, prior to the advent of the science of race, the term race appears as a generalized descriptive category in the informal discourse of travellers' tales. However, its appearance is rare, much more frequent are references to blackes, Moores, Negroes, apes, Aethiopes and the like, attached to whom were the attributes of devilishness, monstrousness, lasciviousness, debauchery, and so on. Similarly, terms most prevalent in the discourses of plantocracy racism are Ethyopians, Blacks, Tawnes, Devils, Beasts, Savages, Negros, etc. The consistent use of the term race commences later, in the eighteenth century (Fryer 1984: 135–146).

Racism before race

For our purposes the main thing to note is that in this earlier period the term race is hardly used, and yet the descriptions are clearly what we would call racist. Thus despite my attempt to be logical and examine the notion of race before that of racism, it appears that racism manifested itself before the invention of race. Or to put it another way, racism did not have to make recourse to a notion of race to activate itself as it had other tools at its disposal. I would explain this in the following way.

In the earlier period 'the Negro' and various 'Others' were not as yet admitted into the category of humankinds, and this allowed them to be treated as beasts. Over time, the progressive collapse of this division under the weight of accumulating evidence, leads to the Negro gaining entry into the category humankind. It is at this moment that the notion of race becomes necessary as the new means of keeping a distance between the 'us' and the 'them'. So now whilst ground is reluctantly given in admitting that Negroes are human, it is asserted that they are a different kind of human – a different race – and so their exploitation can be continued as before. However, although human now, the associations with bestiality are retained, so that they are a bestial human race. Thus we can see that the division of humankind into races, bolstered by 'science', is in a sense a fall-back position.

It will be shown that the movement did not stop here. As the notion of race is progressively found wanting, then the conceptual ground shifts again and now the rationalization for the 'natural' antipathy retrenches itself in notions of culture and ethnicity (Barker 1981). Finally then, when the sociobiologists proscribe a genetic basis for both culture and ethnicity we can see that nothing much has changed. So, despite being called other names, this particular rose smells no sweeter.

Many, including elements of the black nationalist movements, would strongly contest this sort of assertion. They would argue that modern racism is particular and specific, and so different *in kind* from what has gone before, and also different *in kind* from the dynamics around other sorts of divisions – gender, class, and so on. They argue that racism proper begins with the scientification of race. Whilst I would agree that something specifically different is happening in modernity, I think the critical thing is the *functions* that the notions of race serve. This function is the naturalization of power relations by retaining the divisions of humankind. It seems to me that in different contexts the logic of the situation calls forth different instruments of differentiation, be they class, blood, gender, whatever, but that these are secondary to the purpose they are put to.[3] In saying this I am anticipating some of what will be elaborated on at a later stage. The point to be noted for the moment is that something that looks like racism has manifested itself without necessarily making recourse to a notion of race. C.J. Robinson would concur with this idea in general, although he also argues that racism and race had their genesis in the 'internal' relations of European peoples. He says

> At the very beginnings of European civilisation (meaning literally the reappearance of urban life at the end of the first Christian millennium) the integration of the Germanic migrants with older European peoples resulted in a social order of domination from which a racial theory of order emerged . . . positing distinct racial origins for rulers and the dominated. The extension of slavery and the application of racism to non-European peoples as an organising structure . . . retained this practical habit, this social convention
>
> (Robinson 1983: 83)

Miles (1993) and Cohen (1988) also argue that the advent of racism cannot be completely explained through the project of European colonialism because it fails to account for the racism in Europe prior to that, particularly anti-Semitism. The discourse of 'blood' uses a different language and has a different emphasis to that of race, but they both work for the same master – the explanation for the division of humanity into the haves and the must-not-haves.

It can be seen that the discussion on race does not 'behave itself' and is being continually drawn into attending to the idea of racism. The emerging reason for this appears to be the idea that the primary thing is neither race nor racism, but rationales of subjugation. These ideas have an ally in Elias (1994), who will have much to say on this matter later on. We should return to the task at hand – a history of the appearances of the notions of race – and attend to the era where science makes its entry.

Science and religion

But at once there is a difficulty which is, as Banton (1987) reminds us, that until relatively recently the discourses of science and religion were so deeply intertwined that science was readily used to engage with ecclesiastical disputes and vice versa. Science was Mammon's attempt to substantiate and understand the works of the (Christian) God. For example there was the question of the origins of humankind; are humans one species, and therefore all born of one Adam and Eve, or did each race begin separately?

The answers to this dry and remote-seeming cosmological question, were not at all abstract, but full of pertinence to the rationalization of slavery and colonialism. The proponents of *monogenism* argued that the variety of races were the outcome of degeneration of the first perfect race, and that the colour spectrum from white to the yellows and browns ending with black, reflected the degree of degeneration. It was proposed that this degeneration must have taken place very rapidly in order to give rise to such disparate varieties of humans. This was the 'softer' theory of race, as some of its proponents thought that there was some possibility of reversing the process of degeneration. The *polygenists* argued that there was not enough time for the degeneration to take place and so the different races had to have begun separately. In saying that the races were different species, they were saying that they were quite literally different animals (Gould 1984: 39). This meant that God's rules concerning the domain of human relations need not apply to those of other races.

The structure, if not the content, of this dispute continues today in the discourses on race. The structure of the dispute between the polygenists and the monogenists is that between immutability and change. The modern version of this dispute is contained in the division between biology and culture, with biology being the domain of the immutable and culture the changeable.

Whichever line was taken, the notion of the 'Chain of Being' brought all the themes together. The Chain of Being was perhaps the first attempt at a 'Theory of Everything'. It sought to bring together the animate and the inanimate, the varieties of living things, the spiritual and the profane, the body, the mind, the passions, and literally everything else, ordering them into a hierarchy. The Great Chain of Being, as powerful a synthesis as the electromagnetic spectrum from a later time, brought together all the disparate themes, from darkness to light, from evil to good, from beast to man, from impurity to purity, from black to white, from Devil to God.

One could say that the Chain of Being consisted of several separate threads, entwined in such a way that the attributes of one thread could be mapped onto an equivalent place on another; in effect there was an implicit isomorphism between the threads. Thus the range of colours are mapped onto the range of moralities are mapped onto the range of peoples, etc. Even though it has lost its scientific creditability, it has left these connections as residue: as sediment embedded in the structure of language and the psyche. This aspect of the Chain is the precursor to our contemporary habit of layering dichotomies one on top of the other, where the poles of each dichotomy get conflated with others – an idea which will be elaborated in Chapter 3.

Another example of the confluence of science and religion occurs with the use of the structure of the biblical story of Noah in several of the 'scientific' models of diversity. The structure of the story has two elements: first there is a disaster, and second, following the disaster people are scattered over the world. This structure is echoed in Cuvier's nineteenth-century model wherein following a catastrophe three races, distinguished by their colours – white, yellow and black – fled in different directions. In an elaboration of this theory 'Pritchard [1843] ... regarded the three major races as stemming from particular mountain slopes: white from ... Mount Caucasus, yellows from ... Mount Altai, and blacks from ... Mount Atlas' (Banton 1987: 29).

Almost all of the models of race that were put forward between the sixteenth and nineteenth centuries had as their precursor a particular *reading* of another aspect of the tale of the flood – the story of Ham. According to biblical cosmology, all of humanity *had* to emerge from Noah and thus from his three sons: Ham, Shem and Japeth. According to both James (1981) and Jordan (1977) Hebrew tradition used this story to explain the varieties of humankind in saying that the blacks were descended from Ham and his son Canaan, the Jews descended from Shem, and the light-skinned peoples from Japeth.

James then shows how Christianity took over a form of this story and wove it into the episode of Jesus's birth, and the visit by the three Magi. By the thirteenth century the Magi had been transformed into three Kings: Melichor, an old man of sallow complexion, who brought gold (the symbol of earthly kingship) represents the Jews, Balthazzar, a middle-aged man with dark skin, who brought Myrrh (the symbol of suffering and death) represents the blacks, and Jaspar, a young man of 'white and ruddy' complexion, who brought incense (the symbol of divinity) (James 1981: 26). In other words, representatives of each of the three varieties of humankind ordered according to a Christianized hierarchy, come to pay homage to the new messiah.

This legendary diaspora was elaborated on over the centuries by many different groups. First, by the Talmudic tradition (Jordan 1977: 18) in the first few hundred years after Christ. Then by Christian scholars from the sixteenth century (Fryer 1984: 142). But the ideas were mainly popularized by Captain George Best's cogitations in a series of travellers' tales published in 1578.

The science of race

The first formal attempt to classify and differentiate the types of humankind was by Linnaeus in 1758 in his work *The System of Nature*, Linneaus divided *Homo sapiens* into five diurnal and one nocturnal categories. The nocturnal category was said to be the troglodyte whilst the diurnal ones were divided as follows.

1   Four-footed, mute, hairy. *Wild man.*
2   Copper-coloured, choleric, erect. *American* (paints himself, regulated by customs).
3   Fair, sanguine, brawny. *European* (covered by close vestments, governed by laws).

4   Sooty, melancholy, rigid (covered with loose garments, governed by opinions).

5   Black, phlegmatic, relaxed (anoints himself with grease, governed by caprice).

(Linneaus 1758, quoted in Eze 1997: 13)

There are two pertinent things to be noted. First, Linnaeus does not use the term race, he calls each of the categories above a *variety*. Varieties are subsets of species. The interesting thing is that in his description of variety he includes physical attributes (what some call race), mode of dress (what some call culture), and also character types (what some would call psychology). The second point of interest is the extent to which colour is used as one of the main differentiators. Thus, right here in the very first of the formal attempts at classification, all the elements colour, internal character, physical type and culture are all firmly bound together and made integral to each other. In itself Linnaeus has not done anything new, he has formalized, collated and systematized the understood wisdom of the time. It seems to me that those who still argue for the notion of race repeat Linnaeus, albeit in more sophisticated language.

The next influential work was Cuvier's *Le Règne animal* in 1817. In this work Cuvier divided humankind into three major races, the white, yellow and black, and these in turn were organized in a colour hierarchy. C.G. Carus, 1789–1869, a German physician, was dissatisfied with the classification of races purely on physical form, and so positioned the earth's peoples in relation to the sun, and came up with four divisions organized hierarchically

*   the Day People, the purest form of which were to be found in the region of the Caucasus, and were said to have spread over Europe
*   the Eastern Twilight People, the Mongolians, Malayans, Hindus, Turks and Slavs
*   the Western Twilight People, the American Indians
*   finally, bottom of the list were to be found the Night People, namely the Africans and Australians (Banton 1987: 20).

A major writer on race, Robert Knox popularized the idea that external characteristics (mainly skin colour) reflected internal ones (e.g. intelligence). For example 'I feel disposed to think that there must be a physical and consequently, a psychological inferiority in the dark races generally' (Knox 1850, quoted in Banton 1987: 57).

Blumenbach 1865 (German anthropologist) formalized the term Caucasian believing that a particular skull discovered in the Caucasus mountains exemplified the skulls of a particular race, that of Europe. He went on to use colour to divide humankind into five races: Caucasian, Mongolian, American, Malay and Ethiopian.

The list of examples will not be extended as there is sufficient material to draw attention to a particular idea which, although hardly original is central to the developing argument. And it is this: although the number of races varies in the models, as does the names given to them, one thing that remains consistent is *the use of colour not only to refer to the races but also to **name** them*. In fact colour becomes synonymous with the notion of race. The words are used interchangeably. For example, Nott and Gliddons in *Types of Mankind* (1854) state 'those *Races* of men most separated in physical organization – such as the *Blacks* and the *Whites*' (quoted in Banton 1987: 42, italics added). Another example picked at random from many such comments 'When we classify mankind by *colour*, the only one of the primary *races*, given by this classification, which has not made a creative contribution to any of our twenty-one civilisations, is the *black* one' (Arnold Toynbee 1934, quoted in Gould 1984: 41, italics added). Toynbee clearly expects his readers to know what is meant by 'the black one', i.e. that there is a biological category called 'the Black Race' that can be distinguished from the rest of humankind.

So far, attention has been drawn to the correlation of colours with the idea of race. It has also been argued that race is not a biological fact but a discursive category. However, it is a problematic category, because in my mind I also find an *experiential* category which is not unlike the notion of race, i.e. despite myself I find 'automatically' classify people according to the way they look, saying he is African, she is Chinese, he is Indian. What is going on?

Biology of race

Having said that biological races do not exist, I am obliged to substantiate that to some degree. Again I will not do this in any depth here as it has been amply done by many authors (Gould 1984, Barker 1981, Jordan 1977, Banton 1987). For example, in *The Mismeasure of Man* Gould exposes the conceptual fallacies as well as the experimental anomalies that plagued the attempts of scientists. to 'measure' and define the differences between the races.

The modern version of this project is to be found in the discipline of sociobiology. Barker (1981) and Lewontin (1993) have shown that although the language has changed the ideology is the same as that behind the older project of defining the 'types of mankind'. But now, instead of race and groups, the argument is conducted at the level of the gene and an amalgam of culture and ethnicity. The keystone of sociobiology lies in the notion of inclusive fitness. This idea says that evolutionary mechanisms do not work at the level of individuals or groups but at the level of genes. Thus, what evolutionary and selection mechanisms work to promote are behaviours and attributes (at the individual level) that enhance the gene's possibility of replication (Plotkin 1997).

As I have made a fulsome critique of these ideas elsewhere (Dalal 1998), here I will engage more briefly with some of the points via the sociologist van den Berghe's use of sociobiology. He says

> my framework of analysis is specifically biological on only two major points:
> It makes individual inclusive fitness (as measured by reproductive success) the ultimate currency of maximization.
> It identifies nepotism based on proportion of shared genes as the basic mechanism of ethnic[4] solidarity, and it advances commonality of genetic interest as a type of interest distinct from others, such as class interests.
>
> (van den Berghe 1988: 250)

The argument being proposed is that one is genetically programmed to treat one's kin more favourably than those not-kin, because one shares most genes with them. He then delivers the punchline *'ethnicity is an extension of kinship'* (ibid. 250, italics added). In other words certain types of social relations (specifically treating others badly) are given justification through alluding to a biology that has been programmed via evolutionary mechanisms.

Now, I would not want to argue that our biology has not been formed through the evolutionary process, but would argue with this version of the process.

It is now an uncontroversial fact in genetic theory that any grouping (be they defined in terms of race, ethnicity or culture) will be found to share approximately 15 per cent of their genes (Plotkin 1997). To be more specific, it is theoretically possible to find a pattern which will be made up of about 15 per cent of the genetic material, which can be used to differentiate *this* grouping from others. But what this means is that 85 per cent of the genetic material is unremarkable and similar to that of the rest of humanity. By the logic of van den Berghe's own argument which is based on 'the proportion of shared genes', why does the other 85 per cent not overwhelm the 15 per cent?

A much more crucial challenge to this mythology was alluded to earlier, which was the finding that 'patterns of genetic variation that appear at the genetic level cut across *visible* racial divides' (Gutin 1994: 73, quoted in Shepherdson 1998: 53). One then has to ask how is a gene to 'know' that it has a twin in another human being? Even if it could 'look' somehow, as Gutin says there is not much of a clue to be found by looking. Indeed if van den Berghe's argument is to hold water, then all 15 per cent of genes must 'know' at the same time that they all have a counterpart in particular human beings. And if this 15 per cent 'knows' then why does none of the other 85 per cent know?

Another point to consider is that since geneticists tell us that we share 98 per cent of our DNA with chimpanzees why are we not more kindly disposed towards them?

The main point of the argument is as follows. Our genes are so over-whelmingly shared, and the relationship between genes and behaviours are so imprecise, that it is extremely improbable that genes can be directing the kind of ethnic consciousness the sociobiologists and some evolutionary psychologists postulate.

The other critical flaw in van den Berghe's proposition is that the very notion of ethnicity is problematic. As will become evident in the next section, there are multiple and contradictory understandings of what ethnicity is. In conclusion we can safely say that there is no mathematical correlation to be found between 'ethnic solidarity' and 'the proportion of shared genes'.

The effect of this kind of argument is to throw racist 'discourses outside history, making them the static object of a general critique of "human nature" ' (Cohen 1988: 43). In brief, it is a use of biology to explain sociology.

* * *

Despite the evidence to the contrary, the popular imagination continues to use the notion of race as though it were readily understood. Take, for example, a newspaper article in the *Observer* on race, criminality and DNA. The article written by Robin Mckie, the science editor, describes a project which apparently seeks to 'perfect techniques that allow scientists to *pinpoint* a person's race from DNA samples'. Mckie writes of the DNA codes that 'Some are common to all *ethnic* groups, but some are found almost exclusively in one *race*' (May 24, 1988: 13, italics added). It appears from this sentence that race and ethnicity are interchangeable. The races are then delineated, apparently there are three of them 'It is possible to say in some cases . . . that a sample is from a person of East Asian or European or Afro-Caribbean *origin*' (ibid. italics added). What does origin mean in this context? They clearly do not mean where the person was born. The implication is that there are original places where each of the races emerged from, and that this is where they still belong. McKie might not know it but by alluding to a natural belonging he is giving succour to one of the racist theories of the nineteenth century which said that the races are naturally suited to the particular regions of the earth where it was supposed they started from, and that a person risked his life by being in 'climates that nature never intended for him' (Nott and Gliddon 1857: 400, quoted in Banton 1987: 44).

* * *

This chapter was begun with the expressed purpose of engaging in an orderly fashion first with the notion of race before that of culture, ethnicity and racism. The fact that not only has it not been possible to come to any consensus about the notion of race, but also these other terms keep inserting themselves and will not stay removed from the discussion gives us a clue to the problematic nature of each of them and also of their relationships. It suggests that they are all much more entangled with and embedded in each other than it initially appears. This then is the task that I will turn to next, the relationship of the trinity: race, culture and ethnicity.

What is the relationship between the notions of race, culture and ethnicity?

The 'classical' answer seeks to differentiate the three terms on the basis of three domains – how people look, how people behave, and how people think and feel. These three domains are approximately mapped onto ideas of race, culture and ethnicity. Race, according to Fernando (1991: 9–23), is said to describe the biological, physical difference between groups of people. It is a way of grouping people together on the basis of physical characteristics – particularly the colour of the skin. Culture he defines as the social habits, beliefs, the ways of thinking and feeling of groups of people. And ethnicity he says describes the sense of belonging. One can see that this sort of view still contains the concepts of Linnaeus, the difference being that where Linnaeus makes them all part of the same system, the attempt here is to separate them out.

Intrinsic to this sort of model is a further differentiation between 'things' (which are neutral) and the 'uses' they are put to. The first is a fact of nature and therefore biological and the second a fact of culture and therefore sociological. Thus there is the distinction between race (neutral) and racism (not so). This view is expressed by Ruth Benedict who says that race is a neutral scientific category of taxonomy and not in itself to do with racism 'Race is a matter for careful scientific study; Racism is an unproved assumption of the biological and perpetual superiority of one human group over another' (1983: vii).

In contrast to this sort of positivism there is another stream which says that there are no such things as races, and more meaningful descriptions of groups of people are given by the terms ethnicity and culture. Thus it is common practice to put the first term of the trinity – 'race', culture and ethnicity – in quotes (e.g. in Gillborn 1990). The implication of this is that whilst the notion of race is problematic, the other two are less so and exist in a more straightforward way. It will be part of the evolving thesis to show that the other two terms are as problematic as the first, albeit in different ways.

The implication is that if we look *inside* the group, at its contents as it were, we will not be able to find any grounds for race, but we will find a complex of entities some of which we can call culture, and others ethnicity.

In other words it is said that whilst we cannot use race to divide humanity, we can use notions of culture and ethnicity.

But what are ethnicity and culture? Here are some attempts at a definition.

By alluding to ancestry McGoldrick and colleagues (1982) make their definition of ethnicity identical to that of biological race: 'the ethnic group [are] . . . those who perceive themselves as alike by virtue of their common *ancestry*, real or fictitious, and who are so regarded by others' (quoted approvingly by Dwivedi 1996: 8). In contrast to race, Giddens' definition of ethnicity is made identical to culture 'Members of ethnic groups see themselves as culturally distinct from other groupings. . . . Ethnic differences are *wholly learned*' (1989: 243–244, italics added). The anthropologist M.G. Smith makes ethnicity a subset of race 'all ethnic units are sub-divisions of some racial stock' (1988: 188), whilst the psychoanalyst, Zaphiropoulos (1987), reverses this saying that ethnicity is identical to culture and asserts that racial and socio-economic differences are sub-cultural. Thus already all four combinational possibilities are found here. These examples can be multiplied indefinitely.

In a volume aimed at psychotherapists, Carter defines *culture* as 'the transmission of knowledge, skills, attitudes, behaviours and language from one generation to the next, usually within the confines of a physical environment' (1995: 12); *ethnicity* he defines as 'a group with a specific national or religious identity' (ibid. 13); and *race* he says is 'a sociopolitical designation in which individuals are assigned to a particular racial group based on presumed biological or visible characteristics such as skin colour, physical features, and, in some cases, language' (ibid. 15).

The caveats in the definitions (e.g. 'usually within the confines', 'in some cases') are clues to the problematic nature of each of these terms resulting in elements of one sliding into another. He says that 'language' is a differential attribute of 'culture' as well as 'race', so when does language mark out a race and when a culture? On what basis is this decision made? Clearly when something immutable is being inferred then the allusion is to race rather than culture. It seems to me that there is something of significance hidden in the midst of this 'decision' between race and culture, a something that problematizes all the notions: race, culture and ethnicity. The point to be underlined from this example is that despite the attempt to differentiate the terms, race, ethnicity and culture, we can observe how they collapse into one another.

The sociologist Yinger says that his 'preference is to distinguish between socially defined and biologically defined races' (1988: 22). Whilst he neglects to say *how* the two are differentiated, it is clear enough that he does think that *there are such things as biological races*. He then says that the socially defined race is the same as an *ethnie*,[5] and that

> an ethnie exists in the full sense when three conditions are present:
> a segment of a larger society is seen by others to be some different

combination of the following characteristics – language, religion, race, and ancestral homeland with its related culture; the members perceive of themselves in that way; and they participate in shared activities built around their (real or mythical) common origin and culture.

(ibid. 22)

One presumes that the 'race' in the above definition is what Yinger calls biological race. Thus his definition of ethnicity includes race and culture. Having given this definition he then goes on to say that

ethnicity has come to refer to *anything* from a sub-societal group that clearly shares a common descent . . . to persons who share a former citizenship although diverse culturally . . . to pan cultural groups of persons of widely differing backgrounds who, however, can be identified as 'similar' on the basis of language, race or religion.

(ibid. 23, italics added)

The list of tautologies renders this attempt at defining ethnicity meaningless. It seems to me that the bottom line here is that there are groupings, and that pretty much 'anything' is used to differentiate between them and that some other or same thing is used to name a similarity within the group. The name given to this similarity is ethnicity. We now have to ask of Yinger if 'anything' can be used to construct an ethnie, then how and why is one thing being chosen over another? This is exactly the kind of question that prises open this kind of positivist discourse to expose the unnatural phenomena – ideologies – that drive the distinctions between the 'us' and the 'them'.

It is now possible to assert that all attempts to differentiate race from ethnicity from culture fail, precisely because each of the terms is being used to serve the same function – differentiation. By focusing on the similarity that binds a group, the function of the differentiation is being disguised. In effect this is an attempt at naturalizing the differentiation on the basis of an apparent 'natural' difference. These attempts to explain the *differentiations* by looking *inside* the terms ethnicity, race and culture are manifestations of *essentialism*.

The ideas of the social anthropologist Sandra Wallman (1979, 1988) seem to me to give a way through this morass of confusions. We can begin this process by noting that the terms race, ethnicity and culture are all *names* for differences. The allusions to race are meant to indicate an apparently objective and immutable difference. Whilst in Britain ethnicity 'signifies allegiance to the culture of origin and implies a degree of choice' (Wallman 1988: 229). But even here there is a difficulty, for example, what ethnicity is a British-born person whose parents or grandparents were born in (say) Pakistan? Their 'culture of origin' is British, yet they are allocated (by themselves as much as others) a different 'ethnicity' to that of British, or only allowed in with the addition of the prefix *Black* British. Why has this term been introduced? Clearly something complicated is going on – something *not*-objective.[6] As to the notion of 'a degree of choice', whose choice is activating the naming of an ethnicity – the classifier or the classified? Wallman says 'the differences observed and the way they are interpreted say as much about the classifier as about the classified' (ibid. 229). We can add that it also says something about the *intention* behind the classification, as well as the relationship between classifier and classified and the context in which they exist.

Despite the confusions born of the contradictory definitions of ethnicity, race and culture, it is possible to draw out one consistent theme, which is that they hearken to an idea of belonging, and this in turn is linked to some notion of identity. The basis of this belonging might be real or imagined, and it might be attributed from the outside or it might be taken on from the inside as part of a felt self-definition. However, the fact that some identities are self-chosen because they just *feel* right in some self-evident way, is not to imply that this is *authentic* and unproblematic – a kind of true self.

Wallman's way of thinking opens things out and allows us to approach the subject from a different perspective which is a change in focus from what the terms *are*, to the functions they serve. Like van den Berghe she says that pretty much anything can be utilized to mark an ethnic boundary. But where he emphasises the 'naturalness' of the differences, she focuses on their functions, saying 'Differences between groups of people turn into ethnic boundaries only when heated into significance by the identity investments of either side' (ibid. 230).

It is now possible to formulate an interesting question: given that there are always innumerable differences between any two people, how and why does one difference come to be chosen over another? Or to put it another way, *who* is giving significance to one difference and not another, and on what basis? To play with Wallman's metaphor, what is the fuel that is being used to heat the difference?

What is being proposed is a shift in focus, from the difference itself to the use, or function, it is being put to. To anticipate some of the work of future chapters, the use is not one of neutral categorization, but to do with the structure of power relations in which the processes are taking place.

Black and white

Of central interest to the subject of this book is the curious fact that whether it be race, culture or ethnicity that is being alluded to, it is not uncommon to find each of them *named* as black and white. For example, with ethnicity 'the term "black" is used to describe people who share similar experiences of belonging to ethnic minority groups in the UK and *being easily recognizable as such*' (Mehra 1996: 79, italics added). This linkage is in common use as, for example, in the phrase 'blacks and *other* ethnic minorities'. This phrase implies that there are ethnic minorities that are black and others that are not, however it is clear enough that black is a name of an ethnicity.

Compare that phrase to another also common in contemporary usage 'blacks and Asians'. If Asian is used to mean from a geographical place, then black this time must also be a description of a geographical land, presumably Africa. But why not say 'Africans and Asians'? To my mind this is because the phrase is actually a description of culture and history. By implication those designated as Asian have a strong cultural ethos, giving much weight to tradition. In contrast, Africans need only be known by their colour because, by implication, they have no history or tradition behind them. Thus in this phrase black signifies culture, or to be more precise lack of culture. In contrast to this there is also a more positive use of black as in 'black culture', sometimes in simplistic monolithic ways and at other times in more sophisticated ways, for example in the subtitle to Paul Gilroy's book *Small Acts* (1993) which is *Thoughts on the Politics of Black Cultures*. In any case the point made is that cultures too are named by calling them black and white.

Examples of black and white being used to name races have been cited earlier in this text (see pp. 16–18).

What becomes clear is that whilst the terms of reference have changed from race to culture and ethnicity, they are all to some degree reifications. But what has remained the same is the use of black and white to distinguish between different groups. I am not suggesting that this is the only device ever used to differentiate between groups. Indeed, at times these terms are self-conscious attempts to get away from biological race both in terms of genotype, the deep genetic code, as well as phenotype, 'the trivial external' of skin colour. They are attempts to get away from the body and into the deeper territory of internal meanings – territories of psychology. Thus the definition of ethnicity includes characteristics like religion, cultural habits, belief systems and so forth. But what we see is that despite these efforts, the recalcitrant categories black and white somehow find their way back in again, in all sorts of terms like black music, white lie and so on. Let me end this part of the discussion with this quote which, in a grand finale, brings together all the terms in one nonsensical definition 'The term *"Ethnic Minority"* is much debated but includes a wide variety of *races* and *culture* both *black* and *white*' (Bailey 1996: 89, italics added).

* * *

However much evidence accumulates behind the idea that the notions of race, culture and ethnicity are reifications, they continue to be treated as objective (that is measurable) categories. For example, in a paper entitled

'Skeletal differences between black-and-white men and their relevance to body-composition estimates' Gerace and colleagues (1994) seek to measure concrete physical differences between black and white men in order to test their hypothesis that 'Black men have greater bone mass, higher bone mineral density, and longer limbs compared to White men'. They say that they wish to see whether the methods for estimating the amount of body fat are *ethnically* specific. They are silent on the question of the criteria used to distinguish black from white men, indicating that it is taken to be self-evident. We can see then that even in the 'hardest' of the human sciences (biology), the notions of black and white are part of the legitimate currency and nomenclature.

* * *

Let me reprise the argument so far. First, whatever the categories used to differentiate human groups, more often than not the notions of black and white will be found to be implicated in some way. Second, the logic used to enclose the term 'race' in quotes, is also applicable to the other two terms, 'culture' and 'ethnicity'. This is not to imply that there are no such things as cultural artefacts – beliefs and habits – that differ from one part of the world to another. Rather, what is being questioned are the sharp lines drawn between one 'culture', 'ethnicity' or 'race' and another. Third, it is not difference that is problematic, it is the packaging of clusters of particular physical differences into *discrete mutually exclusive sets*. As Rattansi (1992) has pointed out notions of assimilation, multiculturalism and the like, presuppose that there are two or more homogenous 'cultures', separate and different from each other, that need to be or should be assimilated. Miles makes a similar point about the idea of 'race relations', the phrase presupposes the existence of 'races' which are then perceived as 'relating' to each other.

Whatever else these things are (race, culture, ethnicity), at the very least they are an allusion to some notion of identity and identification. Wallman argues that 'ethnicity is the process by which "their" difference is used to enhance the sense of "us" ' (Wallman 1979: 3). What this suggests is that ethnicities and cultures are not internal possessions, but ongoing psycho-social processes that emerge out of larger socio-historic processes. The fact that it is a psycho-social process commits one to the notion that there are power relations inevitably in play between the 'us' and the 'them', and this means that sometimes the identification appears to be self chosen, and at other times inflicted from the outside.

Jenkins uses this power differential to try to make a distinction between ethnicity and race. He says that 'ethnicity is largely a matter of group identification, and "race" or racism one of categorisation' (Jenkins 1988: 177). This is an attempt at salvaging an aspect of identity by allocating it to the region of psychology, and differentiating it from an apparently separate region of power and politics in which more nasty things happen. This kind of division will be found many a time in the theories that are yet to be discussed.

Power

I will not take up the arguments about the relationship between race, class and gender here. This territory has been explored in detail by Banton, Barker, Cohen, Hirschfeld and Miles amongst many others. What is crucial to these commentators is the relationship of these categories to that of power. For example, Gilroy argues for the retention of race as an analytical category 'not because it corresponds to any biological or epistemological absolutes, but [because] it refers investigation to the power that collective identities acquire by means of their roots in tradition' (Gilroy 1987: 149).

Miles agrees with Gilroy to say that the fact that races *per se* do not exist 'does not [in itself] require the denying that the idea of "race" is a constituent element of everyday common sense' (1993: 42). However, 'the issue is whether or not such usage is transferred into the conceptual language that is used to comprehend and explain that common sense' (ibid. 42). This is because the problem with using race as an analytic category is that despite the caveats, the term is used in a 'form which suggests that the human population *is* composed of a number of biological "races"' (ibid. 39).

Racism: a working definition and a proposition

We are faced with the following anomaly: *that although there are no races, there is racism.* This anomaly can be used to formulate a working definition of racism.

> Racism is anything – thought, feeling or action – that uses the notion of race as an activating or organizing principle. Or to put it another way, racism is the manufacture and use of the notion of race.

One can see that the definition of racism is one of *activity*; thus I would say that more useful than the notion of racism is that of *racialization*. From this I would add that racism is identical to racialization, with racialization being the process of manufacturing and utilizing the notion of race in any capacity.

On the basis of this definition let me make a further proposition.

> Racism is a form of organizing peoples, commodities and the relationships between them by making reference to a notion of race.

Racism: the emotions and another proposition

But what both these formulations leave out are the emotions. It is readily admitted that at times powerful emotions of hate and repulsion are involved in racist incidents, for example the lynching of a black man. It is less readily admitted that when no *overt* expressions of hatred and violence are evident, then something that might be called racist may still be taking place, for example in the vicissitudes of the job market. Further, it is possible that although these negative emotions are not evident, they might nevertheless be active, but unconsciously. These thoughts are a prompt to look towards a new territory – psychoanalysis – as it has a lot to say about both the emotions as well as the unconscious. This engagement will be deferred until the next chapter, but for now let me put up one question. If we grant that hate and racism are embroiled in each other, then what is the relation between them? Does hatred drive racism, or does racism mobilize hatred? Or is it the case that something else lies behind both? In a way, the whole investigation is an engagement with these questions, questions that will return periodically but not necessarily in exactly these forms.

On the basis of this discussion, another proposition can be put forward, which is

racism is a form of hatred of one group for another.

It should be kept in mind that it will not necessarily be the case that the mechanisms that drive the first proposition will be the same as those that drive the second. Neither will it necessarily be the case that the two are distinct and different from each other.

***

A danger is flagged up here, which is in saying that racism is any use of race, the definition of racism makes it so that the writings of, say Stuart Hall (1980) are lumped with those of the National Front as both allude to a notion of race. Clearly they are very different and indeed they are the antithesis of each other. I will postpone the substantive discussion on this point until the final chapter, by which time I will have introduced and so be able to use the thoughts of Elias.

At this point I also need to mention the interlinked issue regarding the distinction that some people make between 'prejudice' and 'racism' on the basis of only the latter being a property of power. I will argue later on that, as it is never possible to exist outside the field of power relations, this distinction – based as it is on the two being different kinds of things – is not a viable one.

Some of the difficulties in perceptions of racism are briefly taken up in the next section.

On the ephemeralness of racism

The phenomenon of racism is notoriously difficult to delineate. Depending on how one approaches it, it either appears as a terrifying monolith, or as a chimera that doesn't exist at all.

The problem with the notion of racism is that it is constructed out of the reification 'race'. Thus the effects of racism, which are real enough, are activated by something that in a sense does not exist. This means that as one approaches it in order to study it, it dissolves and disintegrates in front of one's eyes. So what are we left to get a hold of?

This ephemeralness is used by some to flatly deny the existence of racism. In my experience in the psychoanalytic and group-analytic community it is not unusual to find such viewpoints. For example, at a conference some remarks made on aspects of institutionalized racism in psychoanalytic discourse caused some consternation in the membership of two hundred or so delegates. I was challenged: where was the racism to be found in this gathering? I was asked in bemused sort of way: what did I mean by 'black people'? Whilst the absence of the latter at the conference could be seen as a sufficient answer to both questions, I will nevertheless develop a more fulsome answer below.

Manifestations of racism can be located on a spectrum one end of which consists of overt actions like 'Paki-bashing' and 'Jew-baiting', with the other end consisting of more covert and hidden institutional dynamics. The overt racism is more easily dealt with because it is 'self-confessed' and therefore visible to all. The covert racism is problematic precisely because it is invisible, and so is easily denied either consciously or unconsciously. One way of revealing racism is through statistical evidence and analysis. Now psychoanalysis does not, as a whole, pay much regard to statistical evidence and instead relies on the case history – a statistic of one. In contrast, others dismiss the validity of the case study on the grounds that it is a statistic of one, saying it is anecdotal. However, as I will show, both sorts of evidence are also used to deny the general existence of racist phenomena.

The nature of evidence – statistical and anecdotal[7]

When there is a particular piece of overt racism, then it is dismissed as an anomaly, a one-off, something that is an aberration. The fact that this is 'anecdotal' evidence and not statistical is used to render it meaningless precisely because, it is said, that this evidence being one-off is not part of a pattern, and therefore says nothing apart from itself.

On the other hand, when statistical evidence is marshalled to demonstrate that an institution is, say, favouring group A over group B, then this time anecdotal evidence is used to undermine the statistics. It is in the nature of statistical evidence that some of the body of evidence will be contrary to the conclusion. In other words the fact that there are *some* green apples in this basket, does not invalidate the statistical truth that *most* of the apples in this basket are red. Something similar happens when the statistics show that, say, blacks get fewer jobs than whites in a particular sector. Now, the fact that *some* blacks have those sorts of jobs is used to individualize and particularize the issue. The issue is reframed as this sort of question 'if Joe, who is black, got that sort of job, then what is wrong with Harry, Jim and Jack (who are also black) that they didn't get those jobs?' The location of the problem is shifted from that of institutional dynamics to personal psychopathology, from the outside to the inside.

It is part of the complexity of racism, that things have different meanings depending on which side of the fence they occur. An individual racist act on the 'white' side of the fence is easily dismissed as an anomaly. However, when there is an incident in which a black is the perpetrator of a crime, then this particular piece of anecdotal evidence becomes converted into a piece of statistical evidence, from one criminal black to all blacks are criminals. The psychological mechanisms that drive these asymmetries will be elaborated on in the penultimate chapter; for the moment let me note here that Elias will have something to say about the first example and Matte-Blanco about the second.

Summary

This chapter has given an overview of the history of race and its appearance in various discourses, that of science, religion and politics. The attempts to differentiate race from ethnicity and culture were all problematic, and at the very least their status as objective criteria were seriously undermined. It was shown that their meanings and significances were in the main informed by the socio-political, rather than being descriptions of objective reality. The fact that the words 'black' and 'white' are used regularly in a rather vague fashion to name all three, race, culture and ethnicity, reinforces this idea, and prompts one to look more closely at the notions of blackness and whiteness.

It was noted that in moments the ideas of race, culture or ethnicity have the look of a hard reality that appear objective enough to drive huge swathes of human history. At these times they clearly have a critical emotional significance. But yet when one approaches these entities closely, they turn into chimeras and evaporate before one's very eyes. They have an emotional reality which does not calibrate very easily with objective criteria like DNA or even skin colour. Neither is their emotional significance consistent; it ebbs and flows, and at times it has little or no resonance and seems to disappear altogether. In short, the ontological status of race, culture and ethnicity are extremely problematic.

To put it another way, despite the difficulties of race as a *descriptive* category, it wields considerable force as an *explanatory* category. So although one might find great difficulty in detailing coherent objective differences between groups of people, these imagined differences are nevertheless used by people (and their theories) as sufficient *explanation* of their aggressions.

These cogitations led me to propose a definition of racism as *any* use of race (to organize thoughts, feelings or actions). I reasoned that as race does not exist in any objective sense, then racism is the evocation of this construction. The later sections of the book will elaborate and detail the workings of these propositions.

Notes

1 I have yet to define the notion of racism, which I will do shortly.
2 Elements of the following arguments were published in Dalal 1993, 1997a and 1998.
3 This is the reverse of the racist's argument which is that the difference is primary, and the things that take place are *caused* by this difference.
4 The question of what constitutes ethnicity will be picked up in a while.
5 With this new term, ethnicity, which has been an aspect of a thing, has now been turned into a noun – the name of the thing itself.
6 The addition of the prefix only makes sense if the notion of British has already embedded within it a notion of whiteness, and also that of a homogeneity whose basis is this whiteness. The implications of this kind of thinking will be spelt out later on.
7 A version of this discussion was published in Dalal 1997a.

Chapter 2

Psychoanalysis and racism

Cautions and caveats

The psychological sciences are faced with a critical problem, which is that they cannot directly access the subject of their inquiry – the mind. This is also true of the unconscious and the mental life of the neonate both of which play critical roles in all psychoanalytic theories. About the conscious we can at least say that the subject is aware to some degree of its existence. But *by definition* the unconscious is always beyond the realm of the directly known; it can only be *inferred* through clues given via dreams, slips of the tongue and so on. There are similar difficulties with the mental life of the neonate. But even to say the phrase 'mental life of the neonate' is to enter the lists with a position, because some would say that the neonate has no mental life until later in his or her development.

The inaccessibility of these regions makes them particularly available to carry varieties of projection. The point about projection is that it is a way of hiding things from oneself. By definition one is (consciously) unaware of what one is doing or why one is doing it. This is another way of saying that subjects and objects can never be other than deeply implicated and entangled with each other. Psychoanalytic theory offers a further complication to this already entangled situation and it is this: if the mechanisms of displacement and projection are ways of hiding something from oneself, then not only are there always *reasons* as to why they are being hidden, but also the reasons too are hidden from the self.

This insight is true of all disciplines and so applies to the 'body' of psychoanalysis as much as to the patients it treats. All of this is to say that theory is always value laden. Thus, in what follows not only will certain psychoanalytic theories be used to examine racism, but also the phenomena of racism will be used recursively to shed light on what psychoanalysis might be hiding from itself. However, one cannot attend to psychoanalysis *per se* because it is not one theory but a number of different theories each with distinct world views that are often in disagreement with each other. It is because of this that I am going to examine four theories separately. The

four I have chosen are Freud, Klein, Fairbairn and Winnicott. I limit myself
to them because of the importance they are given in the trainings of psychoanalytic psychotherapists in Britain and so will have a bearing on how
contemporary therapists think about the subject when it manifests in their
consulting rooms. I wish to extract theories of racism that are specific to
each of these theoreticians. However, the problem that one is immediately
faced with is the fact that none of them make any direct reference to racism.
I will get round this in the following way. Given that racism is often understood as an expression of hatred, aggression, envy and the like, I will begin
by elaborating how these and other relevant notions arise within the logic
of each of these theories. I will then use these descriptions to *infer* theories
of racism that will be consistent to each of the frameworks.

Using Freud to think about racism

I will organize my discussion on a Freudian understanding of racism around
four main regions: the two theories of the instincts, the Oedipal Complex
and the relationship between the individual and the group. From the first
to the last Freud remained an instinctivist, and each of his theories of the
instincts are major attempts at explaining the fundamentals of *why* human
beings behave in the ways that they do, and *how* they come to do so. Thus
each of these theories lends itself to a different explanation of hatred in
general, and from that, racism in particular. The theory of the Oedipal
Complex and its resolution is the story of the entry of the individual into
society, and as such it gives up another 'take' on hatred and racism. And
finally, Freud has a view that individuals in certain types of *groups* behave
in savage and primitive ways; this too leads to particular Freudian explanations of manifestations of hatred of one *group* for another. I shall begin
with abbreviated summaries of the two instinctual theories, and use these
to catalogue the ways that Freud introduces hate and aggression into his
schema.

The first instinctual theory

The first instinctual duality postulated by Freud consisted of the self-
preservative instincts and the sexual instincts (1910a). The concern of the
first instinct was to preserve the individual self, whilst the concern of the
second instinct was to perpetuate the species through procreation. Freud says
that the two instincts have no regard for each other, and so each unwittingly
finds itself in conflict with the other. Most crudely, this might occur when
the organism's urge to express the sexual instinct puts itself in danger. This
theory encapsulates the idea that the interests of the group are inevitably
and necessarily in conflict with the interests of the individual. What we
have here then, is the idea that conflict is an inevitability structured into

existence itself. However, this conflict is not necessarily the same as either aggression or hate. To find their genesis we have to go a little deeper.

Freud says that the nervous system is designed to move away from stimuli and to reduce the energetic tension in the organism to its lowest possible state; these are all aspects of the Principle of Constancy (1915a: 120). The fact that the organism cannot move away from internal stimuli (known as the instincts) but can from external stimuli, has two crucial consequences. First, it results in the organism's dawning awareness of the distinction between the internal and the external. Second, because the organism cannot directly modify the source of the internal stimuli, it is forced to modify the external world so that the instinct may be 'satisfied', and the internal tension released through this means. This is also the impetus for the genesis of thought itself, thought which is required to engage with the external world in order to modify it.

The other critical component of this theory of instincts are the two principles of mental functioning: the pleasure principle and the reality principle (Freud 1911). Very broadly, the sexual instincts operate under the aegis of the pleasure principle, and the self-preservative instincts under the reality principle. The definition of pleasure is a functional and mechanistic one. The difference between pleasure and unpleasure is the direction of flow of libido. Increase in libidinal tension equals unpleasure, decrease equals pleasure.

Freud now has a problem, which is that both these instincts are 'good' in the sense that both serve a positive purpose, one being the preservation of the species, and the other the preservation of the individual. So he has somehow to derive hate and aggression, he has to find a way to insert 'bad' in his schema. How does he manage this feat?

He allows aggression in, in three ways. First, Freud asserts that love is always mixed with hate, because in the oral stage, the impulse to devour necessarily implies the annihilation of the object. Second, in muscular action, there is implicitly a level of aggression in all movement. The third way is more complex. In the beginning the instincts seek satisfaction auto-erotically, that is from the self. Further, as the instincts seek satisfaction, they do so blindly as 'injury or annihilation of the object is a matter of indifference [to them]' (Freud 1915a: 139). Consequently, as the instincts seek auto-erotic satisfaction, they inadvertently cause the self some pain. Two things follow from this: first, pain has been introduced into the schema and second, Freud says that this 'indifference' of the instincts is in fact the basis of sadism. However, this initial 'sadism' is not a sadism *per se*, but more a not-caring 'the infliction of pain plays no part among the original *purposive* actions of the instinct' (ibid. 128, italics added). This self-inflicted sensation of pain that is felt by the subject, melds with that of 'sexual excitation and produce[s] a pleasurable condition, for the sake of which the subject will even willingly experience the unpleasure of pain' (ibid. 128). However, it 'is not the pain itself which is enjoyed, but the accompanying sexual excitation' (ibid. 129). Now pleasure and pain are joined and we have the advent of masochism. When this masochism is reversed so that pleasure is taken in causing pain to others, then we have arrived at sadism proper.

Racism as an expression of the sadistic instincts

We can use the preceding discussion to formulate the first of the theories of racism. We can say that racist hate, which incontrovertibly has sadistic components, must in part be generated by this same process. However, the fact that initially the object of the instinct is the most variable thing about it, means that the racialized components are not of significance in themselves. The sadism is expressed on some available target, and the self-preservative instincts will ensure that the threat against the self from the chosen target is minimal. However, if the instinct is successfully discharged on the object, then it will progressively come to 'fit' the instinct. As Freud says 'what is most variable about an instinct and is not originally connected with it, but becomes assigned to it only in consequence of being peculiarly fitted to make satisfaction possible' (1915a: 122).

We are caught in a loop. Whilst this might well be a mechanism through which sadism gets expressed on racialized objects, it is not an explanation of how those objects come to be racialized, nor of why sadism *should* be expressed at racialized objects. However, what the theory does say is that instincts become 'habituated' to express themselves at particular objects if they are 'peculiarly fitted to make satisfaction possible'. Thus if one discovers that it is possible to vent one's aggression on black people freely, then they eventually will come to 'fit' this instinct.

Racism as hatred of the external

The other route that hatred uses to enter Freud's schema is on the back of the first division – between the internal and the external. The fact that the external world inevitably stimulates is experienced by the ego as unpleasure. Consequently, during the solipsistic period of auto-eroticism 'the ego-subject coincides with what is pleasurable and the external world with what is indifferent (or possibly unpleasurable, as being a source of stimulation)' (Freud 1915a: 135).

As this process gathers momentum, the ego absorbs and takes in what is pleasurable, rejects aspects of the external which are unpleasurable, and projects aspects of the internal world which are also experienced as unpleasurable 'into the external world ... [which it then] feels as hostile' (ibid. 136).

This eventually leads to the complete mapping of pleasure/unpleasure onto inside/outside 'the ego-subject coincides with pleasure, and the external world with unpleasure' (ibid. 136). Thus at 'the very beginning it seems, the external world, objects, and what is hated are identical' (ibid. 136). If an object turns out to be pleasurable, then it is loved and incorporated into the ego. From this it follows that '[external] objects coincide with what is extraneous and hated' (ibid. 136). In other words all things outside the self are hated, *all things not-self*. Now it is but a small step from a hatred of things outside to a hatred of outsiders.[1]

We can now apply these ideas to two further dimensions of racism which follow next.

Racism as repulsion

So far we have observed that anything that stimulates is hated because stimulation in itself constitutes unpleasure. Further, all things experienced as outside the self and so different from it, are also hated. Freud goes on to say 'We feel the "*repulsion*" of the object, and hate it; this hate can afterwards be intensified to the point of an aggressive inclination against the object – an intention to destroy it' (1915a: 137, italics added).

If the racialized object stimulates (and it must, merely by virtue of it being different and also by being 'outside'), then according to this theory it will be experienced as repulsive. This in turn will lead to hate and the wish to destroy it. This then is an explanation of another component of racism: the feelings of aversion and repulsion against the racialized Other. But once again what these ideas do not address is *why* a racialized Other should stimulate any more than any other Others. Freud does in fact offer an answer to this question through the notion of the narcissism of minor differences, which is where we turn next.

Racism is the hatred that is caused by the presence of racial difference

Here the hatred is triggered *by* the racial difference,[2] *caused* by it as it were. One could say that this is a theory of the hatred of difference, and it is derived from the hate to be found in the self-preservative instincts.

The theory of the hatred of difference is one grounded in the first instinctual theory where 'relation[s] of hate are derived . . . from the ego's struggle to preserve and maintain itself [i.e. the self preservative instincts]' (Freud 1915a: 138). This is his theory of the 'narcissism of minor differences' which he began by noticing that trivial differences precipitated major conflicts 'Every time two families become connected by a marriage, each of them thinks itself superior to . . . the other' (Freud 1921: 101). He explained these antipathies by reference to the self-preservative instincts which, he says, experience anything different from the self as a criticism of the self; this in turn triggers hostility towards the thing that is felt to be doing the criticizing – the thing that is different.

Freud now extrapolates from the consequences of minor differences to those of major differences to arrive at an explanation of racism

> of two neighbouring towns each is the other's most jealous rival. . . . Closely related races keep one another at arm's length. . . . We are no longer astonished that *greater differences* should lead to an almost insuperable repugnance, such as the Gallic people feel for the German, the Aryan for the Semite, and *the white races for the coloured*.
>
> (ibid. 101, italics added)[3]

In sum, in this theory all things different from the self are experienced as criticisms, threats and attacks on the integrity of the self, and this in turn triggers a defensive, narcissistic response of hatred – a hatred of the difference. So according to this theory the triggering of hatred by the presence of difference is inevitable; in fact Freud ascribes to this 'readiness for hatred . . . an elementary character' (ibid. 102).

* * *

We have now a partial answer regarding the variability of the object of the instinct. We can say that the object of the instinct is not completely arbitrary, but aimed at that which is experienced as different from the self. If one does not follow the course of naturalizing some differences over others, then we are left with a problem: given that there are an infinite number of differences between any two objects, why should some of them (e.g. the 'racial' ones) trigger hatred over and above other differences? A partial answer is found in the Freudian notion of group dynamics which we will come to later.

The second theory of instincts

Freud's cogitations led him eventually to put these instincts of sex and self-preservation more or less under the new term 'the life instinct'. Given his attachment to the notion of dualism he was now faced with a problem – what would constitute the other pole of the polarity? He needed something else, something 'beyond' libido and the pleasure principle (Freud 1920). He surmised that organisms sought to destroy themselves because they were driven to do so by an inherent death instinct. Thus life/libido had as its counterpoint death.

The death instinct being endogenous to the organism, in the first instance inevitably acts on the organism itself, thus threatening the extinction of its own life. This threat to the self from an aspect of the self constitutes primary masochism. In order to protect itself, the life instinct uses libido to turn the death instinct outwards on to the external world. Through this process the two instincts are fused and the death instinct is sexualized. Freud names this movement of the death instinct outwards from the organism, *aggression*. This melding of aggression and sexuality is what Freud terms sadism proper. The part of the death instinct that is left behind is 'bound' by libido to protect the self, and forms the basis of masochism. There is a further complication in that the sadism proper can get turned around again, when it becomes a secondary masochism. It is possible to draw out two distinct theories of racism from this theory of the instincts.

Racism as the expression of the death instinct

Once more the variability of the object of the instinct is of pertinence. In order to preserve the self against the attack of the death instinct, it *has* to be projected outwards. According to this way of thinking hatred in general, and racism in particular, is a defensive move to protect the self. However, to the eye this defensive manœuvre *looks* like an aggressive act, and whilst that is precisely its effect it is not in the first instance its motivation. Nevertheless, once the projection has taken place, another complication inevitably follows: the object, now containing the death instinct, is experienced by the subject as something frightening and threatening. Consequently, the object will be attacked again for having the appearance of something threatening and dangerous. It is important to remember that the object is 'innocent', i.e. the threat has been projected into it.

Racism as the organization of hate along racialized lines

This is an idea that says that racism is not about the generation of hate, but a means of managing and modifying its expression *of a pre-existing hate* by diverting its flow along particular channels. Here, racial difference is *used* to manage hatred by siphoning it off. One could say that this is a theory of the racialization of hate. The sequence is as follows: the fact that the instincts are fused means that every gesture of love inevitably carries with it a component of hate, thus every 'emotional relationship . . . contains a sediment of feelings of aversion and hostility, which only escapes perception as a result of repression' (Freud 1921: 101). But the repressed can only remain unconscious if it is projected onto some other object. As Freud says, the conflict 'is often settled by . . . making a change of object and displacing one of the ambivalent emotions on to a substitute' (ibid. 79f). The racialized Other must serve at times as such a substitute. It is being said that the feeling of love for one, *necessitates* the projection of hate onto another.

The other component of the racialization of hate is found in a defensive gesture, a protection of the self. Because in the first instance the death instinct threatens the organism/infant itself, and so in order to survive it is projected outwards into the objects that surround it, these are inevitably the mother and other family members. So now, in order to be able to have a relationship with one's closest objects, these feelings or instincts need to be projected again, further and further out. Thus, the

> advantage which a comparatively small cultural group offers of allow-
> ing this instinct an outlet in the form of hostility against intruders is not
> to be despised. It is always possible to bind together a considerable
> number of people in love, so long as there are other people left over to
> receive the manifestations of their aggressiveness.
>
> (Freud 1930: 114)

So here are two other explanations for the genesis of hatred of one group of people for another. What is not addressed as yet is what determines where one group begins and another ends. In one sense Freud naturalizes particular differences, on the other hand he also gives them a psychodynamic basis. To unpack these complexities we need to move on to Freud's understanding of social groups. This subject is of particular relevance because Freud locates another of the sources of hatred in the transformations that are said to take place to the *individual* psyche as it is *becomes* part of the social.

Oedipus: the superego as a patron of racism

The Oedipal phase arises between the ages of 3 to 5 years. During this time the child is said to feel desire for the parent of the opposite gender and rivalrous with the parent of the same gender. In 'normal' circumstances the boy resolves the difficulty by identifying with the father, and also by renouncing (in the sense of repressing and making unconscious) both his desire for the mother as well as his hatred of the father.

In broader terms the superego consists of the rules of what is and what is not socially acceptable. This ego ideal is the resultant of the gradual gathering up of 'influences of the environment, and the demands that the environment makes upon the ego and which the ego cannot rise to' (Freud 1921: 110). With the resolution of the Oedipal complex and the advent of the superego, the child becomes a social being. As society is taken, the child becomes a part of society.

The fact that the rules are about *social* acceptability does not mean that the superego is conscious. On the whole it operates invisibly, giving the appearance of naturalness to innumerable customs and attitudes. Thus the superego is 'the vehicle of tradition and of all the time-resisting judgements of value which have propagated themselves in this manner from generation to generation' (Freud 1933: 67).

One of the functions of the superego is to constrain and modify the uninhibited expression of the sexual and aggressive instincts.

However, what happens in the situation where the norms of society are such that certain objects (say blacks) are perceived as *deserving* of attack because they are thought of as bad in some way? According to the theory, these attitudes will be internalized and unconscious. The result will be that when it comes to these objects, then the superego will no longer function as an inhibitor of the free expression of the instincts, but would positively encourage the attack 'When the community no longer raises objections, there is an end . . . to the suppression of evil passions, and men perpetrate deeds of cruelty, fraud, treachery' (Freud 1915b: 280). Thus, in a racialized society there would be little or no guilt to inhibit the venting of the instincts against racialized objects, because in attacking something apparently bad, one would be doing a good thing.

Racism as an outcome of group formation

Freud's model of human nature is Rousseauian at one level, and Hobbesian at another. Freud thinks (like Rousseau) that there is a natural state of man that is pre-social, which by implication is that of a solitary individual. However, this natural state is that of Hobbesian man, savage and not so much immoral as amoral. There are two distinct themes to be found in the story of group formation and so each is taken separately.

Exposing the id: the bad group

Through the story of the primal horde Freud (1921) describes the process through which savages became socialized and were able to live with others. But now, when these socialized individuals come together in groups they tend to behave in savage ways again. Why is this? Freud says that at the deep level of the unconscious all human beings are the same; and it is because this region of similarity gets uncovered that people behave in similar ways. So it is that in groups individuality dissolves 'and the unconscious foundations, *which are similar in everyone*, stand exposed to view' (ibid. 74, italics added). When this is added to the fact that within the region 'exposed to view' is to be found 'all that is evil in the human mind' (ibid. 74) then we have arrived at a Freudian explanation for all sorts of group violences, of which the racist ones are a subset. We can also see why it is that the primitive instincts (in both theories) which have been inhibited through the developmental process, are more prone to be activated in their original form when individuals find themselves in groups. Freud quotes Le Bon approvingly 'by the mere fact that he forms part of an organized group, a man descends several rungs in the ladder of civilization. *Isolated, he may be a cultivated individual; in a crowd he is a barbarian* – that is, a creature acting by instinct' (ibid. 77, italics added).

It is this fact, that the group mind is said to be identical to the individual unconscious,[4] which allows all that is repressed there to be set loose in the group.

Replacing the superego: the good group

Having said that the experience of being in a group makes individuals behave badly, Freud and Le Bon also say the opposite: that groups make individuals behave in more civilized ways than they otherwise might. Whilst Le Bon puts it down to contagion, Freud puts it down to a mechanism that concerns the replacement of the superego.

Freud argues that both contagion and suggestibility are akin to a hypnotic state, and that all of them are derivatives of the psychological mechanism of falling in love. He says that being in love entails 'considerable amounts of narcissistic libido' progressively flowing over onto the loved object, until the object 'gets possession of the entire self-love of the ego. . . . The whole situation can be completely summarized in the formula: *The object has been put in the place of the ego ideal*' (Freud 1921: 113, italics added).

Next, this same mechanism gets exploited by the process of group formation, in which the group leader is put in place of the ego ideal. Each member is now in the grip of the illusion that the head 'loves all the individuals in the group with an equal love' (ibid. 94). As it was in the family – where fear of losing the love of the beloved parent led to the transformation of sibling hate, through a reaction formation into sibling love – so it is in the group. Here too one has to inhibit the instincts, because to attack a fellow group member would mean that one would be attacking something the leader loves. This in turn courts the possibility of losing the love of the leader. The psychological solution is for all group members to identify with each other in their egos – become brothers. This then leads to Freud's formula regarding the emotional constitution of groups

> *A primary group of this kind is a number of individuals who have put one and the same object in place of their ego ideal and have consequently identified themselves with one another in their ego.*
>
> (ibid. 116, italics added)

In effect we have arrived back at the dyadic primordial situation: the individualized father leader and the homogenized group.[5] Group formation may be defined as the process through which the operation of the narcissism of minor differences within the group is dissolved, and the self-preservative instincts are inhibited.

> When a group is formed the whole of this intolerance vanishes, temporarily or permanently, with the group. So long as a group formation persists . . . individuals in the group behave as though they were uniform . . . and have no feelings of aversion towards them.
>
> (ibid. 102)

However, this is not the end of the story because the inhibited instincts have eventually to be discharged somewhere. This privilege falls to all things that are not part of the group 'love for all those whom it [the group] embraces; while cruelty and intolerance to those who do not belong . . . are natural' (ibid. 98). There is an exact parallel with the earlier formulations in the first instinctual theory where the ego loved all things within itself and hated all things not-self.

So, we have arrived at another possibility for the explanation of racist violences. The violent instincts are prevented expression within the group by the fact that they are joined by the imagined love of the leader, but objects designated as outside this grouping have no such safeguard and so the 'natural' state will prevail: hatred and intolerance. Additionally, the instincts that *would* have been vented on members of the in-group, will be displaced and discharged on the outsiders, and so they will be doubly burdened by hatred.

There is one last point to do with groups that needs to be mentioned here because it will be referred to later. It is to do with the paradox that groups come to embody both the highest and the lowest possibilities of mankind. Freud resolves this paradox by saying that there are different *kinds* of groups: natural and permanent, and those who come together for short periods of time for some purpose. In the first one *is* already part of something, whilst in the second one temporarily *becomes* part of something.

Freud says that the bad behaviour is the product of the temporary groups, whilst the 'permanent' groups are those that induce civilized behaviour. According to this last thesis, long-established groups (societies) should not act in violent and terrible ways towards its members, which is clearly not the case. Elias will show that the apparent difference between the two sorts of groups is not one of kind, but one of duration. We will also come to see that whilst the apparent good behaviour within a boundaried system has the appearance of a 'pacified social space', violences and subjugations are continued through subtle means institutionalized within psyches and the workings of societies.

Using Klein to think about racism

According to Melanie Klein the instincts of death and life are constitutional and are part of the psycho-biological structure of all infants. The relative strength between the instincts is said to vary between individuals. However, Klein stresses that for all individuals at the beginning of the developmental process, the death instinct is of much more significance than the life instinct *because* it is more problematic. It is not an overstatement to say that in the Kleinian model everything proceeds from the death instinct, that is from the terror of it and also the use of it. Anxiety is the spur to development – it precipitates movement.

Freud explicitly thought and wrote about social phenomena, and directly applied his theories in an attempt to understand the aetiology of social dynamics. Klein makes very occasional and oblique references to social structures, and when she does they are as asides, and *always* as consequences of internal dynamics. For example, she says 'A group . . . consists of individuals in a relationship to one another; and therefore the understanding of personality is the foundation for the understanding of social life' (Klein 1959: 247). The emphasis on the internal in Klein is most evident in her version of the superego. In Freud the contents of the superego explicitly include the social, whereas in Klein the superego is constructed out of an amalgam of elements of the death instinct and unassimilated introjections. These introjections, be they whole (the mother, the father) or part objects (the good/bad breast/penis), are biological and not social – *even though they are external.*

It follows that although racism is observed as a phenomenon of social life, it will be in the study of the internal phenomenology of the individual that any answers or explanations concerning it will be found. We can only surmise that that is how Klein would approach the subject, because although she gives considerable attention to hate, envy and aggression, she never exposes any awareness in her writings of racism as a manifestation of any of them.[6]

Greenberg and Mitchell have pointed out that Klein 'has a tendency to see bad objects as internally derived, that is, as arising from the child's own drives, and good objects as absorbed from the outside, from the ameliorative effect of the parents' ministrations' (1983: 135). In this sense Klein agrees with Freud that it is in the unconscious that all that is evil in humans is to be found. The most she allows from the environment is 'frustration', never any malignancy. This is one of the problematic aspects of Klein's theory: it does not appear to have an explicit conceptual space within its developmental frame that allows for the possibility for some badness to *originate* from the outside. She only goes as far as allowing the outside to fail to ameliorate the internal horror, but never explicitly addresses the possibility of it causing the horror, even occasionally.

Death instinct as a precipitator of racism

One of the differences between Freud and Klein exists in their versions of the relationship between the instinct and its object. In Freud, the object of the instinct is the most variable thing about it, and objects only get attached to instincts through habituation, because they *happen* to satisfy the instinct. Meanwhile Klein suggests that the instincts have versions of the objects that will satisfy them embedded within them in the shape of unconscious phantasy. However, I think that something has been missed. All the objects so embedded[7] are libidinal life-enhancing objects (even though they might arouse anxiety), and so are to do with the life instincts. It would seem that as far as the death instinct is concerned, Freud's dictum about the variability of the object still holds true in Klein 'The fear of the destructive impulse seems to attach itself at once to an object – or rather it is *experienced* as the fear of an uncontrollable overpowering object' (1946: 4). It is a case of any port in a storm.

Thus, the death instinct is malignancy incarnate, the in-born desire to spoil and destroy any and every thing. The fact that the death instinct lashes out at whatever is available results in an explanation of racist hate similar to one of Freud's explanations. In both instances the hatred is endogenous and the racial object is a happenstance. However, given that the death instinct is promiscuous in its choice of objects, there is no reason why it should be aimed any more at one particular grouping, say a black 'them', rather than another grouping. The theory does not say what drives the choice of object.

Envy as a precipitator of racism

With her notion of envy Klein adds a new twist to the death instinct. Envy is said to be a constitutional aspect of the death instinct 'I consider that envy is an oral-sadistic and anal-sadistic expression of destructive impulses, operating from the beginning of life, and that it has a constitutional basis' (Klein 1957: 176). The first object enviously attacked is the breast, because its fullness has the possibility of gratifying the infant's emptiness. The structure of envy consists of a spoiling hatred triggered by the sense of deprivation in relation to the fullness and goodness of some entity. The intention is not to appropriate the goodness but to destroy its source.

For envy to be a precipitator of racism, the racialized Other must be being attacked for some goodness. The difficulty is that the hated racialized Other is more often than not the more deprived of the two. So here is the first point: whilst the breast is envied by the infant because of its 'real' fullness, the racialized Other is envied for their imagined fullness.[8] In other words something good must have been projected into the racialized Other in order to experience them as full. But why would one want to project something good into someone bad? There are two possibilities here – the good can be projected out in order to protect it from the bad within, but if this were the case then one would expect it to be projected into an area where it would be safe. The racialized Other, by definition, cannot be this safe space. How is this difficulty to be resolved?

A possible explanatory sequence is as follows. The amalgam of various psycho-social tides (two of the most important being Christianity and the Enlightenment), inculcated the repression of the passions (particularly sex and aggression) in the European Christian. These repressed elements are bound to be split off from consciousness and projected into a territory which is designated as similarly repellent in some way (enter the racialized Other).

The racialized Other is now experienced as containing not only something desirable, but being desire incarnate. The whole process, being unconscious, leaves the conscious mind feeling perturbed and disgruntled. We may speculate further that the Other is not only envied for seemingly being disinhibited and rampantly sexual, but is also resented because of some hazy realization that this thing that resides with them rightfully belongs to me. This would also go some way to explain why racialized Others are so often experienced as greedy and untrustworthy.

The fusion of the instincts, splitting and object relatedness, leading to a fear of foreignness

Although, according to Klein, the libidinal instincts are said to be object directed prior to experience, this in itself does not constitute an object relation. Object relations proper begin with projection, and once this relation is established then, according to Klein, all the elements of an object relation are intrinsically bound together – the instinct, the object and the subject (the source). This is true of hate as well as love. This interrelatedness allows her to build up a complex picture of internal object relations. Thus, in the paranoid-schizoid position, when the object is split so is the ego, and this *results in a weakening of the ego.*

The split elements are held within different regions of the psyche to protect one from the other. The introjections that are benign are welcomed into the ego. Whilst the introjections that are malign, and so frightening, get distanced from the ego and placed within the superego, these unintegrated internalizations of the endangering aspects are experienced by the depleted and weakened ego as something 'foreign' (Klein 1946: 9n) and 'alien' (Hinshelwood 1991: 106) and also as 'threatening' and 'persecutory'. In effect, the ego fears being overwhelmed and dominated by these unassimilated alien objects.

This is the internal situation. Now, in order to manage it Klein says that an external danger situation is created to echo the internal one, which, if all goes well, is used to modify the internal situation. The child 'displaces its fear of internal dangers into the outer world by projection and finds evidence there to disprove them' (Klein 1932: 242). Klein says that the internal world (internalized and endogenous elements) are hidden from view and so cannot be accessed directly. So the internal is projected into the external, in part, to make it visible and so more accessible (ibid. 116).

This theory leads one to suppose that the fear of the alien Other is really a projected fear that properly belongs in the internal world of the subject. In this way of thinking, the danger is an *imagined* one and to do with unassimilated internalized objects that *feel* alien 'the internal objects act as *foreign bodies* embedded within the self' (Klein 1946: 9f, italics added). The theory suggests that the wish to purge the external (political) body of alien objects is really a displacement of the wish to purge the internal body of the unassimilated objects that one feels persecuted by. Klein says 'this weakened ego . . . becomes . . . incapable of assimilating its internal objects, and this leads to the feeling that it is ruled by them' (ibid. 9). We may also suppose that when this internal state of affairs is projected into the external world and into the 'outsider', then this gives rise to the phenomenon where the majority population, despite being the more powerful, feel in danger of being overpowered and dominated by the racialized (and thus *made* alien) Other. We may conclude that as a way of managing the internal danger situation, the 'aliens' in the external world are suppressed, oppressed and marginalized, in much the same way as the internal aliens are suppressed and marginalized.

The fear of the death instinct

This is the mechanism where the death instinct is projected into an external object as a defensive act – a way of distancing it from the self. Whilst these acts of splitting and projection initially result in a weakening of the ego, over time with progressive re-introjections of the external object one eventually achieves an increased ability to tolerate anxiety,[9] with the result that one is less likely to evacuate hostility unthinkingly. In this way the benign external world gets incorporated into the internal world, and so moderates it. But things can go wrong in one of two ways.

First, things get stuck sometimes because the weakened ego cannot take in the evacuated aspect without feeling completely overwhelmed by it, so it remains outside, ominous and threatening. If the object cannot be taken in, then life and love are not taken in either – there is only fear. Fear prompts projection, prompts anxiety, prompts aggression, and so on endlessly, Klein calls this 'the vicious circle' and says that when 'these parts have been projected excessively into another person, they can only be *controlled* by *controlling* the other person' (1946: 13, italics added). This then could be taken as the Kleinian explanation of the source of the impulse to dominate and control other human beings; it can even be thought of as a partial explanation for the cruel dominations that take place in the colonial situation and slave societies. But once again the fact of race is not of particular significance in itself. The racialized situation is a subset of the more general situation where one group or person dominates and controls another.

The second way in which things might go wrong is considered next.

Guilt increasing persecution

Having caused hurt and pain to another, it is possible that the ensuing guilt does not lead to reparation but to further persecution in the following way.

Guilt is an uncomfortable emotion. At times, quite unfairly, the injured object is blamed for 'causing' this uncomfortable feeling. This results in one feeling persecuted by the injured object, and so one attacks it in turn. There are two further reasons why guilt might not lead to reparation. First, it is occurring when paranoid-schizoid mechanisms predominate, and so one is not yet able to feel depressive anxiety. The second interlinked reason is that the death instinct in the shape of envy is too strong to allow the reparative gesture 'one of the consequences of excessive envy is an early onset of guilt. If premature guilt is experienced by an ego not yet capable of bearing it, guilt is felt as persecution and the object that rouses guilt is turned into a persecutor' (Klein 1957: 194). And as we have seen, if the ego feels persecuted then it persecutes in turn and so spirals back down into the vicious circle.

The epistemophilic instinct leading to a hatred of those who speak foreign tongues[10]

According to Klein, the epistemophilic instinct, the desire to know, is activated during the Oedipal phase.[11] She describes the genesis of this instinct in this way. At the onset of the Oedipal tendencies the ego is very weak because of splitting. One aspect of the Oedipal phase is the awakening of sexual curiosity. Not only does the infant have no answers to these troubling questions, it is also without a language in which to formulate the questions or to understand any of the answers that might be forthcoming. This situation is very traumatic for the infant and Klein says that

> in analysis both these grievances give rise to an extraordinary amount of hate. Singly or in conjunction they are the cause of numerous inhibitions of the epistemophilic impulse: for instance, the incapacity to learn foreign languages, and further, *hatred of those who speak a different tongue.*
>
> (1928: 188, italics added)

One of the interesting things about this formulation, is that it naturalizes a hatred of Otherness. What is being suggested is that the explanation of a *sociological* behaviour – hatred of those who speak a different tongue – is to be found in the universal *biological* developmental process which *all* infants must inevitably go through (according to this theory that is). Whilst Klein is not saying that foreignness *causes* hatred, she *is* saying that this particular difference, foreignness, is hated *because* it reminds one of a terrible time, a time where one suffered because one did not have language.

There are at least two critiques we can make of this theory. First, the speakers of different foreign languages are not all hated equally. Indeed speakers of some foreign tongues are desired and admired. For example, in my experience there are clear differences in the attitude towards someone speaking English with an Italian accent and someone speaking English with a Pakistani accent. Clearly something more than an 'experience of a difference' is happening.

The second point concerns the fact that in this theory the difference that is hated is not one of sight but one of sound. If this idea were right then one would expect black Britons born in Britain, speaking the English tongue not to be the recipients of racist hatred. The evidence does not bear this idea out in any straightforward way. The situation is very complex and one cannot engage in any simple mapping of language and accents onto hatred. Of course language and the way it is spoken, is critical to social positioning. For example, it would appear that black Britons speaking 'Queen's English' are much more likely to appear on the BBC, than those who speak 'black' English or who have regional accents. Until recently, the latter was very true of whites as well. The main point being made here is that hatred of the foreigner is due to much more than the fact that they might speak a different tongue.

Klein says that the timing of the genesis of the epistemophilic instinct has some further interesting consequences for 'the whole of mental development'. The fact that this impulse arises at the time when anal and urethral sadism are said to be at their height, problematizes this instinct. She argues that it is not libido that brings this instinct into being, but sadism. The child desires to plunder, *and so desires to know what there is to plunder.*

> the child . . . dominated by the anal-sadistic libido position . . . impels him to wish to *appropriate* the contents of the body. He thus begins to be curious about what it contains. . . . So the epistemophilic instinct and the desire to take possession come quite early to be most intimately connected with one another and at the same time with the sense of guilt aroused by the incipient Oedipus conflict.
>
> (ibid. 188, italics added)

But then there is a complication, which is that the infant, whilst it plunders, is inflicted with guilt because it is attacking a loved object. The anxieties set off by this guilt are partially responsible for driving the infant outwards from the mother (in order to protect her) and into the world. For Klein the world is always in some way a substitute for the first primary object, the mother's body, or more precisely, the breast. Anything that is not-mother is symbolic of mother and interactions with her. Thus all cultural artefacts, however complex and sophisticated they may appear, from mathematics to mountaineering to gardening are 'substitutes for the relation to the primary object' (Klein 1952b: 83).

One can see then the process by which a sadistic urge to appropriate, plunder and dominate the world is generated, by slipping along a line from the breast to mother to *all* other objects. One could read this as giving biological substantiation and 'naturalizing' imperialisms, colonizations, and the harsh manner in which these are usually conducted.

Extending Klein: from the paranoid-schizoid to a pseudo-depressive position

If we are to use Klein's theory to think about racism as something pathological,[12] then we are straight away led to the paranoid-schizoid position. This is because the mechanisms of racism are very reminiscent to those of this position, in which the world and self are violently riven into two – the good and the bad. Paranoid-schizoid mechanisms work by distancing ambivalent elements from each other partly by exaggerating the properties of each (denigration and idealization), and partly by the various mechanisms of splitting and projection.

But now we hit a snag. If racism is a manifestation of pregenital modalities, then we would expect very young infants whose mode of functioning is said to be primarily paranoid-schizoid, to be particularly racist and feel terrorized by the Other. The research evidence contradicts this prediction, for example Goodman (1964) and many others have found that racial awareness begins at around the age of 3 years. Can we make another use of Klein to explain this 'late' onset of racial awareness? There are two lines of possible resolution.

First, Klein does leave a space for the external to impact on the internal and *change it fundamentally*. She allows the outside to penetrate and impress itself on the inside, making changes in the unconscious *structure* of the psyche.[13] It is true that the changes that she is referring to are always benign ones, that of the external moderating the death instinct and so on. But what if one of the changes is a malign one? For example, for the racist structure of society to be incorporated and become part of the psyche. Although she never takes up this possibility, it seems reasonable and necessary to do so. In other words, as the child internalizes more of the world, the more racist it potentially becomes.

A second explanation for the late genesis of racialized awareness can be constructed from Klein's descriptions of the early life of the neonate. She says that all uncomfortable sensations, fears and frustrations are experienced by the infant as attacks by foreign and alien objects. The infant must give these objects some sort of shape, it must *imagine* them in some way. Klein suggests that the first object that the infant thinks is attacking it is the bad breast. Now we can try to extend Klein and postulate a two-stage projective process.

Initially, the infant projects its hostile objects and so creates the bad breast. But when the infant comes to realize that the breast that it has been hating is also the one that has been loving and providing, then it is stricken by guilt and sets about repairing the imagined damage – the depressive position. However, this does not always take place. Sometimes the task is felt to be too big for a variety of reasons – the predominance of the death instinct, too weak an ego from too much splitting and projection – and this results in the infant remaining in a primitive mode of functioning. At this point there are two possibilities

1   the infant continues to attack the breast and spirals into the vicious circle
2   the infant denies what it has done.

One way of denying is to project out the damaged and dangerous bad breast into some other object; in effect to hide it there. This other object could be the Other, the black. The Other is then experienced as dangerous on two counts: as a container of the bad breast, and as the container in which something shameful is being hidden, the knowledge of the injury one has caused the primary object.

If we follow this line then we would predict that although racisms are paranoid-schizoid mechanisms, they would start to manifest during and after the depressive position, which is actually the case, i.e. after the age of 3 years. We could go even further and say that in a racist society the depressive position is a pseudo-depressive position. The suggestion here is that in the depressive position, things appear to be more whole and wholesome at the level of the individual by virtue of the fact that the Other is utilized as a container at a societal level. Thus the individual comes to feel 'clean' as he or she fits in with the social norms. The hurts and violence continue, having been relocated at a higher level of organization in the social structure.

Using Fairbairn to think about racism

Fairbairn's theory inverts Freud and Klein on four critical counts. First, 'libido is object seeking and not pleasure-seeking' (Fairbairn 1943: 78). Second, aggression is not active automatically at birth, and only ever activated by frustration. Third, the infant is orientated towards the external world from the beginning, and that it is only driven inwards to first construct and then inhabit an internal world when difficulties arise in the external relationship. And finally, the Fairbairnian infant *begins* with whole-object relations, which get rendered into part-object relations following external-whole-object-relational difficulties. One can see then that where the Freudian and Kleinian infant moves from an internal world to an external world, and from part to whole objects, Fairbairn's infant moves from the external world to an internal one, and from whole to part objects. I would say that although Fairbairn's is an object-relations theory, it is an object relations that is grounded in an instinctivism: after all it is *libido* that is said to be object seeking. Nevertheless, Fairbairn's theory is sufficiently innovative to challenge many of the core concepts of the psychoanalytic theories of his predecessors.

The vicissitudes of aggression in the Fairbairnian schema – group formation

Fairbairn's description of group formation echoes that of Freud; both describe a two-component process with libido residing inside the group to cohese it, and aggression being cast outside it. However, the sequence followed by Fairbairn is different to Freud's and this in turn generates differing descriptions of racism.

Fairbairn allows aggression in two ways: out of the capacity to bite and as a consequence of frustrations in the libidinal relationship with the mother. This frustration and the consequent aggression then set off a chain of events which constitute his version of the developmental process. To cope with the frustration the infant internalizes a pre-ambivalent (whole) object, which it then splits and represses. As with Klein, it is an *object relation* that is split and repressed. The good pair is named the Libidinal Object and Ego and the bad pair is named the Rejected or anti-Libidinal Object and Ego. Both these pairs are repressed, leaving the Ideal Ego and the Ideal Object in consciousness. At a later stage these internal objects (particularly the bad ones) are evacuated and projected into the external world. Initially, the exciting object is projected onto the parent of the opposite gender, and the rejecting anti-libidinal object is projected onto the parent of the same gender.

The thing to note is that it is the nature of the anti-libidinal object to attack and aggress all libidinal relationships in the internal as well as the external world. Thus, the anti-libidinal object having come to reside *within* the family system, now threatens to destroy it by attacking the libidinized relationships through which it is constituted. So in order to protect the family from fragmentation, the aggression is projected again into a region outside the family into another equivalent structure – another family – leaving libido behind to 'bind' the family.

However, family structure is not only threatened by the presence of aggression, it is also threatened by the nature of libido acting in two 'directions', upwards and downwards. The tendency of libido is to be inclusive, and so it tends to expand and join up things 'and for the group to become correspondingly more comprehensive' (Fairbairn 1935: 238). This causes a movement upwards, for families to dissolve and cohese into clans, and later for clans to cohese into tribes and then nations. However, each structure, say the clan, is equally threatened by too much libido being bound up in the structure 'below', the family, which would work towards the fragmentation of the clan (ibid. 237) into a number of families.

To change the language a bit, all these dangers constitute a threat to a particular level of identity.

A Fairbairnian theory of racism[14]

So, once something becomes a 'whole' (i.e. parts are joined up by libido), then it is obliged to project out aggression in order to survive and retain the sense of 'wholeness'. In effect, it is a sequence in which hatred is deposited in a container called 'them' in order not just to protect, but to *manufacture* the 'us'. We can now say 'where libido is present, there aggression cannot be'. At least that is how it looks, but what has happened in fact is that the aggression has been projected outwards into another group. We can then say that the work of libido gives the appearance of dissolving aggression, whereas it has in fact displaced it elsewhere. This rendition begins to give us a pictorial representation of the manifestations of racism: aggression is seen to be present outside the boundaries of the designated 'us', and if this boundary is a racialized one then this aggression/hatred can be called racism. The argument can be summed up in a Fairbairnian formula: *racism begins where libido ends.*

In this theorization Fairbairn echoes an aspect from each of Freud's instinctual theories. From the first theory is the idea that the original aggression is 'innocent' of malice, and from the second theory the idea that a difference is used as a container to deposit the aggression.

'Natural' and 'artificial' groups – a deconstruction

Although, like Freud, Fairbairn naturalizes certain levels of grouping, the family, the clan, and so on, it seems to me that this model in fact lends itself well to a post-modernist rendering of groupings where things are much more fluid. Thus the level of grouping one 'fixes' at, is dependent on the outcome of an instinctual arithmetic between libido and aggression. There are echoes of Klein here. For her the relative amounts of life to death instinct determine the type of experiences one has. Similarly, in Fairbairn the relative strengths of libido to aggression will determine the grouping level at which they will resolve themselves into a state of equilibrium. Thus the grouping level would be of no particular significance in itself, it would be the consequence of an instinctual arithmetic. This way of thinking ascribes an arbitrariness to the grouping level at which the forces of libido and aggression come to rest. It is a version of the Freudian dictum that the object is the most variable thing about an instinct.

Fairbairn too says that there are two sorts of groups, natural and artificial. Natural groupings do not need a purpose, they just occur in nature. Meantime the artificial groupings are said to need a reason for their existence, and when the reason is no longer of significance, the grouping dissolves.

One of the ideas being posited in this book is that there are only the second kind of groups, and that whatever has the appearance of a naturalness, has to be examined and deconstructed. The attribution of naturalness will be a consequence of an ideology. We can catch a shadowy glimpse of ideology at work in this statement of Freud's 'the tendency which proceeds from the libido and which is felt by all living beings *of the same kind*, to combine in more and more comprehensive units' (Freud 1921: 118, italics added). What makes for a 'same kind'? When and how is it that we come to feel and say 'they are not our kind of people'? Fairbairn might answer that the level that the 'us' forms at is the outcome of the resolution of the forces of libido and aggression. But as we will see, the factors that determine where these levels are, are much more than biology.

Creating otherness

I shall put up a hypothesis here, which I will substantiate progressively through the book.

The purpose of the grouping is the critical element that drives the motivation for the grouping, and so is of more significance than the nature of the grouping itself.

In proposing this I am, in fact, following Fairbairn. His strategy has been to continually reverse Freud and Klein. Where they see causes he sees consequences. Fairbairn has moved the focus from the subject – the instinct itself – to the other end, to object relating. His criticism of Freud and Klein is that they mistake techniques for causes. He says that the vicissitudes of the instincts are not the cause of types of relationship, rather it is the desire to relate that utilizes the things called the instincts to achieve this end.

It seems to me that this change in focus from the apparent beginning of the process to its apparent end is helpful when it comes to the formation of groups. If we do not take a particular grouping level as a 'natural' one, then the question we are confronted with is 'what is driving the group to coalesce at a particular level?' The answer that will be proposed in Chapter 9 is that, in part it is dependent on the power relations and power struggles going on in the socio-political milieu. In brief, out of the pragmatics of the situation I will argue that the logic of the power relations in certain socio-political milieus drives towards a racializing tendency. The racializing process is a means of creating a grouping that is said to be 'of the same kind'. If it is 'of the same kind', then that is mistakenly taken to be an explanation in itself – both necessary and sufficient – for the existence of the grouping: it is seen and experienced as 'natural'.

It is now possible to say, with the help of Fairbairn, that racist hate is the displacement of the aggression from within a racialized 'us' into a racialized them. As we have seen, Fairbairn adds the intriguing dimension that the 'us' is threatened by both love and hate. Hate and aggression threatens the 'us' from within through fragmentation, and libido threatens the 'us' either by attaching itself to a lower level of organization (a version of splitting), or by absorption into a bigger 'us'. In summary, identity is threatened by hate towards the self and by love towards another.

These Fairbairnian formulations give us our first glimpse of an idea that will eventually be central to the arguments being developed. The idea is a reversal of the contention in which difference is said to be exploited in the service of projection; what the preceding discussion is beginning to suggest is that *projection is a way of generating difference*. In other words, rather than the Other being used as a container to carry evacuated aspects of the 'us', what is being said is that the impression of Otherness is *created* by the projection of these elements.

Desire and the forbidden

The fact that libido is continually seeking to extend its kingdom means that the work of aggression is constantly being undermined. So even as a part of the 'us' is hating the 'them', another part of the 'us' is seeking to join with 'them'. This, in itself, must evoke prodigious amounts of anxiety because here it is not hate that is the internal saboteur but love. This formulation goes some way to explaining the phenomenon in which the racialized object is simultaneously sexualized as well as hated. It also sheds light on the mythology that says that 'they' are the oversexed ones, and it is 'they' who want to have sex with 'us'. The theory suggests that this imputation of sexuality in the 'them' is a projection of something (libido) that belongs to the 'us'.

There is another avenue to be found in Fairbairn that leads us to the same territory to reinforce the ideas above. The way in is through this statement 'The Oedipus situation must exercise a profound influence upon all socio-logical developments' (Fairbairn 1935: 242). The Oedipus situation, as envisaged by Fairbairn, is the projection of the anti-libidinal object onto the parent of the *same* gender, and the exciting object projected onto the parent of the *different* gender. This leads to the startling assertion that difference will be found to be attractive, which is the reverse of the preceding argu-ments. So in keeping with his formulations of the Oedipal drama, let us assume that the exciting object is projected onto the Other, who by defini-tion is 'different'. Fairbairn calls this a paranoid externalization. Now, it will be remembered that in the internal world, the anti-libidinal ego attacks the internal libidinal relationship. It would follow then that anti-libidinal ego would also attack the externalization of the exciting object, i.e. it would attack the Other *because it is enticing*. This formulation seems to be quite promising as it starts to weave in some of the complexities of forbidden desire, as well as explaining how and why something exciting should be hated and attacked.

So this is the predicament. The exciting object, which was initially a part of the internalized bad object, is projected onto the Other. The different relationships that the two repressed egos have with this object complicate matters: the libidinal ego desires the Other, and the anti-libidinal ego attacks it because it contains the tantalizing. The split inner world is maintained as a closed system. It is repressed and projected onto the external world. Thus the external situation is experienced in the light of internal (bad) object relations. In other words the Other is experienced not so much for themselves, but in terms of what has been projected onto them – things from the inner world.

One of the aims of therapy is to breach this closed system of the internal world, to allow in the reality principle. The outcome would then presumably be that the Other will be experienced for themselves, freed of the projection from the internal world. Thus the anti-libidinal ego would not have need to attack them, as they are no longer a repository for the exciting object.

Using Winnicott to think about racism

Winnicott is of the school that we are born good and made bad, and this idea allies him with Fairbairn, in contradistinction to Freud and Klein. Winnicott is famed for saying that at birth there is no such thing as a baby, there is only the nursing couple. From this we might suppose that the first note of his infant developmental theory is struck by relatedness. It is, but only in a particular sense, because at the beginning of life there is not yet an Other to relate to. Winnicott's infant begins existence in a 'oneness', an unexcited state of quietude, which he calls the Being mode. The elements that are operative here are the female elements. In the beginning there is no difference because all is me. Within this quietude there arises the beginnings of a movement. 'Here is a baby with developing instinct tension. There develops an expectancy, a state of affairs in which the infant is prepared to find something somewhere, not knowing what' (Winnicott 1988: 100). This movement is the basis of the Doing mode, and is the kernel around which the True Self forms. The movement itself also constitutes the basis from which a 'me' starts to differentiate from a 'not-me'. The beginning of the movement is the me, and at the end of the movement, the thing that it meets is the not-me. But sometimes the movement is initiated in the environment. In which case the environment impinges on the infant, and the infant is forced to react to something outside itself. One could say that here what is constructed is Environment and Not-Environment. This is the Being-Done-To mode, and is the basis of the False Self. Thus Winnicottian developmental theory consists of the interplay of three processes – being, doing, and being-done-to. It is of some significance that these are descriptions of interpersonal dynamics which only later become descriptions of intrapersonal states.

Other elements of his developmental theory will be introduced as they are needed in the following discussions. In order to begin using Winnicott to discuss racism, Winnicottian theory is divided into two parts, one located in an individualism and the other concerning groups and transitional phenomena. Once more, because Winnicott does not speak of racism, I will track the genesis of aggression, destructivity and hate in his schema, and take racism to be specific racialized versions of these.

Six models of aggression and hatred in Winnicott-the-instinctivist

Winnicott derives aggression in several contradictory ways. In some of his models aggression and destruction are given an a priori status, in other models they are derived from 'experience'. However, he *never* allows hate to be primary. Envy too is never primary according to him, and is only possible once there is an inside to be contrasted with an outside, 'an empty' with 'a full'. In Winnicott-the-instinctivist, when hate and envy appear in adult life, it is almost always as a consequence of some developmental failure, and not because of any a priori status. This Winnicott would say that racial hatred is a pathological phenomenon and a sign of something gone wrong. He strongly asserts the unified nature of humanity.

> Human nature does not change . . . what is true about human nature in London today is also true in Tokyo. . . . It is true for whites and blacks, for giants and pygmies, for the children of the . . . Cape Canaveral scientist and the children of the Australian aboriginal.
>
> (Winnicott 1963: 93)

He now has to explain why, if we all have the same human nature, one group should virulently hate another. On what is this hatred based? In fact Winnicott tends not to talk so much about hatred but levels of aggression and destructivity. It is possible to delineate six distinct instinctivist trajectories for the emergence of aggression and destructivity in his work.

The first of these is a description of aggression as a covert attempt to get help. Here aggressive acts are understood as an attempt to provoke the environment to look after one, and so set in motion a healing and reparative process.

The second similar dynamic is found in Winnicott's version of the Oedipus Complex. Winnicott says that guilt is inherent in all triangular relationships. This gives rise to the difficulty that one feels guilty and has a sense of having done wrong, and yet one does not know what this is. Because one cannot reach the cause of this guilt then it can never properly be assuaged. One solution is to commit a crime and then be punished for it, and by this measure gain some temporary relief.

The third aetiology concerns the need to feel real. Motility, the physiological capacity and urge to move is used to drive the erotic instinct. This motility is the precursor of aggression. When motility is used in this way *then* there forms a fusion of the instincts which is the basis of the True Self. Here, aggression is put in the service of the erotic instinct. Now, only a part of the motility gets used in this way and so some is 'left over'. This 'unfused motility . . . *needs to find opposition*. Crudely, it needs something to push against, unless it is to remain unexperienced and [so] a threat to well being' (Winnicott 1950–1955: 212, italics added). This opposition is provided by the environment – as it inevitably impinges on the infant. But when the impingement from the environment is severe then the infant is forced to utilize its motility defensively, and this time the erotic is drawn in secondarily. Now the normal fusion has been reversed to form an 'eroticization of aggressive elements' (ibid. 213). One outcome of this is that 'the individual feels real only when destructive and ruthless' (ibid. 213). A dire consequence of this is that not only does the individual seek opposition to feel real, he or she actually *creates* opposition so that aggression/motility may be discharged.

Unused motility also features in the fourth schema, a malfunction in the developmental mechanism called the benign circle. When the infant reaches the depressive position it discovers that the object mother on whom it has vented the instincts and the environmental mother are one and the same. The infant feels concern and eventually makes some reparative gesture. A consequence is that the infant is now a little less frightened of its instincts: they may cause damage but that can be put right. In Winnicott's words 'a benign circle is set up which forms the basis for infant life over a considerable period' (1988: 72). However, if the benign circle breaks down for whatever reason, then one is left with a residue of untransformed aggression. One possible consequence is that the individual inhibits their aggression resulting in depression. Another possibility is that once again external opposition is sought out to discharge the aggression against, resulting in an asocial individual.

The fifth mechanism delineates the emergence of aggressivity during the healing process. In one version of ill health (introversion) the child defensively keeps good objects in the internal world and bad objects in the external. With recovery, the child turns towards the external world where it is faced with 'an external world full of persecutors, and at this point in his recovery the child regularly becomes aggressive' (Winnicott 1950–1955: 208).

The sixth explanation for the manifestation of aggression is derived from the internalization of quarrelling parents. In this scenario it is the bad that is internalized in order to gain control over it. Winnicott describes several possible consequences

1   the internalized bad relationship can take over and the child becomes aggressive as though possessed by the quarrelling parents
2   the child might engineer quarrelling around him in order to have a place into which to project his feeling of badness
3   the child can attack the bad within by attempting suicide or becoming accident prone.

Having outlined these mechanisms through which aggression and destruction are generated, we might then say that racialized versions of these constitute explanations of particular instances of aggression towards racialized others. However, these mechanisms say nothing about the processes of racialization nor do they say anything about group hatreds. It seems to me these mechanisms are possible explanations of why particular individuals might be behaving in hateful ways to others because of their particular individual developmental histories. As Winnicott says 'if society is in danger, it is not because of man's aggressiveness but because of the repression of personal aggressiveness *in individuals*' (ibid. 204, italics added).

Group formation: the name of the enemy

With his theory of groups, Winnicott allows aggression a new route into existence. This time it is not to do with the instincts but with a notion of identity. Here, the first aggressive note is struck at the beginnings of existence itself – at the very moment in which a group is created. A group is a spatial structure, that is something with a boundary, an inside and an outside.

Winnicott says that groups form using a similar process to the formation of individuals. In individual development, the first moment of self-consciousness, the first 'I AM' moment occurs at the point when the infant gathers up and integrates elements of itself. He says 'the newly integrated infant is . . . the first *group*. Before this stage there is only a primitive pre-group formation' (Winnicott 1965: 149, italics added). At the moment of the formation (one might say creation) of individuals and groups, there also comes into existence a paranoia. 'A group is an I AM achievement, and it is a dangerous achievement, [because] the repudiated external world comes back at the new phenomenon and attacks from all quarters and in every conceivable way' (ibid. 149). In other words, there is a fear that the elements that have been excluded from belonging will attack the 'me' or the 'us'.

How does the infant know which elements on its experiential horizon belong to itself, to the me, and which to the not-me? Presumably it comes to 'know' as a consequence of the uses of its motility as discussed above. However, when it comes to group formation *per se*, then it is not at all self-evident which elements 'belong together' and which do not. I would say that it is this uncertainty about belongingness that gives rise to the paranoia.

Given that the 'us' may be formed out of an amalgam of any number of attributes, giving rise to an infinitude of types of 'us', we are always faced with the question as to which elements are to be included and which excluded. The answer to this question must be dependent on the reasons for the formation of a particular sort of 'us' over and above another. Where does one group begin and another end? Winnicott does not address these questions. Nevertheless Winnicott is saying something very interesting about the consequences of group formation. He is saying that in the very moment a group names itself, it also names for itself what it fears – the anti-name. If 'Serbian' is the designated name, then one will fear those designated as 'not-Serbian'. We can see that the multicultural notion of 'equal but different' is beginning to be problematized. So, according to this line of thinking, if the name of the group is a racialized one then the group will inevitably fear a racialized other, and fear, as is well known, is often a trigger for hostility and violence. Whilst this existential formulation is a very promising one, as yet it is asocial in that hostility is said to be of necessity triggered by the mere structure of existence, i.e. we cannot not form into an 'us'. But before the social can be built into the theorization, we will require the presence of Foulkes, Elias and Matte-Blanco. At that point Winnicott's theory of transitional phenomena will be found to have a critical role.

In the meantime we can say the following: given the varieties of names it is possible to have at any one moment, then group identity is bound to be precarious. This vulnerability is countered by anchoring it in some aspect of external or internal reality, for example belief systems, geography, history, 'race' and skin colour. The anchor in part always contains elements of rationalization, and so the boundary needs to be bolstered continually, and particularly when there is danger of collapse or merger.

Summary

The writings of the four psychoanalysts either made no mention of race, or took it to be a self-evident category of nature. Their writings did not address racism directly, so their theories of hate and violence were used to make *inferences* about possible theories of racism that were consistent with their world views. In all of the four theories racism is to be understood as a subset of revulsion, hatred and violence in general.

Each of Freud's instinct theories gave up a distinct theory of the relationship between hatred and difference. In one, difference triggers hatred, and in the other difference was used to deposit a pre-existing hatred. He also said that there was no natural connection between instincts and their objects, and that they became attached to an instinct over time by virtue of repeatedly *satisfying* that instinct. His work threw up three interesting sets of questions.

1   Given that there are an infinite number of differences, why is one particular difference more likely to trigger hatred than another? Or in terms of the second theory, why is one difference deemed to be a better receptacle in which to store hatred than another?

2   If established groups cohere by evacuating their aggression into marginal groups, how is it decided where one group begins and another ends? An answer that Freud gives to this last question is that there are in fact natural groups, and so their boundaries are self-evident. This then allows us to ask the third question.

3   What makes one group natural and another not?

All in all we can perhaps bundle together all these concerns into one: just *what* is a group?

These questions are extremely useful ones and will be taken up progressively as they will help us lay bare some of the structures of racism.

Moving on to Klein. Her instinctual object-relations theory offered five possible aetiologies of racism, each of which is a vicissitude of the death instinct. It was argued that in a racist society the depressive position was a pseudo-depressive position, because real reparation to the damaged (white) object had not taken place; following the logic of Kleinian theory, it was proposed that knowledge of the damaged white object was denied and projected into the black object; from this it would follow that the black object is simultaneously hated and distanced.

Fairbairn's work inverted the instinctivist theories of Freud and Klein. He said the mistake they made was to assume that the aim of the instinct was more important than the object. He argued the reverse, to say that it was the object relation that called forth the instincts in particular shapes and forms. He concluded that they mistook *techniques* for *causes*.

As far as a Fairbairnian theory of racism goes, it was found in his elaboration of the Freudian theory of groups. Although Fairbairn based his theory of groups on the outcome of instinctual arithmetic, his work was used to undermine the notion of a 'natural' group. The logic of his theory suggested a new definition of racism: *racism begins where libido ends*. Fairbairn's idea that the instincts were secondary to the object relation was extended to say that the *purpose* of the grouping would determine at which level the conflicting instinctual forces would find their resolution. The most exciting element to emerge from this reading of Fairbairn is the proposal that (paraphrasing him) *difference is a technique, not a cause*. In other words difference is activated to achieve particular ends. This in turn led to the idea that at times projection is used in the service of differentiation, i.e. in order to *create* difference.

Winnicott's corpus was divided into two, an instinctivist one and a relational one to give each a greater internal coherence. Winnicott-the-instinctivist has a much more benign view of the human condition than

Freud and Klein. His view accords with Fairbairn's to say that whenever aggression and hostility make their appearance, it is always a secondary phenomenon born out of frustration. What was particularly intriguing was the idea that existence inevitably precipitated aggression. He shows how precarious group identity always is, and the only thing that it really has to hold itself together is a name. It was argued that the name of the group and the name of the enemy were intimately bound together; that the name of the group named the enemy and that the group needed the name of the enemy to give itself existence.

Notes

1 Whether this is a legitimate step or not is another matter, but this sort of move is commonplace in psychoanalytic discourse.

2 In the discussions that follow we will be obliged to (temporarily) accept the notion of race as a reality, because this was Freud's view. We can glean this from innumerable statements made by Freud on any number of subjects, for example 'Each individual . . . has a share in numerous group minds – those of his race, of his class, of his creed, of his nationality, etc.' (Freud 1921: 129). Here, Freud is being careful to include, and differentiate, all the levels of human existence that he thinks exist: these are those of biology (race), economics (class), spirituality (creed) and politics (nationality).

3 I have described the logical contradictions inherent in sliding from a theory of minor differences to one of major differences in Dalal 1997a, 1998.

4 'A group is impulsive, changeable and irritable. It is led almost exclusively by the unconscious. . . . It cannot tolerate any delay between its desire and the fulfilment of what it desires. It has a sense of omnipotence; the notion of impossibility disappears for the individual in a group' (Freud 1921: 77). 'A group is extraordinarily credulous and open to influence, it has no critical faculty, and the improbable does not exist for it. . . . The feelings of a group are always very simple and very exaggerated. So that a group knows neither doubt nor uncertainty. It goes directly to extremes; if a suspicion is expressed, it is instantly changed into an incontrovertible certainty: a trace of antipathy is turned into furious hatred' (ibid. 78).

5 The illusion 'that the leader loves all of the individuals equally and justly. But this is simply an idealistic remodelling of the state of affairs in the primal horde, where all of the sons knew that they were equally *persecuted* by the primal father, and *feared* him equally' (Freud 1921: 124–125).

6 I have found one reference to the 'coloured races', that appears in the context of her description of a child's phantasy life 'For Fritz numerals in general are people who live in a very hot country. They correspond to the coloured races, while letters are the white ones' (Klein 1923: 67). She does not elaborate how or why these associations should have arisen.

7 The penis, the vagina, the primal scene, the breast, etc.

8 There is the more general question of whether it is legitimate to take the structure of an element from infant development, and apply it to relations between adult people in later life. The task here, however, is to use the theory in its own terms.

9 This happens because as the good internal object gets increasingly stronger, it is less likely to be overwhelmed by the bad.

10 A version of the following discussion appeared in Dalal 1997a.
11 For Klein, the Oedipal phase occurs in the first 6 months of life.
12 Which might not necessarily be how Klein would think of it.
13 'when the infantile neurosis has run its course. . . . the balance in the fusion of the life and death instincts . . . has in some ways altered. This implies important changes in unconscious processes, that is to say, *in the structure of the superego and in the structure and domain of the unconscious (as well as conscious) parts of the ego*' (Klein 1952: 88, italics added).
14 A version of this discussion appeared in Dalal 1998.

Chapter 3

Peeking into the consulting room[1]

This chapter serves as a contrast to the previous one on at least two counts: if the last chapter focused on theory and the past, this chapter will focus on practice and also make the inquiry more contemporaneous. This chapter asks questions regarding how contemporary psychoanalysts think about, and understand the subjects of race, prejudice and racism when they make an appearance in the consulting room.

But before we proceed on to the subject itself, two questions about methodology need to be addressed. First, the conventions of clinical discourse make the individual case study paramount. Whilst this method throws up certain kinds of useful information to do with the *particulars* of an individual history, other existential aspects escape this kind of individualized analysis. To explain: racism and prejudice are group phenomena, they grip large numbers of people at one and the same time. As we noted in Chapter 1, whilst racism is a group phenomenon it does not operate on all individuals homogeneously, thus there are always variations with instances going against the general trend. It is my contention that certain facets of racism and prejudice *only* make their presence known when the field of view is a broad and general one, and that the device of focusing on the particular is a means of negating its presence. Thus any examination of racism or prejudice has to include a *number* and range of the items so that the generalized norm might come into view. Thus this chapter consists of an examination of a collection of papers.

Next, given the variety of psychoanalyses and plethora of texts, where should one look for material that properly reflects the 'culture' of psychoanalysis? I was fortunate to be provided with a ready made sample, this being the set of journals found on the CD Rom[2] published under the auspices of the main psychoanalytic institutes in Britain and the USA. These then are the establishment's choice of journals, and so are validated by them. In the main, these journals also happen to be read, and contributed to, by practising clinicians.

Thus the articles in these journals provide a window onto the conversations that take place in the psychoanalytic community, and in particular the clinical community. To this group of journals I have added one other, *The British Journal of Psychotherapy*, as it serves the same purposes for those designated as psychotherapists in the British context.

* * *

To begin with I will give an account of the metapsychologies implicit in these papers as this will shed light on how 'differences' are thought about. This will be followed by grouping the papers according to the kind of explanation that they give for prejudice and racism, for example Oedipus, envy, etc. Next, I will give some evidence for the existence of racism in psychoanalytic discourse. In what follows I will not detail every pertinent paper as I have done this elsewhere (Dalal 2001a), but I will use one or two examples to illustrate each of the points.

Metapsychologies: human nature

Despite the variety of psychoanalyses, the overwhelming majority of the papers treat the topics of racism and prejudice as a symptom, that is, they think of it as the *effect* and expression of internal psychological dynamics. These types of formulations are due in some degree to the metapsychological foundations that permeate positivist psychoanalytic theories. In this world view there is a categorical split inserted between the internal world and the external world, between the individual and the group, and between biology and society. Additionally, the first term of each dichotomy is prioritized over the second – the internal over the external, the individual over the group, and the biological over the social. Another facet of this metapsychology is the view that that which takes place in the external world is thought of as an outcome and *expression* of what is taking place in the internal psychological world. Thus the 'real' thing is the latent content; the manifest is a happenstance – the shape that the 'real' happens to take. In sum, the psychoanalytic model found in these papers is a surface–depth model, in which depth is valued over surface.

At this point it will be helpful to tabulate the dichotomies to show their relation to each other (see Figure 3.1).

Norbert Elias has shown that these associations are not inevitable, but have been generated over centuries by the struggles between figurations of

External	Group	Social	Manifest	Surface
Internal	Individual	Biological	Latent	Depth

Figure 3.1 The relationship of dichotomies

power in what was to become Europe. Thus the conflations and associations between these dichotomies are not peculiar to psychoanalysis, but are found there because they permeate the larger consensual world view within which psychoanalysis is located. He says that in certain cases (e.g. the brain within the skull)

> we can say clearly what is the container and what is the contained. . . . But if the same figures of speech are applied to personality structures they become inappropriate . . . there is no structural feature of man that justifies our calling one thing the core of man and another the shell.
>
> (Elias 1994: 212)

As will become apparent, the thrust of this belief system results in the external manifestations of racism and prejudice being treated as the 'manifest', and therefore requiring less attention than that which is thought to lie below it, the 'latent'. One can see then how it is that this way of thinking comes to view racism and prejudice almost entirely as *effects*, and so seeks to look for the *causes* within biology (the vicissitudes of the instincts) and *individual* development (the vicissitudes of the developmental process). Because the movement in much psychoanalytic theory is from the inside to the outside, much is made of projection in these papers and little or nothing is said of introjection. In the main these papers argue that some internal malfunction causes internal distress which is then projected out in the shape of racism or prejudice, *in order to ameliorate the internal distress*.

The point is borne out by Gordon (1993) who researched psychotherapy training organizations in London to find that on the whole they took little or no cognizance of issues of race, colour and the like, suggesting that much clinical practice proceeds as though it were taking place in a sociological vacuum.

Any discussion about prejudice or racism *between* groups presupposes a theorization of the nature of a group: where and how does one group end and another begin? Clearly differences have a critical role to play in the process of differentiation, but what is the nature of these differences? In the main these papers do not give thought to how groups are manufactured and not just found, which leads them to speak of races, ethnicities or cultures unquestioningly as self-evident, universal, natural categories, but in idiosyncratic ways: not only do the number of races vary, so do the attributes used to define the so-called races – colour, geography, religion, culture, etc. The external social world is portrayed in simplistic terms, whilst the portraits of the internal world tend to be much more intricate. This difference is an outcome of the values allocated to the external and internal in psychoanalytic discourse.

Not only does the confusion about what constitutes a sufficiently relevant and significant difference play a critical role in all the papers, but so

External	Group	Social	Manifest	Surface	Difference
Internal	Individual	Biological	Latent	Depth	Similarity

Figure 3.2 In which the similarity between individuals is emphasized

does the question of where the difference is located. The majority of the papers may be divided between two belief systems. One of these says that at our deepest levels we are the same with our differences created by culture, and the other says that at our deepest levels we are different – that is unique – and it is culture that makes people the same. The following sections take each in turn.

We are all the same (yet different): multiculturalism in psychoanalysis

The ethos of the papers that locate similarity in the domain of the biological, the individual and the internal, can be broadly described saying that whatever the appearances are, at bottom we are all the same. This viewpoint is represented in Figure 3.2.

But now there is the question of the nature of this sameness. In some psychoanalytic renditions this sameness is said to be a primitive layer wherein one will find all that is destructive and malevolent in humankind. This represents the Hobbesian view of human nature. On other occasions this biological domain of similarity is perceived in a more benign light. This latter view is broadly akin to a multiculturalist philosophy in which differences between cultures are thought to be the source of misunderstanding between groups which in turn are said to set off hatreds between them. The set of papers that focus on the contents of cultures underline the importance of a therapy being culturally sensitive. Whilst this is a commendable aim, they do tend to homogenize the internals of each culture, and this leads to problems in their formulations. Here are two examples of papers that make lumpen generalizations about cultural groups.

The first is Davidson who says that the East is a shame culture whilst the West is a guilt culture, the outcome of which is that 'Socio-politically the West is ideologically democratic with much freedom to openly criticize authorities. In the East authorities may be influenced only through polite suggestion, indirect statements or manipulation' (1987: 664). One can witness the conflation of dichotomies taking place in this formulation: *shame* is a *public* process and therefore its domain is the *external* and the *group*, whilst *guilt* is a *private* process and therefore its domain is the *internal* and the *individual*. The implication of this formulation is that people in the East would try to get away with as much as is possible as long as they are not found out and so shamed. Those in the West meanwhile, police themselves internally and behave properly whether they will be found out or not. If someone from the West acts in a criminal way, then it is a *particular* individual that is doing so, whereas if someone from the East acts in a criminal way then they do so because it is part of their *general* ethos of life. There is also the additional problem of treating the whole of the East as *one* culture, and the West as *one* other culture.

The second example is Traub-Werner who says that within 'the context of group psychology the Jew is experienced as a threat because in an indefinable way he is different, has defied oppression throughout centuries in spite of cruel persecution, and has *refused to assimilate*' (1984: 407, italics added). There are many things to be said about this. First is the moot point of whether Jews exclude themselves or whether they are excluded. Second, the sentence structure reveals that the author is at the centre of this 'group psychology' (implicitly gentile), and its normativeness to him means that it does not have to be described further. Third, the Jewish group has been homogenized; many Jews have quite consciously assimilated. The notion of assimilation cannot be answered without taking up the question, what is being assimilated? What *is* Jewishness? The fact that Traub-Werner says that the difference is indefinable gives a clue to the problematic nature of what is being described – indefinable yet somehow indelible.

Devereux (1953) too follows the notion that deep down people are the same, but then uses this to build an opposing argument wherein the content of cultures count for little. In his model the nature–nurture division resides *in* the psyche; a universal, biological part that is said to be prior to culture, and an acculturated differentiated part that is formed through sublimation. He then says that personality disorders are drawn from the universal, presocial part of the psyche and therefore are the same in all cultures. Thus the really *deep* psychological work conducted in this region has no need to know of a person's cultural configurations because the region is prior to culture; this work he calls psychoanalysis. Meanwhile the shallower work of engaging with the effects of particular cultures takes place in the social part of the psyche, and this work he calls cross-cultural psychotherapy. Notice the status allocated to each of the tasks by the use of the terms psycho*analysis* and psycho*therapy*.

We are all unique: essentialism in psychoanalysis

Those who propose that one's true nature is *unique*, something each individual is born with, argue that to preserve this internal sanctum, the external has to be resisted 'if the demands of the biological forces within the

External	Group	Social	Manifest	Surface	*Similarity*
Internal	Individual	Biological	Latent	Depth	*Difference*

Figure 3.3 In which the uniqueness of each individual is emphasized

individual are denied, much of individuality goes, and we are only what our culture makes us' (Axelrad 1960: 184). In this and other similar accounts, difference is a good thing and similarity is a bad thing. This is because the processes of socialization are said to work in the direction of making people 'the same' which consequently erodes the differences which constitute the unique true self (Figure 3.3).

This kind of thinking leads to the suggestion that individuals behave badly to others because they have been unable to resist being taken over by an external ideation – an ideation that is not their true (internal) belief. There are two sorts of explanations given for why this happens to certain individuals: the instinctivists propose that people succumb to the external because of a constitutional weakness to do with the instincts, and the formulations grounded in relational theories say the reason is to do with some developmental malfunction that has left them in a weakened state and so unable to resist the external.

Although versions of these belief systems are to be found in all the articles discussed in this chapter, the point will not be laboured. In what follows the articles are grouped according to the kinds of explanation they offer for prejudice and racism.

Models of racism and prejudice

From differentiation to difference to hatred

Birth, the first separation, is the kernel around which some theories of racism and prejudice are formed. The main idea behind these theorizations can be summarized in this formula: contemporary *differences* are said to be hated because of the consequences of an earlier *differentiation*.

One such attempt is that by Tan (1993). There are two steps to his argument. First, he says that difference is difficult to bear and so one works towards making the self and the object the same by denying differences between them. He then proceeds to define racism as the 'denial of difference', and this in turn leads into problematic waters. It seems to me that the denial of difference is not the racism but the *defence against racism*. All the examples of racism that I am aware of consist of an inability to accept *similarity*. What the racist seeks to do is to reinforce difference, and indeed turn any difference into an absolute one.

Splitting and projection

Other psychoanalytic texts make much use of the trinity, splitting, repression and projection to 'explain' racism. For example, Timmi begins by acknowledging that psychoanalysis has not taken into account historical and social reality when addressing racism. But thereafter the paper makes no further mention of these elements and very early on reveals its true thinking 'racism develops out of internal paranoid schizoid splits' (1996: 183). Timmi places the source of racist feeling in the psychotic and primitive layers of the mind. The basis of this, he says, is the same as that used by the infant who cannot bear the thought of being separate from mother. This then is magically made the basis of racism. Magically, because the two themes are never actually connected, they are just put together. Look at these two concurrent sentences

> [the infant] uses phantasies of controlling the object at the same time as identifying with it, in order to ward off painful feelings of separateness and difference. Cultural and particularly racial differences are in this respect fertile areas for projections.
>
> (ibid. 184)

To spell it out he begins by saying that the infant cannot be separate from its mother so identifies with her. He then says racial differences are fertile areas for projections. Whilst there is truth in both statements what have they to do with each other? The second statement is a non-sequitur.

Stranger anxiety

Basch-Kahre (1984) says that feelings of aversion *inevitably* arise in the transference and countertransference when the analyst and analysand are from different backgrounds. The basis of this is said to be found in infantile stranger anxiety, which is said to arise in the following way. The appearance of the father's face represents a puncturing of the fantasy of endless symbiosis with the mother. The baby hates the father and defends against the realization of the reality by 'not recognizing' the father, i.e. by making him unknown and therefore a stranger. This repressed memory is reactivated with the appearance of any strangers, which results in the old hatred towards the father being projected onto the stranger. Basch-Kahre says 'This happens when confronted with people and cultures in which we can discover no similarity with ourselves' (1984: 62). She defines strangeness as a difference in socio-cultural background, and by this she means 'when we can discover no similarity with ourselves'. Clearly this is an impossibility – that there is 'no similarity' between analyst and analysand. We have to ask of the analyst a deeper question – how does the analyst manage the feat of experiencing 'no similarity'?

What this sort of analysis leaves out is the fact that strangeness *per se* does not inevitably evoke fear and hostility. A stranger knocking unexpectedly at the door will elicit quite different associations and emotions depending on whether 'the stranger' is a young black man, or a white man in a suit. It will also depend on who is opening the door and where the door is. All of this is to say that the socio-political context cannot be meaningfully left out of the analysis.

Oedipus and envy

Many of the papers make the failure of a proper resolution to the Oedipal complex the basis of prejudice and racism. One such is Bird (1957) who provides a novel theory of prejudice. The essence of his thesis is that the mechanism of prejudice is the same as that found in the Oedipal situation, where the attack on the desired parent is displaced onto the less desired one. Thus

> the cause . . . of prejudice should be looked for not only in the relationship existing between the subject and the object of prejudice, but *mainly* the cause should be looked for in an unsuspected rivalrous relationship to a third party – a more fortunate or desired third party.
>
> (ibid. 494, italics added)

This then leads Bird to assert that prejudice is a middle-group phenomenon and its basis is envy. The sequence is as follows. A middle group feels inferior and envious towards a better-off group. This envy is repressed and projected onto a lower group. This lower group is now experienced as enviously desiring and is hated for it. Bird concludes 'the oppressed race is attacked, for something it has not done, by a race which really has nothing against it, using a hatred it does not own' (ibid. 502). He is saying that Jew and Negro are not really hated at all. They are incidental to the main play – the middle and upper classes – which is where the real relationship lies.

Bird concludes that successful people will not be prejudiced because they will not have anyone to envy. Similarly, those who have no hope or ambition will also not have envy and therefore have no need of the mechanism of prejudice. He also suggests that to be available to be used as an object of prejudice, the group must

> harbour envious wishes and active drives to better itself. *There is no prejudice against people who know their place* . . . Negroes who engage in personal-service employment, *who devote themselves to their employer, and who show no signs of ambition, are not held in any way as objects of prejudice.*
>
> (ibid. 507, italics added)

Oedipus and difference

Chasseguet-Smirgel (1990) says that the basis of racist ideology is found in a universal structure she calls the archaic matrix of the Oedipus complex. She suggests that there is a primary wish in *every* newborn to strip the mother's body of its contents in order to merge with it. The contents of the mother's body are akin to difference – the thing that gets in the way of becoming one and *the same* with mother. Thus the archaic matrix is a resistance to differentiation, and when in this state then one hates all things different to the self. Over time, through the developmental processes, the archaic resolution comes to be supplanted with the 'proper' resolution of the Oedipus complex in which difference is allowed to exist and be utilized.

Chasseguet-Smirgel then makes a causative link between the archaic matrix and Nazi ideology. She says that the structure of the Nazi ideology is the wish for the body of the German people (the Aryans) 'to become one with the body of the Mother (the German homeland, the whole earth' (1990: 171). For this merging to proceed, the body of the German people has to be made pure, homogenized 'in order to form a single body, its constituent cells must be identical, purified of all foreign elements liable to impair its homogeneity' (ibid. 171).

The problem with this as with other universalistic and individualistic explanations is that it does not explain the *group* phenomenon of genocide. For this sort of theory to work, it has to be the case that a whole nation of individuals fall prey to the archaic matrix at one and the same time, and at a later time simultaneously complete the proper resolution of the complex. Further, the argument takes as a given what is meant by '*the* German people'. It does not engage with the mechanisms through which certain constituent groups *come to be defined* as foreign and not-German.

The individual and the group

The other main explanation for prejudice and racism is located in an essentialist model of the relationship between individuals and groups. The basis of the argument is the belief that groups are primitive in themselves, and when individuals get into groups then they behave in these primitive ways because they are part of (primitive) group culture. An example is found in Zilboorg who says 'There is a psychopathology of prejudice, an individual psychopathology which is put in the service of an unjust, immoral, but apparently normal, or at any rate nonpathological social reaction' (1947: 307). In other words he is saying that an *individual sickness* is used in the service of a *normal social phenomenon*. Another example is found in Traub-Werner, who seeks to marry the findings of the social sciences with psychoanalytic observations and says

> The *content* is culturally bound and will determine 'who I hate', while
> the defensive structure of the *process* will answer the question 'why I
> hate' . . . the interaction between the individual psychopathology and
> group psychology, will determine the *form* that the process takes, i.e.
> 'how I hate'.
>
> (1984: 408)

The critical slip, which is easy enough to miss, is the elision of 'individual
psycho*pathology* and group *psychology*'. This is one of the powerful effects
of conflating the individual–group dichotomy with the nature–nurture
dichotomy. Prejudice is made the property of particular individuals where
it is said to be a pathological phenomenon because of faulty development.
However, the prejudice expressed at a group level is not pathological but
said to be normal because *group nature* is bad.

The problem of the external, and the 'underlying' internal

In tune with the conflation of dichotomies presented earlier, these papers
give more weight to the internal than the external. Whilst there is nothing
untoward in this *per se*, what is extraordinary is the degree and number of
ways in which this happens.

First, many of these papers are unable to give the external social world
any role in the *structuring* of distress. For instance Basch-Kahre says that
the explanation for her black African patient's 'deep feeling of being worthless whenever the theme of the stranger was brought up, . . . [was found
in] his experience of weaning and with his oedipal conflict' (1984: 65).
The fact that the patient was unable to advance in his job was explained by
this feeling of inferiority, in other words the state of his internal world.
Whilst his particular experience of weaning no doubt played a significant
role in the structuring of his feelings of worthlessness, no space is given to
the possibility even that *components* of his feelings of worthlessness might
also have to do with particular experiences of living as a black man in
Sweden.

Second, engagements with the external are denigrated either as an acting
out, or read as an expression of pathology. For example, Myers (1977)
understands his black female patient's increasing involvement with black
militant groups as a flight from her rage with him. It seems to me however,
that the patient's *new* capacity for involvement with Black militant groups
is in itself a sign of increasing health and self-esteem. Ironically, Myers
reports that the patient's self-esteem does indeed increase following this
involvement as revealed in her dreams. However, Myers is unable or
unwilling to give *any* credit to the patient's involvement in the external for
the changes in her; he ends up saying that her increase in self-esteem was in

part 'real' because of the analytic work, and in part 'false' because it was due to the *repression* of her 'degraded black self-representation' (1977: 70).

Third, the introduction of certain social facts (such as colour) into the therapy by the analysand, tend to be experienced by the analyst as resistance (e.g. Goldberg *et al.* 1974). Myers understands his black patient's doubts and suspicion towards him 'as a transference resistance' (1977: 165). In saying such a thing Myers is implying that the suspicions of a black patient towards his white analyst have no basis in social reality, or that if they have such a basis they are irrelevant to the analytic project which deals somehow in exclusively internal matters.

Schachter and Butts (1968) say that there is a 'real' transference which is to do with significant others, and there are the effects of racial stereotypes. They go on to say that the presence of colour or 'racial' difference in the patient's material is a transference resistance to expressing instinctual material; their interpretations, therefore, are designed to dissolve this difference so that the 'real' analytic work can take place. The general view in these papers is that the increasing absence of colour from the patient's material is an indicator of the analysis succeeding, for example 'As the analysis progressed, the analyst was generally perceived as not having any specific colour' (Goldberg *et al.* 1974: 499).

I do not wish to argue that social facts are *never* used by patients defensively, which would be a ridiculous claim. The point I wish to make is that these social facts are uniformly and *only* understood as resistance by these authors.

Racism and prejudice in psychoanalytic discourse

Polzer (1991) describes her shock at discovering virulent racist views in Groddeck's untranslated writings

> It is bad enough that our time allows for marriage with foreigners, but miscegenation with coloured people is a crime which ought to be punished at least by depriving such couples and their offspring of their rights. He who betrays his blood does not deserve to be a citizen. I understand that certain chemical reactions of the bloodstream . . . show that the blood of Malaysians is nearer to that of the apes than to that of man. One ought to prove the same fact for the Chinese and the Japanese, and to affix it on all street corners in order to arouse shame, and respect for God's gift of pure blood.
>
> (Groddeck 1984: 183, quoted in Polzer 1991)

The thing of interest is not so much the discovery of these passages but the fact that Polzer finds it incomprehensible that Groddeck can hold such views in the light of his other thinking. She wonders whether they can be put down to an 'infection' from the zeitgeist. In calling these thoughts an infection they are made something alien and foreign to the body and mind of the 'real' Groddeck. An attempt is being made to salvage a sanitized good Groddeck from contamination by a bad Groddeck infected by racism. This is an attempt at splitting, if not amputation. Perhaps the worrying thing for Polzer is the thought that if Groddeck is so unexpectedly infected then perhaps so is the whole body of psychoanalysis: practitioners black, white and all.

It would appear of the authors gathered here, that they see themselves and their discipline, psychoanalysis, as outside and beyond the tides of history and ideology. This is curious because as the psychoanalyst Cushman refreshingly says

> It seems noteworthy that a discipline that prides itself in unflinchingly confronting the ambition, greed, power-hunger, perversity, and murderous rage of individuals can unquestioningly accept a disciplinary history devoid of similar influences. . . . We routinely expect our *individual* patients to exhibit prejudice and practice self-deceit, and we believe *individual* practitioners to be capable of the same foibles. But when we write history we seem to consider our discipline, as a discipline, beyond such practices.
>
> (1994: 809, italics added)

Difficulties in the analyst

Analysts, no less than their patients, imbibe the world view that is endemic to the society that they grow up in. This means that associations endemic to that world view are taken at times to be 'natural'. If they are natural, then anything else is in a sense *un*-natural, and so needing interpretation. Thus in some of these papers it would appear that the associations between black and bad, and white and good are so deeply embedded in the analyst's unconscious as obvious and self-evident, that when the situation arises when patients reverse these associations, they are experienced as anomalous by the analyst. For example, when a black patient of Myers (1977) associates the colour white with death, Myers explains the 'anomalous' association by her interest in Chinese art – wherein white is the colour of mourning. It would appear that the analyst cannot bring himself to think that the association of white with something threatening in the patient's mind is not just from Chinese culture but also from her experience of life as a black person in contemporary USA.

Book reviews

Psychoanalytic discourse, like all others, may be divided into a formal one which is guarded and careful, and an informal one that is expressed in unguarded moments, idle conversations in corridors, slips of the tongue, etc., and it is through these that some of the ideologies embedded in psychoanalytic discourse are occasionally revealed. The book reviews that were found in this trawl for papers are interesting for precisely this reason. Amongst other things, book reviews are invitations to state one's personal opinion, hence their language and tone are often less guarded. Also of interest here are some of the 'defences' put up by the reviewers on behalf of psychoanalysis against charges of racism and the like. One example is Boesky's (1974) review of Thomas and Sillen's book *Racism and Psychiatry*. Boesky allows the authors an authority to speak on the experiences of being black. However their charge of racism in psychoanalysis and psychiatry is summarily dismissed thus 'My own reading suggests not racism, but conceptual confusion and methodological error' (ibid. 144). Even if it were just confusion and error, surely what a psychoanalysis would have to ask is why does the confusion and error occur? What are the unconscious forces that drive the errors in particular directions? The power of the psychoanalytic method is such that it leaves no territory for the merely innocent – not even for itself.

Some of the defences of psychoanalysis consist of what philosophers call the intentional fallacy – wherein one interprets the state of mind of the person, rather than engaging with the arguments. This is after all the psychoanalytic method, however its use outside the consulting room is questionable. Whilst reviewing Badcock's book *The Psychoanalysis of Culture*, Stein (1984) attacks not the arguments for relativism, but the state of mind of those who put it forward as a philosophical proposition. Stein says that the psychological basis for the belief in relativism is to be found in the developmental themes of adolescence, thus those that hold to this view are by definition maladjusted in some way because they are stuck in their own adolescence. The manœuvre is one of pathologizing the state of mind of one who holds an alternative view.

Although McDonald's paper (1974) is not a book review, it is located here because of the type of argument it puts up. McDonald wishes to explain why the story *Little Black Sambo* is so vilified because, according to her, the story is not racist at all. She claims that the story is in fact a disguised description of childhood sexuality which is universal to all human beings. Given that it is universal, she takes the fact that blacks, more so than whites, have expressed a strong antipathy to this story, as an anomaly that needs to be interpreted. She proceeds by saying that the story reassures the 'white reader . . . that the sexual . . . feelings of childhood belong just to primitive black people from the jungle, not to civilized white Americans' (ibid. 527). However, this denial does not work for the black reader because the story 'assigns the forbidden sexuality specifically to people with their own black skin color. Thus the black reader's rejection of Sambo resembles the impassioned rejection which greeted Freud's discovery of infantile sexuality' (ibid. 527). In effect she has pathologized the antipathies stirred up by this story and particularly the 'impassioned reaction' of blacks, by calling it a defence against knowing. McDonald ends her paper with a plea, saying that consciously the author of the story was not prejudiced, and that she should not be criticized for the unconscious projection of her childhood sexual feelings onto black skin colour. There is a double movement here: the black anger is problematized, and the racist projection sanitized.

Against the grain

Against the general reductive trend of these papers a few exceptions stand out. They do not form a coherent body in themselves but each has a vital point to make.

Of the clinical accounts, the papers by Beisner (1988) and Fletchman Smith (1993) stand out in trying to hold on to the internal and external complexities in a non-reductive fashion. Papers by Bernard (1953) and Meers (1970, 1973) are unusual in that they focus on the actual *effects* of racism and deprivation on the black in contemporary USA. Bernard goes one step further than the multiculturalists in that she acknowledges not only difference but also status differentials. In her view a successful analysis does not entail going past visible differences rendering them meaningless, instead she says that the true deep meanings of the difference become apparent. White (1991) makes the vicissitudes of identity formation and retention the basis of prejudice. Da Conceição Dias and De Lyra Chebabi's (1987) paper is unusual in its attempt to tie together psychoanalytic ideas with historical trends without reducing one to the other. Blum (1994) contextualizes the analysis of Dora's dreams within a socio-political framework, gives a historical dimension to anti-Semitism, and even dares to comment on the anti-Semitism of Jones.

Butts (1971) describes some findings following a research questionnaire to white psychiatrists, taking up many themes that are now commonplace but were not so at that time. The research uncovered a generally held view amongst white psychiatrists that the black psychiatrist was better able to treat working-class patients and black patients, in effect those who pay lower fees.

The difficulties and limitations in the psychoanalytic theorization of racism

The fact that the clinical work of psychoanalysis addresses the internal world of patients, might make it appear that the criticism of psychoanalysis as 'internalist' is a bit pointless as the psychoanalytic take is self-consciously intended to be partial, focusing on one aspect of the subject – the internal.

Whilst I would agree with the first part of the statement, I think that a conflation has taken place. There is a distinction to be made between the location of a disturbance and how it came to be there in the first place. I think that in many of the papers the fact that the disturbances are located *inside* individual patients is mistakenly used to surmise that the disturbances find their genesis there. This makes the analyses not so much partial, as reductive to say that group hatreds are *caused* by internal difficulties, for example 'the entire evidence we have presented in this paper leads us to believe that anti-Semitism, like all other group hostilities, presents *a reflection of a conflict in* the prejudiced person' (Ackerman and Jahoda 1948: 259, italics added).

The ethos of the psychoanalytic method – as represented in the majority of these papers – is to focus on the internal domain at the cost of the external social domain. If and when the external social is given a role at all it is secondary, in that it is said to give a particular shape to the expression of these internal dynamics. The result of this is that the papers focus on the internals of the racist subject to such an extreme degree, that the object of racism – the Semite, the black, and so on – are made incidental to the proceedings.

Many analysts would undoubtedly say that these papers do not reflect their view of this subject, nor do they reflect how they work with this material in the consulting room. I am sure that is the case. However, it is interesting as to why alternative viewpoints are not reflected in the literature. There are no papers published in the psychoanalytic journals that are *directly* critical of previously published articles on this subject. We might suppose from this absence, that on the whole the psychoanalytic community agrees with them. Further, the fact that these articles are subjected to reviews by peers for suitability prior to publication, gives them an institutional stamp of approval. There are of course occasional articles that go against the general reductive trend, however these cannot be used to dissolve the overwhelming statistical truth that the majority treat notions of race and racism as secondary phenomena and not of import in themselves.

I will now summarize the limitations and difficulties with the psychoanalytic thesis as it stands.

1 The overwhelming majority of the papers treated the topics of racism and prejudice as a symptom – as the external effect and social expression of internal psychological dynamics. If and when the external social is given a role at all, it is secondary in that it is said to give a particular shape to the expression of these internal dynamics.

2 The two Freudian theories of difference and hatred are never delineated in the papers, and depending on what the author is trying to argue, one or the other is used.

3 The fact that some papers locate difference in biology and others in culture is unregistered by the authors and exploited to the full to argue contradictory positions.

4 The papers that lean on the notion of splitting tend to 'mistake techniques for causes' (paraphrasing Fairbairn). By stripping these papers of their elaborations, their thesis is starkly exposed, which at its baldest is 'racism is caused by splitting and projection'. But as Littlewood and Lipsedge said 'projection is a mechanism not an explanation' (1989: 29).

5 Some of the papers ground their theories of racism in highly abstract notions like 'separation', 'difference' or 'the stranger'. However, they are used in ways that are curiously asocial, as though all differences or separations were equivalent. The question that many of the papers neglects is why should one sort of difference be more pertinent than another?

6 The next problem is to do with the fact that these are said to be universal explanations. In other words they are said to pertain to all human beings. But if they do pertain to all human beings, then we would expect to see much more homogeneity in the world, because everyone would be equally projecting into everyone else. But instead of homogeneity, we see powerful asymmetries – men subjugating women, whites subjugating blacks, Christians subjugating Jews, Jews subjugating Arabs, and so on. According to these theories, the only way such an asymmetry can come about is for one group of humans to be more prone to developmental failures, or more prone to instinctual projection than another. And always these will be the more powerful ones. But why should one group be more prone to projection? What happens to the consequences of the archaic matrix in women, Jews and Blacks, where do their projections go?

7 This leads to the seventh problem which is that these theories focus almost entirely on the racist subjects themselves, the objects of racism are curiously absent from the drama. They are incidental to the proceedings. When the objects feature at all they do so as containers, screens and vehicles for the projections of the racist subject. Ironically, they are made so incidental that they are not even hated in their own right, the main play is always going on somewhere else.

8 Another question is how do these aggressions get to be aimed at particular groupings in the first place? To answer this all these theories make a central division. They say that the energy or cause for the conflict comes from the internal world and the conflict finds itself being expressed on socially sanctioned targets. Thus the instinctivist says that the cause of racial conflict is the vicissitudes of the instincts, and the developmental theories say that the cause is something in early childhood. These disturbances are then said to be vented along socially sanctioned channels. However, the critical question that we began with has been avoided: how do these targets come to be socially sanctioned in the first place? The argument takes as a given a pre-existing racism

in society, which is said, secondarily, to be exploited by these internal mechanisms. Whilst this might be an explanation of the process of the management of internal difficulties, it avoids the question of the actual genesis of racism.

9   A further critique concerns the models that explain racial hatred as a consequence of developmental failures of some kind. Take Chasseguet-Smirgel's (1990) notion of the archaic and normal Oedipal formulations. For her theory to work at the social level, it would have to be the case that a whole nation of individuals fell prey to the archaic matrix at one and the same time failing to complete the proper resolution of the complex. And then miraculously, at a certain later time, much of the nation simultaneously came to resolve the matrix. For this kind of theory to work, the developmental process of a large number of members of a society must be finely synchronized. Surely this is not a realistic scenario. Something more must be going on.

10   A supplementary problem found in Chasseguet-Smirgel's paper and also in others, is to do with an idea of the 'natural' group. In her analysis she talks about the wish for the body of the German people to become one with the body of the Mother, and for this to occur alien elements (like Jews) need to be expunged. But if we ask what attributes are utilized to include and exclude parts of the population from belonging to the name German? We can see at once that the notion of German is not at all a natural one, and that one has to do some work to exclude Jew or homosexual from the category German. Returning to point 9 above, given that the notion of German included both Gentile and Jew, how did it come about that it was the Gentile and not the Jew that fell prey to the archaic matrix?

In fact Elias was reputedly asked during his old age whether, as a child, he felt more a member of the Jewish community or of the wider German society, Elias said that the very question reflected events that have unfolded since then. At that time the issue did not arise. He knew as a child he was both a German and a Jew. The issue of how and why the question comes to be asked in the first place is worked through in the latter half of this book.[3]

11   The developmental theories that make past experience the basis of contemporary cruelties are faced with the following conundrum that they cannot resolve: if it is the case that people behave cruelly to others in adult life (and racism is one version of this) because they have been dealt with cruelly or suffered some kind of trauma in their earlier life, then we would expect those who have had a happy childhood with no trauma, not to act in cruel ways to others. This is self-evidently not the case. And even if it were the case, then once again it would be an explanation of the how and why of a particular individual's behaviour. The other possibility is that a large number of children in a whole

society were traumatized in a particular way at more or less the same time. Whilst this does on occasion happen, through war for example, one cannot say with any conviction that contemporary Britain is traumatized by some calamity. Some instinctivists take this difficulty as an opportunity to argue their case. The instinctivists who hold a Hobbesian view of human nature (raw in tooth and claw), say that if humans can get away with it, they will behave badly at every opportunity because it is in their nature – basically, they do not need something bad to happen to them for them to behave badly. But neither of these ways of thinking satisfactorily account for the fact that one does not witnesses uniform bad behaviour. People live as neighbours and friends for decades, and then suddenly something happens and they are at each other's throats. It will be shown that this something has more to do with the vicissitudes of power relations rather than the instincts.

12 The fact that the papers do not consider the possibility of racism also being a cause as well as an effect means that they do not consider how racism might actually structure the internal dynamics. This has rather serious consequences not only for the techniques of psychotherapy and psychoanalysis, but also on how the 'treatments' are experienced by patients. For example, psychotherapy clinics and trainings in the UK are increasingly asking of themselves why it is that more black people do not come forward for either psychotherapy or to train as psychotherapists. The findings of this review go some way to answering this question: they suggest that it is because aspects of the actual troubled experiences of the marginalized and dispossessed are not understood for what they are, they are instead dissolved by a series of analyses that locates their source in the patient – either in instinctuality or in an asocial, personal, developmental process.

13 In sum, all the theories just described, the developmental and the instinctual, are beset by the same set of difficulties, in that whilst they might go some way to explaining the aggression and hatred of particular individuals, they fail to address group hatreds. The exception to these are the group theories of Freud, Fairbairn and Winnicott, and in my opinion the most promising of these is Winnicott's. But even when these group theories are used in these papers, the group–individual dichotomy is always in play, and it is said that decent individuals do bad things when they get into groups because when in groups the primitive within them is let loose to wreak havoc.

In my opinion, the problems thrown up in this territory shed light on a more general difficulty in some psychoanalytic theories; a difficulty born of a false distinction made between the *developmental* and *socialization* processes. Foulkes and Elias have gone some way to disentangle these conflations. But before we attend to them there are a couple of gaps in the psychoanalytic corpus still to be filled and this is the work of the next chapters.

Notes

1 A version of this chapter was previously published in Dalal 2001a.
2 The Psychoanalytic Electronic Publishing (PEP) 1998 Archive 1 (1920–1994), published by Psychoanalytic Electronic Publishing Inc., London. This contains the journals *Contemporary Psychoanalysis, International Review of Psychoanalysis, International Journal of Psychoanalysis, Journal of the American Psychoanalytic Association, Psychoanalytic Quarterly, The Psychoanalytic Study of the Child.*
3 Ironically, at a recent conference in Berlin where I was giving a talk on this very subject, it was my intention to tell the Elias story and discuss why the question should be asked of him. But even before the talk, several colleagues on meeting me for the first time at that conference, asked me exactly this: did I feel British *or* Indian? It struck me that I was being asked (or forced?) to choose because in the questioners' minds the two were mutually exclusive categories.

Chapter 4

Other psychoanalytic theories of racism

There exist a small number of additional explicit psychoanalytic theorizations of racism. However, most of them have not emerged from within the British context, nor have they been taken up directly in the main psychoanalytic trainings here, with the result that their influence on the *practice* of psychotherapy has been marginal if not negligible.[1] Whilst these last reasons throw most of these works out of the remit of this book, they will be mentioned none the less, albeit in a highly condensed fashion, otherwise the survey would be a lopsided one.

The contributions of note are those of Adorno and colleagues (1950) who speak from within a broadly Freudian tradition, Kovel (1988), Wolfenstein (1981, 1993) and Fanon (1982, 1983) who in their different ways seek to conjoin Freud with Marx, Rustin (1991) who draws his inspiration from Klein and Bion, and the group analyst de Zulueta (1993) whose thesis is framed within a broadly relational schema. Dollard and colleagues' (1939) ideas are more difficult to locate in any straightforward way, they have affinities with the relational schemas as well as with those of group analysis.

Rustin and de Zulueta write from within the British context. Fanon's concern is colonial Algeria, whilst Adorno, Dollard, Kovel and Wolfenstein are located in the USA. The forms of racism found in each of these contexts are specific to them, emerging as they do from particular histories. However, the differentials between these forms will not be traced here as the current task is a much more limited one of noting the kinds of explanations each of these theoreticians generate from within the particular psychoanalytic traditions that they subscribe to. The importance of Fanon is such that he will not be included here in these brief summaries, but be given a chapter to himself.

Dollard: frustration-aggression

Dollard and colleagues developed the frustration-aggression hypothesis, which was renamed the Scapegoat hypothesis. This theory has affinities with the metapsychology of the Independents – Fairbairn, Winnicott, etc. – in which aggression is not a primary phenomenon but emerges after frustration. The theory suggests that when frustration cannot be expressed in immediate aggression then it is displaced onto a safer target; further, this is particularly likely to happen when the frustration is caused by those in authority and power. This aggression is then equated with prejudice and racism.

What this sort of theory cannot do is explain the emergence of prejudice and racism when there is no prior frustration in evidence, of which there are a great many instances. Adorno's solution to this difficulty is to say that the source of the problem is to be found in the past, in developmental history.

Adorno: the authoritarian personality

This change of focus into the past made Adorno and colleagues' formulations explicitly psychoanalytic. They posited the idea of an authoritarian personality syndrome. They suggested that a child brought up by harsh restrictive parents who secure the emotional dependence of the child by the manipulation of love and its withdrawal, results in a love–hate relationship with authority. This sort of childhood is said to result in an adult who has a strong id and superego with a relatively undeveloped ego. The ego being weak is unable to mediate between the two and resolves its difficulties by splitting the two components: love is projected on to power figures resulting in rigid obedience to them, whilst hate is displaced on to weaker targets which can be hated without danger. This theory (like Dollard's) is drawing on the psychoanalytic notion of *displacement* of the hate and aggression towards something too powerful (and so frightening) on to substitute targets consisting of weaker social groups.

The difficulty in this attempt at explaining racism as a consequence of harsh child-rearing practices, is that it cannot account for the existence of racist and prejudiced *individuals* who have grown up in a non-authoritarian milieu. This same difficulty occurs in the work of de Zulueta.

de Zulueta: relational schemas

de Zulueta's thesis is encapsulated in the title of her book *From Pain to Violence* (1993) in which she posits that the roots of violence are to be found in previous traumas. There are two sorts of trauma that she refers to, those experienced in childhood during the developmental process which impact on the attachment processes, and those experienced by adults through accident or war. It is said that the pain of these traumas leads their victims to be violent to others. One of the forms that this violence takes is racism. She says

> Racism . . . begins, as all acts of dehumanization, by a distortion of perception . . . This cognitive process *originates* . . . from the experience of abuse which the infant or child attempts to ward off by identifying with the aggressor. It can also be culturally transmitted through learning and modelling, but it is my belief that *such learning only takes place where the psychic template of dehumanization already exists: the seeds of . . . racism . . . are sown in the emotional wounds of the abused and traumatized.*
>
> (ibid. 244, italics added)

So, whilst she agrees that these 'cognitive sets' can exist in culture, she says that before they can take root within an individual, they need psychic ground previously made fertile by trauma. I would go a long way with de Zulueta's formulations. However, in my opinion it does not hold at its limit wherein she asserts categorically (above) that those not traumatized could not become racist.

Rustin: racism as psychosis

Rustin begins his analysis by noting that as there is no evidential basis for the idea of race, it is an empty category. His preoccupation is the same as that of this book – how is it that something so empty 'is one of the most destructive and powerful forms of social categorization' (1991: 57). He argues that it is the very fact that it is an *empty* category, that makes it particularly available to being *filled* with projected unconscious fantasies, and that it is these fantasies that render racism its power and potency.

Rustin says that the intense feelings aroused by race 'are akin to psychotic states of mind' (ibid. 62). His view (following Klein and Bion) is that all minds have psychotic aspects to them, which under certain conditions of fear and anxiety get activated and become primary. Paranoid-schizoid modes of operation predominate in these psychotic states of mind in which ambivalence and difference cannot be tolerated, and so the primitive defence mechanisms are activated to manage them. These primitive mechanisms are paranoid splitting into the loved and hated, followed by projection and projective identification. The ultimate aim of these mechanisms is to evacuate 'unwanted states of feeling' (ibid. 63) into those of other races, and this is racism.

The fact that these unconscious mechanisms are universal to all of humanity, does not make racism an inevitability in his account. He notes that children first become aware of 'racial' differences during latency, and concludes that 'racial feelings among children seem to be a product of group life and culture, not instinctual nature' (ibid. 59). But whilst racism is not born of instinctual nature, the capacity for it is inherent in all human beings, the 'psychic roots of racism are to be found in the primitive mental associations . . . of racist thinking' (ibid. 67). Ultimately racism is said to consist of the use of paranoid-schizoid mechanisms to 'organize' difficult *internal* feelings through splitting, and 'distribute' them through projection and projective identification. Rustin says

> Dichotomous versions of racial difference are paranoid in their structure, since they function mainly not as cognitive devices intended to identify facts, but as ways of channelling and condensing basic feelings of positive and negative identification.

(ibid. 66)

In this state of mind all bad feelings (or to be more exact, feelings that make one feel bad), are evacuated 'Disgusting and degraded aspects of the self . . . are dealt with by . . . being ascribed to . . . unwanted groups' (ibid. 67). This mechanism tends to generate a vicious circle (c.f. Klein) of increasing hate, for example Rustin says that as 'cultures of domination . . . are founded on greed . . . [they] have many . . . hateful states of mind to get rid of' (ibid. 66). This hateful state of mind of the dominating (greed), which is in fact the generator of domination, is denied and projected into the dominated. Now, as the dominated contain this hateful substance they appear to be hateful *per se*, and so stimulate even greater hate in the dominating, which gets evacuated once again, and so on endlessly.

Rustin evokes Bion to describe another mechanism of racism. He says 'The schizoid mechanisms described by Klein in the context of infantile life . . . have also been described as processes in the mental life of groups by Bion' (ibid. 67). Rustin then extends this idea to the societal level to say that it is the same mechanisms that are the basis of racist hatreds found between 'members of imaginary collectivities' (ibid. 67).

Given that Rustin says that race is an empty category, it might seem curious that he does not engage with the conundrum of how racial groups come to be formed in the first place. He answers this charge by saying that the question is outside the remit of psychoanalysis which cannot give a *complete* explanation for racism, and that one has to acknowledge the 'enormous role of imperialist domination in creating conditions for, and legitimizing, racial domination' (ibid. 70).

Although he goes so far as to call racial groupings 'imaginary collectivities', in the main what he does is to describe the activation of certain internal primitive mechanisms that are said to exploit a pre-existing racial differentiation in 'society'. It would be fair to say that he describes how racism is sustained, not its construction.

Kovel: anality

Kovel's thesis is the most developed expression of a Freudian theorization of racism. The criticism that Kovel himself makes of this viewpoint (in the long introduction to the 1988 edition) is that it derives its basis almost exclusively from instinct theory (ibid. xciv). If his error in the book itself (first published in 1970) is that he relies too heavily on instinct theory and fantasy, then his error in the introduction to the 1988 edition is that he lays the blame for racism almost exclusively on capitalism. In doing so he does rather romanticize The East as well as The Past, as more wholesome times and places.

Kovel says that the psychology of prejudice emerges from racism, whilst racism itself is said to be the historical expression of underlying symbols and fantasies. These symbols and fantasies are said to be primary and 'are rooted in a timeless biological striving' (ibid. 100) – and their expression in the world is secondary. Thus he says 'Race fantasies are applied only at second-hand to races; they are actually generated in the universal setting of childhood' (ibid. 47). He continues 'the full range of meanings involved in race fantasies just cannot be understood unless their *infantile root* is taken into account' (ibid. 47, italics added). He defines fantasy as 'a form of knowing based upon wish and desire – i.e. upon the internal mental state of the person' (ibid. 47), and adds the caveat that this infantile desire can never be satisfied completely. Thus racism, according to Kovel, is a *system* which facilitates the expression of infantile desire, *without conscious knowledge* (ibid. 99). In other words, it is a kind of 'acting out'.

This leads us on to the next questions: what are these infantile fantasies and from where do they emerge? The answers are linked to two kinds of racism (as defined by Kovel), dominative and aversive, and we shall take each in turn.[2]

Dominative racism

Dominative racism is the explicit enactment of racism like that which manifested in the southern states of America in the time of slavery. Here, there is no shame in brutalization, lynching and the like, they are part of the norm of society. Kovel finds the basis for this racism in the Oedipal drama. He argues that diverse aspects of infantile desire get split off, repressed, and get projected onto the black. All these aspects are elements of the id 'the black man represent[s] both father and son in their destructive aspects' (Kovel 1988: 71), the father with the enormous penis, and the son that lusts after the mother. Kovel says that in attacking and dominating the black, the white wins both ways – the father castrating the (black) son, and the son castrating the (black) father. Thus dominative racism is a means of defeating the Oedipal complex by the hidden but continued expression of infantile desire. This explanation throws light on the conundrum of why it is that

> these same black men, so debased and humiliated in actual life, should be invested in white men's fantasy life with the most prurient of wishes

and the most prodigious of sexual capacities and should be in fact the subject of profound envy by those who dominated them.

(ibid. 70)

They are being envied for still possessing (in the fantasy of the white) the id elements no longer available to the white.

Aversive racism

Kovel glosses over the move from dominative to aversive racism, saying that the aversive racist 'abandoned the wish for directly dominative racist activity in exchange for material gain' (1988: 60). The difference between them being that whilst the dominative racist feeds off the fantasies around sexuality born of the Oedipal stage, the aversive racist feeds off fantasies of dirt located in the anal stage. Kovel makes the point that although aversive racism is an 'evolution' in that it is a later historical development and that it looks 'cleaner', it is in fact based on earlier more primitive fantasies than that of dominative racism, and is therefore all the more powerful.

Kovel now relies on Erikson's (1958) and Brown's (1960) tracking of the evolution of the body–mind divide in Western culture – in particular through Protestantism. The name of the game here is the quest for purity. In this quest all matter is designated as bad. Thus the task becomes to get further and further away from all material things, and increasingly towards mental and spiritual things. Excrement becomes the apotheosis of all material things, and the dirtiest of all material things. Thus, the feelings and fantasies attached to faeces are able to migrate across to black people because of the 'fact' that both are said to be black.

Psychoanalysis teaches us that the nature of the repudiated is such that one desires even that which is repudiated. Thus faeces are divided into the acceptable and the unacceptable. The acceptable is only acceptable by being disguised (e.g. property). In contrast, that which is unacceptable is designated as dirty. However, even property has to be purified further – to get it away from the material realm (which as we have noted is dirt incarnate). This process of purification, Kovel says, consists of the process of abstraction and the most abstract form of any possession is money.

Wolfenstein (who will be dealt with in more detail below) develops this theme in an interesting direction. He says that as 'white people disburden themselves of their emotional excrement, they empty themselves of their sensuality at the same time. Hence their peculiar double attitude towards blackness. They both despise and lust after it' (Wolfenstein 1993: 337). Next, he invokes Bion's assertion that the group stirs up unconscious fantasies about the contents of the mother's body, to say that the black somehow perceived as being constituted by lumpen groupishness, becomes associated with the mother's body. Thus 'blackness signifies the maternal body, whiteness the collective self that yearns for union with and is terrified by this most profound and unchangeable of beings' (ibid. 345).

Kovel draws on Norman O. Brown to build on another explanation of why faeces are hated. He says that there is a primary alienation that occurs inevitably in the development of any individual – the formation of the I and the repudiation of the not-I – towards which there is bound to be an ambivalence. This leaves a wound, the agony of individuation. The rage that this gives rise to is displaced onto expelled excrements as they signify separation. And by association, this hatred is transferred onto black people.

* * *

By dint of repetition the linkages between blacks, hate and faeces have become a self-evident commonplace. The fact that Kovel supposed that the fear and hatred of blackness was 'natural' because of its association with faeces led him to say (incorrectly) that black was 'the color that had *always* horrified the West' (1988: 21). He says that the European was shocked to see a material manifestation of something that they had already learnt to loathe independently, blackness, because it signified badness via black faeces. 'The devil was a construct in Western thought before the Westerner encountered black people . . . The devil is black; and so, Europeans noticed, were Africans – if not absolutely black, at least mightily dark' (ibid. 62). In this last formulation it does seem that the white's hatred of the black is an inevitability. What he does not take up is the fact that if these are indeed universal phenomena, then presumably black people too would have found blackness loathsome from times immemorial. In other words they would be doomed to self-loathing as a natural and inevitable thing.

Thus, whilst Kovel notes that the races have been constructed by the ideology of racism, he does not notice that the notion of blackness is also constructed, and that both faeces and people have been blacken*ed*.

Three central components of his analysis are not borne out by the evidence of the later chapters of this book, and because of this the Kovelian analysis falls.[3] The first of these is the association of hatred with blackness, the second is the association of faecal matter and blackness, and the third is the shame and repulsion attached to excrement and the act of excreting. In his argument all of these are transhistorical and natural. But what Elias will show is that the shame attached to the faecal functions have not always followed the course prescribed by twentieth-century psychoanalytic theory, and that the shame and repulsion attached to them vary according to which historical epoch one is discussing. Further, the semantic history of 'black' and 'white' will show that the associations of blackness with dirt and hatred are also recent historical events – and also not natural by any means.

Wolfenstein: epidermal fetishism

Wolfenstein's work is an elaboration of Fanon's psycho-social cogitations from a more rigorous Marxist perspective. This world view construes human beings as 'sensuous beings' that are *objects* 'receptive and responsive to the impact of external reality', and also *subjects* that 'respond actively to the realities' (Wolfenstein 1981: 348). The alienating objectification process inherent in capitalist structures is said to generate a false consciousness embedded within an alienated character structure

> The character structure of the individual in bourgeois society becomes a foundation for self-alienation, for a divided self who judges the rationality . . . of his actions against the standard of his alienated reality, and who therefore acts so as to reproduce that reality.
>
> (ibid. 351)

By explicitly locating Freud's formulations within a sociological milieu, Wolfenstein goes that one step further than Winnicott to remind us that if there is no such thing as an infant, then neither is there such a thing as a mother–infant couple outside of the power relations that constitute the social. Wolfenstein talks about race through a conception of an emotional group which, through the processes of introjection and projection, result in the 'in-group . . . [being] narcissistically aggrandized while the out-group is contemptuously devalued' (ibid. 352–353).

Thus racism is an

> intergroup relationship [which] is . . . an externalization of the divided self. But the divided self results from the internalization of primary family relations, which are themselves the product of the family's social situation. The group relation is therefore a re-externalization of these relations, or, rather, it is their split and duplicated re-creation.
>
> (ibid. 353)

This recursive process is almost identical to Freud's, with one significant difference: the cycle starts with introjection and not projection.

Wolfenstein argues that the possibilities of character structure are constrained by a) social structures, and b) where one is positioned within them. The hierarchical relationship between black and white has particular consequences for each of them. The 'black race serves as a mirror in which white people see reflected their own unconscious repressed or alienated selves. . . . The black person is what the white person is not. He is the alienated white self' (ibid. 354).

Whilst the white becomes 'the incarnation of both right and reason, as civilized humanity' (ibid. 355), for a black individual the story is more complicated: like Elias and Fanon, Wolfenstein is cognizant of the fact that those lower in the power hierarchy are obliged to identify with the oppressors to some degree and so

> the character structure of black children will be partially formed in the oppressor's image. White power defines reality (is the reality principle); [and] white authority fuses with black parental authority in the formation of conscience.
>
> (ibid. 356)

There are two possibilities now before the black individual: conformism through complying with the 'good negro' stereotype, or rebellion through accepting the 'bad nigger' stereotype. In either case 'each individual is trapped in the vicious circle of self-destructive aggression' (ibid. 356).

Class interests cut through the black body, with the result that the middle classes are more prone to conformism, and the masses to violence – but both are alienated from some notion of a true racial consciousness which can be recovered through revolutionary activity. Whilst there is much of value in this sort of formulation, it renders the world more simple than it is – a singular dichotomy between true and false, it also feeds the fantasy that there is a singular truth that can be accessed if the conditions were right.

Nevertheless there are many points of consensus between the ideas being developed in this thesis and Wolfenstein's work, which is not surprising as both draw their inspiration from Fanon. Whilst Wolfenstein relies on Marx, this book draws on Elias and Foulkes, thus approaching the same territory but from a different direction.

A summation of the journey through the psychoanalytic scene

The journal articles were, on the whole, disappointing as they did not build on the rich possibilities contained in the four theoreticians of the previous chapter, and instead tended to oversimplify the complexities therein. Perhaps the most striking thing about the journal collection is its difficulty in thinking about social phenomena as something other than the outcome of the projection of internal difficulties. Variations of this difficulty were also found in the ideas of Dollard, Adorno and de Zulueta. To repeat myself, these theorizations work at the level of explaining why particular individuals might behave in hateful ways to others, but they say little about the phenomena of group hatreds. Rustin, meanwhile, made no pretence of psychoanalysis being a 'complete theory', and in the main described how racism is sustained within a previously established racialized context. Kovel and Wolfenstein's work overcame several of the previous difficulties in engaging with social, with Wolfenstein's conceptualizations having significant affinities with the ideas being developed in this book.

Now it is time to meet Fanon.

Notes

1 Concrete evidence for this can be gleaned from the fact that these works are hardly ever cited as references.

2 There is also a third stage of racism which is said to come after aversive racism – metaracism. In this stage the racism is perpetuated by the social system itself without the explicit actions of any individuals; in modern parlance it is known as institutional racism. Whilst Kovel does not say much about it, the latter part of the book will develop some ideas around this theme.

3 The Kovel that wrote the preface to the Morningside edition would agree with this.

Chapter 5

Fanon: the colonial context

The Fanon chapter is located here, at the 'edge' of the psychoanalytic chapters, as he begins to answer many of the limitations previously delineated. It also launches the theorization of racism that will be developed here, a theorization that will eventually weave Fanon in together with previous elements from psychoanalysis, Foulkes, Elias and Matte-Blanco.

In many ways Fanon is the progenitor of this work. Many of his thoughts, formulations and asides have served as subliminal prompts to influence the structure and proclivities of the book. His work is important on many counts. First, he was writing about the effects of society on psyche from deep within the colonial context, a context when things black and white are brought into their sharpest focus. Second, he was writing about the effects *on* the psyche of the colonized, and as has been noted previously, most of the psychoanalytic accounts concern themselves with racist subjects rather than racialized objects. Third, the fact that he himself was a 'black' psychologist gave him a perspective on the colonial situation that was radically different from the 'white' mental-health establishment of the day.

Anticipating much of what is yet to come, Fanon's 'take' on the relationship between psyche and society is remarkably close to the Eliasian world view. Both give an importance to language in its role and function in the maintenance of the social order and the impact that this has on the formation of psyches. Fanon's critique of the view that would locate the causes of the psychological problems of the colonized, *in* the colonized, predate Foulkes' formulations regarding the *location* of illness. These reasons and the fact that notions of blackness and whiteness are everywhere in his account, are why his work is presented here.

Fanon's concerns begin and end with the colonial situation – with its strategies for sustaining itself and with its consequences on the psyches of the colonized. Fanon says that 'With the exception of a few misfits within the closed environment, we can say that every neurosis, every abnormal manifestation . . . in an Antillean is the product of his cultural situation' (1982: 152). And by cultural situation he means the colonial situation. So right here at the beginning, Fanon has differentiated himself from the previous psychoanalytic ethos in two dramatic ways. First, he has reversed the ethos in which the social comes second on to the stage; and second, he has dissolved the distinction between psychological development (primary) and socialization (secondary). As we will see later, these ideas form the basis of the radical theory of Foulkes as well as Elias. Although much of what Fanon describes is from a different age and place, its pertinence lies in the fact that he is describing a legacy that we are still firmly in the grip of.

Fanon describes how colonialism constructs its own discourse and perpetuates itself through it. There are two elements to this. First is the rigid and powerful divide made between the colonizer and the colonized. And second is the number of devices and strategies that are used to bolster and sustain the divide. These strategies range from the dissemination of ideology to brute physical force.

Ideology

Let us begin here with ideology. It seems to me that there are two elements to ideology – one more conscious and the other unconscious. The first of these, mythology, is reminiscent of Eliasian gossip, and the second of the Foulkesian unconscious. Mythology consists of several elements, one of which consists of the day-to-day sayings that are perpetuated through unthinking repetition. Examples of these are the well-known ones of blacks as bad, noisy, stupid, dirty and so forth. The power of mythology and gossip is such that it becomes part of the belief system of those that it denigrates – and it is repeated and perpetuated by them too. Another aspect of colonialist mythology is the appropriation of history. The myth here is that 'the settler makes history; his life is an epoch, an Odyssey. He is the absolute beginning: "This land was created by us"; he is the unceasing cause: "If we leave, all is lost, and the country will go back to the Middle Ages"' (Fanon 1983: 39–40). To have a history is to have a past as a self-reflective being. In other words it is to be human, and what is being said is that the colonized is not human and having no history or culture is part of nature. The idea of nature here is to be contrasted with culture – which is a human activity. This makes the 'native', as a part of nature, fair game for capitalism and also Marxism as both declare their task to be the domination and exploitation of nature in the service of human beings 'under the German occupation the French remained men. . . . [meanwhile] The Algerians, the veiled women, the palm-trees and the camels make up the landscape, the *natural* background to the human presence of the French' (ibid. 201, italics added). Thus there are occasions when one might meet a German who speaks French badly, and whilst one might speak to them with gestures one is nevertheless aware of the fact that the German has a history and culture. But when 'it comes to the case of the Negro, nothing of the kind. He has no culture, no civilization, no "long historical past"' (Fanon 1982: 34). Thus the mythology that colonialism constitutes itself by is that it is a civilizing project of humanizing of the primitive native, and so disguises its true intentions which are exploitative and economic. Much of Fanon's work consists of exposing this lie for what it is.

The second element of colonialist ideology, which is unconscious, is to be found embedded in the structure of language. Language is given a critical role to play in Fanon's account – the fact that he introduces it in the very first sentence of his book bears testimony to that 'A man who has a language consequently possesses the world expressed and implied by that language' (ibid. 18). Like the structuralists, Fanon thinks that the structure of language imposes a particular order and hierarchy on the world – and gives it the appearance of something self-evident and natural 'to speak means . . . above all to assume a culture, to support the weight of a civilization' (ibid. 17–18). Embedded in this language are definitions of what is human (the colonizer) and what is not (the colonized), what is good and what is bad, and so on.

> The torturer is the black man, Satan is black, one talks of shadows, when one is dirty one is black – whether one is thinking of physical dirtiness or of moral dirtiness. It would be astonishing, if the trouble were taken to bring them all together, to see the vast number of expressions that make the black man the equivalent of sin.
>
> (ibid. 189)

The etymological research presented in Chapter 8 was prompted by this statement.

The colonialist imposes a language which introduces new status differentials through which everything in the indigenous is denigrated 'Every colonized people – in other words, every people in whose soul an inferiority complex has been created by the death and burial of its local cultural originality – finds itself face to face with the language of the civilizing nation' (ibid. 18).

Cultures as monoliths

Before going any further it will be useful to spell out a couple of problems in Fanon's work. On the whole Fanon talks in a way that suggests that cultures are discrete monoliths, and that there are only two of them – the colonialist culture and local culture. Additionally he has a notion of 'authentic' culture which he equates with a true national culture. This leads him into essentialist territories. He is at times aware that he is homogenizing, and says 'there are Negroes whose nationality is Belgian, French, English; there are also Negro republics. . . . The truth is that the Negro race has been scattered, that it can no longer claim unity' (Fanon 1982: 173). However, one can see that even whilst Fanon acknowledges a heterogeneity in the present – he also hearkens back to a time when there was an imagined unity – a kind of pure 'race' of Negroes before the Diaspora.

I suppose that Fanon was forced to take this position because of the pragmatics of the situation; as he says 'Wherever he goes, the Negro remains a Negro' (1983: 173). One could take this to mean that what ever heterogeneity exists it is irrelevant in a racist context. The only thing of relevance being the 'race' of the person. If that is so then that is the only thing to be understood about 'race', it has no other intrinsic meaning. Another way of understanding this globulalization in Fanon's work is to see it as a consequence of colonialist discourse that allows no 'in-betweens' between 'us' and 'them'; it is an either/or world. As Fanon says, the colonialist's world is a Manichaean world that is rigidly divided into two absolute regions – good and bad, white and black, colonizer and colonized. Thus Fanon is forced to argue within the terms already set out by colonialism. As we will eventually see, he seeks to go beyond them, but takes some of this essentialist legacy with him.

The psychological consequences

In reading Fanon the first thing that one learns is that like the external colonial situation, the internal world of the Negro is inevitably and deeply divided 'The black man has two dimensions. One with his fellows, the other with the white man . . . this self division *is a direct result of colonialist subjugation*' (Fanon 1982: 17, italics added). One of the means by which the colonized's psyche gets divided is through the absorption of the colonizer's language. Another is the drip drip drip of everyday experience

> With the exception of a few misfits . . . every neurosis . . . in an Antillean is the product of his cultural situation. In other words, there is a constellation of postulates, a series of propositions that slowly and subtly – with the help of books, newspapers, schools and their texts . . . work their way into one's mind and shape one's view of the world of the group to which one belongs. In the Antilles that view of the world is white because no black voice exists.
>
> (ibid. 152)

The colonial discourse is such that the definition of being human is made identical to the colonizer and his entire world system. The colonized, the Other, is something not human. Or if he is allowed to be human then it is only so far as being an 'early' human in the shape of a child or a primitive. Fanon describes a curious and terrible phenomenon – that in his mind the Antillean sees and thinks of himself as white. At the very least he does not think of himself as (to use Fanon's term) a Negro. That dubious privilege is reserved by the Antilleans for the Senegalese, or other 'Africans', and they of course are to be looked down upon.

The fact that the Antillean thinks of himself as white, Fanon says is an abnormality. Fanon then asks the interesting question – how does the Negro become abnormal when 'very often the Negro who becomes abnormal has never had any relations with whites' (ibid. 145). He answers, that the abnormality is caused by a *collective catharsis*. By this he means that the whole system of thought, of education, of the very air that is taken in, all work in the same direction 'the black schoolboy in the Antilles, who in his lessons is forever talking about "our ancestors, the Gauls", identifies himself with the explorer . . . the white man. . . . *There is identification* – that is the young Negro subjectively adopts a white man's attitude' (ibid. 147, italics added). With these powerful statements Fanon draws close to Foulkes by anticipating the notion of location which says that the ill individuals are symptoms of malfunctions in the network of human relations; he also anticipates the notion of the social unconscious with his idea of 'collective catharsis'. Consequently, Fanon has distanced himself from some of the exclusively internalist accounts that we came across in Chapters 2 and 3 where the causes for abnormalities are limited to the constitutional and the early personal experiences of individuals.

This hallucinated white structure is shattered 'once [the Negro] goes to Europe; and when he hears Negroes mentioned he will recognize that the word includes himself as well as the Senegalese' (ibid. 148). He gives the example of watching a Tarzan film while in the Antilles versus in Europe 'In the Antilles, the young Negro identifies himself *de facto* with Tarzan against the Negroes. This is much more difficult for him in a European theatre, for the rest of the audience, which is white, automatically identifies him with the savages on the screen' (ibid. 152–153n). Fanon concludes 'The Antillean who goes to France in order to convince himself that he is white will find his real face there' (ibid. 153n).

The point of all this is that the abnormality is not an individualistic phenomenon

> It is not just this or that Antillean who embodies the neurotic formation, but all Antilleans. . . . Hence we are driven from the individual back to the social structure. If there is a taint, it lies not in the "soul" of the individual but rather in that of the environment.
>
> (ibid. 213)

Psychopathology

Towards whiteness: construction of the internal divide

The fact that everything of consequence is white, means that the colonized has to do everything in his power to make himself white, inside and out.

This is another way of saying that power relations structure the content and direction of desire. This notion will be developed in the penultimate chapter, but if one accepts this idea for the moment then one can understand why it is that the colonized person agrees with the colonizer and denigrates everything home grown and desires all things from the 'mother country'. The point is that the 'Negro of the Antilles will be proportionately whiter – that is, he will come closer to being a real human being – in direct ratio to his mastery of the French language' (Fanon 1982: 18).

The external divide is profound; on one side of the divide is the human and on the other side nature 'raw in tooth and claw'. Thus Fanon is quite right when he equates race with species – it is not an unthinking conflation. 'When you examine at close quarters the colonial context, it is evident that what parcels out the world is to begin with the fact of belonging to or not belonging to a given race, a given species' (Fanon 1983: 31).[1] The sometimes hidden and sometimes explicit purpose of racialization is to determine who is human and who is not. Once this divide is made and accepted the consequences are inevitable: there is going to be a rush to get over to the human side of the divide. The use of the word 'accepted' (and 'choose' in the quote below) makes it appear that the sequence is a matter of choice, and that the colonized could as easily not choose to accept the imposed hierarchy. There is a degree of truth in it, but only a degree, because as Elias will show power relations *constrain* choices. Fanon counters the charge that the Negro makes himself inferior, by saying that he is *made inferior*.

Fanon then describes how this divide is interiorized 'The Antillean has therefore to choose between his family and European society; in other words, the individual who climbs up into society – white and civilized – tends to reject his family – black and savage. . . . and the family structure is cast back into the id' (Fanon 1982: 149). Now the external structure is institutionalized in the psyche rendering the superego white and the id black. Henceforth this Antillean has a phobia against blackness.

Now there follows yet another complication. In the normal course of events a phobic will distance themselves from the thing that they are phobic about. But here the black person does not have the possibility of withdrawing from their black skin and this in turn leads to alienation. The sequence is as follows: Freud and Winnicott describe the necessary developmental stage of discovering oneself through and in the eye of the Other. In the colonial situation the black person has to look in the white man's eyes to give himself substance, to find himself, but instead of himself he finds the white man's perception of himself. In effect, he is torn asunder and becomes an object to himself 'The black man has no ontological resistance in the eyes of the white man' (ibid. 110). He becomes 'sensitive', that is excruciatingly aware of himself as he is seen and experienced in the eye of the beholder

> when I had to meet the white man's eyes . . . an unfamiliar weight burdened me . . . in the white world the man of color encounters difficulties in the development of his bodily schema. Consciousness of the body is solely a negating activity. It is a third-person consciousness.
>
> (ibid. 110)

The black person is alienated from their black body.

Policing and sustaining the divide

Although the Antillean seeks to hallucinate away this reality, the colonizer never fails to remind him by various strategies of his status, saying 'you are not one of us'. One of these strategies consists of the French colonial's habit of talking in 'pidgen-nigger' to the Antillean – whatever their level of mastery of the French language 'to talk pidgin-nigger is to express the thought "you'd better keep your place"' (Fanon 1982: 34). Fanon says, when the black man is accepted it is 'on one condition: You have nothing in common with real Negroes. You are not black, you are "extremely brown"' (ibid. 69). These constant 'reminders' contribute to the creation of the inferiority complex.

Another innocuous seeming but powerful device for sustaining the divide is the continual usage of the terms 'black' and 'Negro'. Thus Aimé Césaire is not known as a poet but 'a Negro poet with a university degree'. Even compliments serve the same function, for example André Breton saying of Césaire 'Here is a black man who handles the French language as no white man today can' (quoted in Fanon 1982: 39). Meanwhile, all Fanon knows about the author Paulhan is that he writes interesting books.

Nothing in Fanon can be understood without taking cognizance of the fact that there is a profound power differential between the colonizer and the colonized. As Elias will show, it is the more powerful that define the world and the rest are obliged to swallow it 'Willy-nilly, the Negro has to wear the livery that the white man has sewed for him' (Fanon 1982: 34). What would one do if not flee from the black self. In such a context *not to want to flee would in itself be something pathological.*

Horizontal violence

There are several consequences that follow out of this identification with the white. One of these is what Paulo Freire (1972) called at a later time 'horizontal violence'. Fanon says that the subjugated native is full of anger and aggression. Whilst Fanon does not engage directly with the psychological sources of this anger, we can nevertheless tease out several themes from his writings.

First is the fact that the colonized is divided. This means that as the white subjugates the black externally, so the 'white' part of the native subjugates the 'black' part within. We have already considered this theme previously in the discussion on identification.

Second, we can presume that the anger is located in the subjugated black part of the psyche. When this anger is externalized it is first of all aimed at other blacks. Fanon gives two explanations for this is, one concerns the defence of his identity and the other concerns patterns of avoidance. In order to survive the native has to acquiesce to daily assaults and humiliations perpetrated by the colonizer. He dare not stand up to him. This pent-up rage erupts at the slightest provocation, real or imagined from a fellow native 'for the last resort for the native is to defend his personality vis-à-vis his brother' (Fanon 1983: 42). Second, the native preoccupies himself in a local dispute because there he has a semblance of autonomy, and this helps him avoid his castrated reality 'By throwing himself . . . into the vendetta, the native tries to persuade himself that colonialism does not exist, that everything is going on as before, that history continues' (ibid. 42). In addition to these mechanisms Freire suggests that the oppressed attack each other, because they see in each other the internalized oppressor, and that this imago is the true target of their aggression.

The fact of the matter is that not only is the colonizer venerated, he is also *feared* because of his power. Thus the aggression, which cannot be expressed 'upwards' because the consequences are too threatening, gets turned either inwards or outwards in a horizontal direction. Fanon says that another way of avoiding the expression of rage and despair is by turning to religion and superstition as a way of making the situation more bearable

> the native manages to by-pass the settler. A belief in fatality removes all blame from the oppressor; the cause of misfortunes and of poverty is attributed to God. . . . In this way the individual accepts the disintegration ordained by God, bows down before the settler and his lot, and by a kind of interior restablization acquires a stony calm.
>
> (ibid. 42)

The family and society

Another trajectory towards pathology is found in the relationship (as envisaged by Fanon) between family and society. Whilst Fanon gives priority to the social over the individual, peculiarly he seems to give the family ontological priority over both 'The society is indeed the sum of all the families in it. The family is an institution that *prefigures* a broader institution: the social or the national group' (Fanon 1982: 149, italics added). Society is said to be made up of an aggregate of families, and the shape of society is said to reflect and echo the shape and structure of the family. When the two are in harmony with each other then there is health 'the family is a miniature of the nation . . . the characteristics of the family are projected onto the social environment' (ibid. 142). However, if there is a radical difference between a family structure and the social structure in which it is situated, then this will lead to pathology 'a normal Negro child, having grown up within a normal family will become abnormal on the slightest contact with the white world' (ibid. 142–143). This particular formulation is essentialist with the 'essence' located in the family.

Corruption

The colonial powers explain corruption and criminality, which are endemic in the colonial and post-colonial situation, by the mythology that says it is part of the *nature* of the colonized: the Algerian is a born criminal. Unsurprisingly, Fanon provides an alternative analysis of criminality and corruption 'The Algerian's criminality, his impulsivity and the violence of his murders are . . . not the consequence of the organization of his nervous system nor of a peculiar trait in his character, but the direct product of the colonial situation' (1983: 250).

There are two corruptions to be found. A good one that is put to the service of liberation, and a bad one that is used to hamper liberation. The first of these comes about because in the colonial context the judicial and administrative machine work for the enemy, the oppressor. Thus to cheat the state is a sensible and ethical course of action because one is cheating the enemy and undermining the structures of oppression. Fanon brings a similar analysis to bear on the criticism that the native is lazy and a good for nothing. He says 'is it not the simple truth that under the colonial regime a *fellah* who is keen on his work or a Negro who refuses to rest are nothing but pathological cases?' (ibid. 237). The 'bad' corruption belongs to the native bourgeoisie who, as we will see later, use it to further their own interests rather than as an instrument of liberation for the whole community. In a sense it is a corrupt corruption.

Naturalizing psychopathology: the work of Mannoni

Mannoni serves the function of a foil in Fanon's work, giving him the opportunity to develop arguments against colonialist explanations that seek to naturalize the colonialist project as something preordained.

Mannoni begins with the idea that in the colonized there is a dependency complex 'Not all people can be colonized; only those who experience this need [for dependency] . . . [the] coming [of the European colonizers] was unconsciously expected – even desired – by the future subject peoples'

(Mannoni 1964: 85–88). Mannoni continues to say that whilst the native accepts this position and lets himself be dependent, then all is well. However at some point he starts demanding more, but, when he is given more, it does not feel enough and so he demands even more – he is insatiable. This is because however much he is given he cannot become the equal of the white man as he *is* inferior. This then is the basis of the inferiority complex, which is said to be a *real* inferiority. Mannoni leaves no space for the colonized between the alternatives of the dependency complex and the inferiority complex.

In effect Mannoni is saying that the position the colonized occupies is because of his psychological predisposition and constitution and says that the germs of these complexes are '*latent* in him from childhood' (ibid. 40). Fanon counters the genetic constitutional argument with a neat analogy saying that it is as nonsensical as suggesting that 'the appearance of varicose veins in a patient does not arise out of his being compelled to spend ten hours a day on his feet, but rather out of the constitutional weakness of his vein walls; [as though] his working conditions are only a complicating factor' (Fanon 1982: 85).

Liberation

In Fanon the process from colonialism to liberation goes through three stages, the first is unqualified assimilation, in the second there is a move, but into the past, and the third stage is the fighting phase. I will take each in turn.

The first stage: unqualified assimilation

In this time the colonialist powers pretty much have everything their own way; the native has little or no alternative. Almost all are convinced that the colonial situation is part of the natural order of things. In this stage having swallowed the mythology whole, the native believes that he *needs* to be looked after and contained by the colonizer. He is relieved by and grateful for the settler's presence.

So powerful is this mythology that even now in India (and no doubt other places) some 50 years after independence, one can still hear some people saying that life was better under the British. But the people that one hears saying this sort of thing more often than not belong to the 'bourgeoisie'. And this brings us to the next important point, which is that the settler does not treat the entire colony in the same way. Certain sections of the population are elevated and privileged over the rest. These are the middle men who are allowed to prosper because of the help they give the settler in his exploitation of the colony. As we will come to see these self-same middle men, having literally taken the 'King's shilling', go on to play a critical role in sabotaging and perverting the liberation process.

The second stage: the resurgence of tradition

As we have seen the settler has set about destroying the historical past of the colony, and claimed history begins with the advent of the colonizer. This fact has dire consequences for the colonized in that it precipitates an existential crisis. Because there is no sense of 'we', the individual is left rootless and is constantly forced to ask 'who am I?'

So, the first step in the liberation process is to retrieve and reclaim this lost history, one could even say invent a history. This task serves three functions. First, it is the beginnings of an answer to the 'who am I?' and 'who are we?' questions. Second, it counters and provides an alternative reality to the colonialist's mythology, and in doing so it serves the third function which is to build a new psychological anchor in preparation for the moment when the colonized cut themselves adrift from the colonialist's world system. In effect, this is the time of building a psychological, cultural and ideological home.

But when the native looks into his past he finds little to compare to the 'occupying power's civilization' because the ideological system of colonialism still prevails and continues to designate what is and is not of value. The native is still looking at himself through the eyes of the colonizer and so finds himself wanting. Another strategy is then put in place, which is to celebrate the very qualities that are denigrated by the settler

> the poets of Negro-ism oppose the idea of an old Europe to a young Africa, tiresome reasoning to lyricism, oppressive logic to high-stepping nature, and on one side stiffness, ceremony, etiquette and scepticism, while on the other frankness, liveliness, liberty and – why not? – luxuriance: but also irresponsibility.
>
> (Fanon 1983: 171)

This strategy is limited in what it can achieve because although the attempt is to turn the tables on the settler, it retains the settler's definition of the native.

Whilst in a sense this strategy is a dead end, it is a very necessary dead end because it triggers an internal change in the colonized '[In order] to escape from the supremacy of the white man's culture the native feels the need to turn backwards towards his unknown roots. . . . This tearing away, [is] painful and difficult . . . [but] necessary' (ibid. 175). Fanon appears to be saying that this psychological shift in which the state of being in thrall to the colonizer is broken, is a *necessary* precursor before the actual business of physical revolution can take place.

There is also a resurgence of a problem we have touched on already, which is that it is the colonizer that defines the terms of the battle. Thus because the colonizer uses an idea of 'race' to divide and rule, the colonized are obliged to answer in the same language initially. Because it is asserted that there is no 'Negro culture' or 'Arab culture' it becomes necessary to prove that there is such a thing. Fanon sees and names the danger: culture is being racialized and so colonialist ideology is still being perpetuated. But this too is a necessary cul-de-sac *'This historical necessity* in which the men of African culture find themselves to racialize their claims and to speak more of African culture than of national culture will tend to lead them up a blind alley' (ibid. 172, italics added).

The third stage: the time of action

Violence

Like many revolutionaries Fanon locates purity of action in the peasantry and not the proletariat because 'they have nothing to lose and everything to gain' (1983: 47). For Fanon the act of revolution is necessarily an act of violence, and this is so for several reasons. First, pragmatics: the colonizer has no wish to relinquish his power and possessions and so they must be torn from him. The second reason is to do with the fact that violence is endemic in the colonial situation. The first word spoken, the act of colonization, the act of appropriation, was an act of violence. Following this, in the period of colonization violence was freely and continually utilized to bolster the structures of colonialism and exploitation. So Fanon says, as it was in the beginning and in the middle, so will it be at its end 'He of whom *they* have never stopped saying that the only language he understands is that of force, decides to give utterance by force. In fact, as always, the settler has shown him the way he should take if he is to become free' (ibid. 66).

In Fanon's account the violence of the native has another purpose – paradoxically it is a means of reclaiming dignity and of finding their humanity once more 'the "thing" which has been colonized becomes a man during the same process by which it frees itself' (ibid. 28).

During the time of liberation the direction of violence changes from the horizontal to the vertical, from attacks on the self and others like the self, to attacks on the oppressor. This shift from depression and self-destruction to anger constitutes the beginnings of psychological health 'Armed conflict alone can really drive out these falsehoods created in man which force into inferiority the most lively minds among us and which, literally mutilate us' (ibid. 237). It would appear that the peaceable transition of power is not possible and, as we will see, if it is possible then it is not meaningful.

Culture as activity

In this time the notion of culture takes on a new form, the focus changes from content to process. As we saw in the second stage culture took the form of looking backwards and deifying the past. Although important, it is not nearly enough because it is trying to find succour in something dead. There is now a shift from the dead towards something alive, the struggle to take part in the future. Now, the central elements of culture are revolutionary *activities*. This view of the notion of culture is anti-essentialist; now, culture is not a 'thing' or a collection of 'things', but *activity* and *process* 'A national culture is not a folklore, nor an abstract populism that believes it can discover the people's true nature. . . . A national culture is *the whole body of efforts* made by a people in the sphere of thoughts to describe, justify and praise the action through which that people has created itself and keeps itself in existence' (ibid. 188, italics added).

Ideology: the concealment of violence

But even now colonialist ideology weighs in on the side of the status quo. The new vertical violence (as was the previous horizontal violence) is taken by the colonizer as evidence and a substantiation of colonialist mythology which says that the native is a violent primitive animal that needs to be controlled. Thus it is said that as there is no external justification or reason for this violence, it must be the outcome of either their childlike or bestial natures. And as they are beyond reasoning, the only means one is left with to control them is unfortunately violence – the white man's heavy burden.

Fanon argues an Eliasian line in his discussions concerning the differences regarding strategies of oppression between capitalist and colonized countries. In the colonial context violence is naked, whilst in the capitalist context it is masked and internalized. In capitalist countries ideologies

> create around the exploited person an atmosphere of submission and of inhibition which lightens the task of policing considerably . . . [and] a multitude of moral teachers, counsellors, and 'bewilderers' separate the exploited from those in power. In the colonial countries, on the contrary, the policeman and soldier, by their immediate presence and their frequent and direct action maintain contact with the native and advise him by means of rifle-butts.
>
> (Fanon 1983: 29)

The predicament created for the native by colonialism is such that it leaves the native *no alternative* save violence. The predicament that the native continually finds himself in constitutes a kind of delirium 'The settler keeps alive in the native an anger which he deprives of outlet; the native is trapped in the tight links of the chains of colonialism' (ibid. 42). The only question the native has to deal with then is what he is to do with this anger – turn it against himself or against the oppressor.

But when the anger is turned against the oppressor then colonialist ideology manages to give the appearance of causes to that of effects and vice versa. It is made to *look* as though the violence of the oppressor is a response to the colonized's violence and not the cause of it. The violence of the colonizer has either been sanitized or completely hidden; it is as though it does not exist 'soon we shall have had seven years of crimes in Algeria and there has not yet been a single Frenchman indicted before a French court of justice for the murder of an Algerian' (ibid. 73). In the same breath the activities of liberation are delegitimized by designating them as terrorism, mindless hooliganism or childlike. Fanon quotes a judge saying 'We are wrong in believing this whole revolt to be political. From time to time that love of a scrimmage that they have has to come out!' (ibid. 243n).

The role of psychotherapy

Fanon finds a role for psychotherapy in the revolutionary process, which is to expose and undermine the dominant ideologies of the colonizer which obfuscate and distort not only external reality, but also internal reality. He approaches the subject through the dream of a Negro in which he travels exhausted and finally enters a room where 'there were white men, and I found that I too was white' (Fanon 1982: 99). It is known that the Negro has problems in his career, and from this Fanon deduces that the dream fulfils an unconscious wish. However, Fanon does not stop there, he says 'I have to incorporate my conclusions into the context of the world' (ibid. 100). His analysis is as follows. 1) The patient is suffering from an inferiority complex. 2) His wish to be white is derived from the social structure 'he lives in a society that makes his inferiority complex possible, in a society that derives its stability from the perpetuation of this complexion . . . the superiority of one race' (ibid. 100). 3) What is required is something two-fold, a combined action on the individual and the group: help the patient become conscious of his unconscious wish, and act in the direction of changing the social structure 'As a psychoanalyst, I should help my patient to become *conscious* of his unconscious and abandon his attempts at a hallucinatory whitening, but also to act in the direction of a change in the social structure' (ibid. 100). In contrast to the two options that the colonizer offers the colonized, turn white or disappear, Fanon advocates the destruction of the mechanisms that generate and perpetuate this dichotomy.

Bewilderers: the use of individualism against the native

In contrast to Fanon's version of psychotherapy, the psychological institutions of the time weigh in on the side of the colonizer by designating all attempts at protest and liberation as pathological.

The philosophy of individualism is used to undercut social cohesion and thus undermine the mechanisms of liberation 'The colonialist bourgeoisie had hammered into the native's mind the idea of a society of individuals where each person shuts himself up in his own subjectivity, and whose wealth is individual thought' (Fanon 1983: 37). This is a divide and rule strategy that tries to ensure that the colonized do not join together to form groups, because it is sensed that the formation of groups spells danger for the status quo. This danger and fear is rationalized to form another thread woven into colonialist ideology. It becomes a commonplace that groups are bad, primitive and dangerous. It should be remembered that le Bon's views on groups were formulated at exactly this sort of time – the French revolution. Thus when the oppressed group together, it is once more seen as evidence of their primitive nature, because according to this ideology groups are more primitive than individuals: the modern person is individuated and stands somehow outside and beyond society and the influence of groups. Native groupings are denigrated as 'breeding *swarms*, of foulness, of spawn, of gesticulations . . . "the yellow *multitudes*" and black, brown and yellow *masses*' (ibid. 33, italics added).

The dichotomy between individual and group is a battle for the mind. It takes time for the native to free his mind and discover the virtue of groupings '[the] colonized intellectual . . . dusted over by colonial culture, will . . . [eventually] discover the substance of village assemblies, the cohesion of people's committees, and the extraordinary fruitfulness of local meetings and groupments' (ibid. 37).

In contrast to this idea of groups as a bad thing, there is a group structure that is deified by the colonizer, because it is necessary for sustaining the colonial divide. These are the structures known as 'races', and it is to these we now turn.

Racialization: the activation of difference by the colonized

Fanon is faced with two things: tribalism, which existed before the advent of the colonizer, and racism, which was invented by the colonizer. Fanon despises them both and sees them as part of the same thing. Colonialism takes what is available – tribalism in this instance – and turns it to its own uses. Fanon says 'By its very structure, colonialism is separatist and regionalist. Colonialism does not simply state the existence of tribes; it also reinforces and separates them' (Fanon 1983: 74). The point is that racism is taken up as a strategy by the colonized no less than the colonizer. However 'those who are most responsible for this racialization of thought, or at least for the first movement towards that thought, are . . . Europeans' (ibid. 171).

Like the colonizer, the colonized use 'race' as a strategy in two domains – the socio-political as well as the psychological. In the socio-political domain it is used to differentiate between those who are allowed to approach the honey pot and those who are not 'for the mass of the people in the towns competition is represented principally by Africans of another nation . . . in Ghana they are the Nigerians; in Senegal they are the Sudanese' (ibid. 126). In the psychological domain it is used to bolster and sustain a notion of belonging to the group of humans; in effect it becomes a core element in the notion of identity.

At the boundary between the colonial and post-colonial era, there is a resurgence of intra-national racism. This comes about from two directions. First, the national bourgeoisie who had been privileged by and served the colonial powers, take over wholesale the colonialist's strategy. They continue the job of disorientating the people by fanning internecine flames of 'racial' divisions. They do this in order to preserve the economic structures put in place by the colonialist powers in order to exploit them for themselves. The imminent departure of the colonizer leaves a power vacuum which gives rise to the second generator of racism which is caused by the 'aggressive anxiety to occupy the posts left vacant by the departure of the foreigner' (ibid. 128). Religious as much as 'racial' rivalries are activated to this end.

We can see what is occurring. There is a cynical activation of particular sorts of differences which are used to lay claim to positions of power and privilege 'Old rivalries which were there before colonialism, old inter-racial hatred come to the surface' (ibid. 128). Here, Fanon is perfectly in line with the main ideas being developed in the book. He notes that 'In regions where Catholicism or Protestantism predominates, we see the Moslem minorities flinging themselves with unaccustomed ardour into their devotions' (ibid. 129). In other words, which difference will be thought to be significant will be dependent on what is taking place in the socio-political context. Fanon does not think that some differences are intrinsically more significant or meaningful than other differences. What is of significance is the service the differences are put to, which is the same in all cases: the appropriation of power.

Fanon chastises the national bourgeoisie for not educating the masses, and instead encouraging the activation of ancient rivalries. Fanon observes these phenomena and is filled with despair

> everywhere that the national bourgeoisie has failed to break through to the people as a whole, to enlighten them, and to consider all problems in the first place with them . . . we observe a falling back towards old tribal attitudes, and furious and sick at heart, we perceive that race feeling in its most exacerbated form is triumphing.
>
> (ibid. 127)

We have seen how and why culture starts getting racialized by the colonized in the infant nation and that this move, although inevitable, is in fact a blind alley. Fanon's way out of the predicament of racism and the racializa-tion of culture is to change the central terms of the game: his solution is to counter racism with nationalism.

Nationalism

Here, at the heart of Fanon's vision of hope, is a confusion and it is this: what precisely is a nation? Some of the time Fanon speaks as though the nation were a natural category, at other times he speaks in a way that suggests that the idea of nation is constructed by, and forged out of, the revolutionary efforts of the people, and on another occasion he contends that nation is a contingent and pragmatic category that is a necessary stage in order to participate in the international arena.

The beginnings of this confusion lie with the colonizer. Remember the colonizer had asserted two things, one being that there was no history or culture in Africa, and because of this that there was no differentiation amongst the people of Africa. The only thing of significance about them, the way they were known, their name, was their 'race' – black or Negro. This apparent lack of culture is what is said to make them not only pre-historical but also not quite human. The perceived differences between African groupings being named tribal (this is a sophisticated version of the 'they all look the same to me' idea).

The first move against this assertion is the contrary one that says that there is a Negro, black or African culture. However, this move retains the racist homogenization of the continent of Africa.

In contrast to this strategy, Fanon seeks to incapacitate colonialist ideo-logy by undermining its central tenet – racist homogenization – by cultural and national differentiation. In effect he is saying 'no we are not all the same. We have differing histories, cultures, languages: we are different nations'.

One can see then why the idea of nation is so important in this context – it is a claim not only to modernity but also humanity. Fanon describes the beginnings of political differentiation in the following way 'Negro and African-Negro culture broke up into different entities because the men who wished to incarnate these cultures realized that every culture is first and foremost national' (1983: 174). But the question reappears – what is national? Where do the boundaries that contain the nation come from? Are they made or do they already exist?

When Fanon talks of a 'whole people' he implies that the nation already exists. In which case the question returns: what makes for wholeness and completeness thus making a nation discrete and distinct from another? In other places Fanon speaks like a post-modernist saying that nationhood is constructed through its revolutionary efforts and activities, and that these efforts are what constitute culture. What is important in this formulation is the fact that culture and nationhood mutually construct each other and are part and parcel of the same thing 'If culture is the expression of national consciousness . . . it is the national consciousness which is the most elaborate form of culture' (ibid. 198–199).

The third way that Fanon uses 'nation' is different again. One assumes that in this next passage he is arguing against those socialists who say that nationalism is a dead end. In response Fanon says nationalism is not just an introspective turning away from the world. The internationalists are mistaken in trying to skip the national period because 'National consciousness, which is not nationalism, is the only thing that will give us an international dimension. . . . Far from keeping aloof from other nations, therefore, it is national liberation which leads the nation to play its part on the stage of history' (ibid. 199).

The argument that Fanon is putting forward is very reminiscent of what Lal from the Chicago School of Sociology calls the 'ethnicity paradox' in which the dispossessed emphasize the very difference that has been used to marginalize them. This theme is elaborated on more fully in Chapter 9.

Post-colonialism

Fanon is very conscious of the fact that the story does not end with independence 'The atmosphere of violence, after having coloured all the colonial phase, continues to dominate national life, for as we have already said, the Third World is not cut off from the rest' (1983: 60).

One reason for this is that more often than not the economic superstructures set up by the colonial powers are not disbanded but are retained. The difference now is that instead of the colonialist it is a national that sits in the seat of power. So the same mechanisms and structures that were used to maintain the divide between the haves and have-nots in the colonial era, continue to be used in the post-colonial era for exactly the same purpose.

As with violence so with racism

> The national bourgeoisie . . . [having] totally assimilated colonialist thought in its most corrupt form, takes over from the Europeans and establishes in the continent a racial philosophy. . . . By its laziness and will to imitation, it promotes the . . . stiffening of racism which was characteristic of the colonial era. Thus it is by no means astonishing to hear in a country that calls itself African remarks which are neither more nor less than racist, and to observe the existence of paternalist behaviour which gives the bitter impression that you are in Paris, Brussels or London.
>
> (ibid. 130)

The corruption and criminality that were once weapons of liberation in the colonial era, continue to proliferate in the post-colonial era. But now they undermine the very thing that they once were fighting for.

The struggle goes on.

Note

1 Recently the English 'comedian' Bernard Manning defended his view on television that black people, although born in Britain, *really* belong elsewhere by saying that a dog born in a stable did not make it a horse. Compare this with some of the rationales for race in Chapter 1.

Chapter 6

Foulkesian group analysis

We have seen that, in the main, the explanations that psychoanalysis has to offer for racism are couched at the level of the individual and so cannot begin to engage with the group phenomena of racism. Whilst elements of Fairbairn's and particularly Winnicott's explications do begin to engage with groups, they do so in way that takes no account of the context in which groups are located – the social world. The works of Kovel, Wolfenstein and Fanon form a bridgehead into this domain, with the second two authors managing this more successfully than the first.

I will now turn my attention to the psychoanalyst and group analyst S.H. Foulkes. His work is of interest precisely because of the central role he gives to the social in his developmental theory, particularly with his notion of the social unconscious. The fact that his intellectual odyssey began as a Freudian psychoanalyst meant that he could never quite shake free from individualism even whilst he tried to develop a theory of human beings that gave primacy to the social group. By using the *device* of abstracting two sorts of theories from his works, each with a greater internal coherence, I was able to disentangle many of the contradictions in his writings (Dalal 1998). The first theory I called 'orthodox' as it remained within an individualistic frame and proclaimed itself Freudian. I will not refer much to the work of orthodox Foulkes here as his contributions are poor facsimiles of Freud's thoughts, and these have already been described in some depth. I called the other theory 'radical' in order to signal the fact that this theory subverts many of the metapsychological assumptions within much of psychoanalysis, particularly those of the instinctivist schools.

Radical Foulkes' difference with psychoanalysis may be illustrated in the following way. Where Winnicott says that 'the clue to social and group psychology is the psychology of the individual' (1958: 15), Foulkes would reverse the statement to say that the clue to individual psychology is to be found in the psychology of the social and the group. Thus Foulkes' dictum is that it is in the understanding of social life that the foundation for the understanding of the individual personality is to be found.

Initially, some Foulkesian group analytic concepts will be introduced, and following that we will see what they offer towards understandings of racism.

Elements of Foulkesian theory

Belonging

Foulkes and Anthony say that in 'the most asocial and antisocial individuals, one can discern the wish [to belong], which is tantamount to saying that, fundamentally, man is a group animal' (1957: 157). Foulkes uses the fact that man is a group animal to give the social group a formative role in the developmental process 'each individual – itself an artificial, though plausible, abstraction – is basically and centrally determined, inevitably, by the world in which he lives, by the community, the group, of which he forms part' (1948: 10).

Foulkes is saying that the fundamental drive is not as Freud suggested, instinctual discharge, but the drive to belong. This brings Foulkes close to Fairbairn's idea that libido is object seeking rather than pleasure seeking. Attachment and belonging are now the primary psychological motivational principles. We may now reframe the developmental process from being an expression of the vicissitudes of the instincts, to that of the vicissitudes of belonging.

Communication

The mechanism of belonging is communication. Communication is central in Foulkesian theory; not only is it the glue that holds the group together, psychological illness itself gets to be defined as a malfunction in the communicational field. Foulkes is continually inviting us to focus on interpersonal space, rather than the internals of persons. He is putting forward the idea that things only exist as an emergent property of processes, and that they have no independent existence of and by themselves. For example

> At the centre of all our thinking about communication in groups is the concept of the group network or group matrix. . . . The group is a matrix of interpersonal relationships, and the events which occur in it are interpersonal phenomena. These relationships and these events exist literally in between two and more people; they do not occur in one person or in another, but *can only come into existence through the interaction of two or more people.*
> (Foulkes and Anthony 1957: 258, italics added)

Mind and matrix

At his most radical, Foulkes asserts that mind itself is located in the inter-actional field 'what is called "the mind" consists of interacting processes *between* a number of closely linked persons, commonly called a group' (Foulkes 1973a: 224, italics added).

In contrast to Freud, who supposed that mind was precipitated in order to manipulate the world to facilitate discharge of the instincts, Foulkes supposes that mind was precipitated to facilitate communication. Foulkes is keen to point out that the thing called mind – be it group or individual – is not an entity *per se* but a reification, something abstracted out of ongoing processes. There is no such thing as a group mind because the group does not have a mind. The group consists of a series of individuals. Nevertheless, by some means, the group does influence, inform and constrain what takes place in individuals. This is a paradox. How can it be that something that does not exist *per se*, not only gives the impression of existing, but also has such a powerful determining effect? And where exactly does this 'agency' exist and what form does it take?

Whilst we might be readily convinced that a group mind does not exist, we would be much more reluctant to give up an idea of an individual mind: our powerful subjective sense of our beingness. In fact, this is exactly what Foulkes invites us to do 'I do not talk of a group mind because this is a substantiation of what is meant and as unsatisfactory as speaking of an individual mind. The mind is not a *thing* which exists but a series of events, moving and proceeding all the time' (ibid. 224). As George Herbert Mead has said 'the mechanism of thought . . . is but an inner conversation' (1913: 146). When conversation stops, then mind is no more. Instead of group mind Foulkes introduces the term *matrix*.

> The network of all individual mental processes – the psychological medium in which they meet, communicate and interact – can be called the *matrix*. This is of course a construct – in the same way as for example the concept of traffic, or for that matter, of mind.
>
> (Foulkes 1966: 154)

The matrix is a concept and not a thing. One could say that the matrix is the repository of culture, but as yet it is not clear in what way.

Illness and location

Foulkes' theorizations become increasingly systemic. Thus, whilst one person might be 'ill', this 'mental sickness has a disturbance of integration *within the community* at its very roots – a disturbance of communication' (Foulkes and Anthony 1957: 24, italics added). Consequently, although it is particular individuals that express ill health – neurosis – they are in fact symptoms of some malfunction in the larger communicational field: the illness is *located* elsewhere in the system.

> [It is] axiomatic that everything happening in a group involves *the group as a whole* as well as each individual member. In what precise way it involves any of them, or even which aspects of each are actually mobilized, is a matter of paramount interest. . . . [An] unending variety of configurations . . . can be observed, [and is described by the notion of the] *location of a disturbance*.
>
> (Foulkes 1964: 49)

But now having come so far Foulkes balks at the last hurdle, the jump into the truly social. Thus although he talks of 'networks' and 'communities', for him they consist of 'family members, work associates, friends, lovers and others' (ibid. 133). Like Winnicott and Fairbairn, Foulkes has moved past the individual into the domain of *relationship*, but then fails to locate it in a socio-political milieu. Nevertheless Foulkes provides us with another notion – the social unconscious – and this does in fact take us more clearly into the social.

The social unconscious

Let me begin with Foulkes' central thesis

> the group, the community, is the ultimate primary unit of consideration, and *the so-called inner processes* in the individual are internalizations of the forces operating in the group to which he belongs.
>
> (Foulkes 1971: 212, italics added)

There are two important claims embedded in this sentence. First, he has reframed the things that look like the instincts as internalizations of group processes. Second, if one thinks of the instincts as motivational devices, then he is describing how it is that the instincts are acculturated. The important thing here is that the notion of the instincts, which up to now have been thought of as an internal agency *par excellance* have been given an external and sociological basis. This idea cuts the Freudian metaphysic to the quick, a metaphysic in which the instincts are prior to culture.

The social in the unconscious

The language of the instincts is a way of explaining the manifestations of desire. In contrast to the instinctivists who say that we are driven from within towards or away from objects by the vicissitudes of the elemental instincts, with his notion of the social unconscious Foulkes is putting forward a mechanism for *the social construction of desire*.

Earlier we saw that Freud too allowed the social to impact on the structure of desire, but in a limited way. For him desire (that is the instincts) is a pre-existing biological predisposition, the expression of which is *modulated* and *modified* by the internalized social (the superego). This formulation retains the division between nature and nurture (located as they are in two different structures – the id and the superego), and is accepted by orthodox Foulkes who says

> the group-analytic situation, while dealing intensively with the unconscious in the Freudian sense, [also] brings into operation and perspective *a totally different area* of which the individual is equally unaware . . . the individual is as much compelled and modelled by these colossal forces as by his own id and defends himself as strongly against their recognition without being aware of it. . . . One might speak of a *social or interpersonal unconscious*.
>
> (Foulkes 1964: 52; italics added)

Thus what we have here is something like the social *made* unconscious, or the unconscious social, or the social *in* the unconscious, and as such is a repetition of Freud.

The social as unconscious

Radical Foulkes differentiates himself from Freud in allowing the contemporary social to enter territories that were prohibited to it before – the id itself. For example, he says 'what in later development can be usefully abstracted as superego, ego *and id* arise from a common matrix, beginning at birth or perhaps even prenatally' (Foulkes 1973b: 236, italics added). And here he says 'the superego and the ego develop *pari passu with the id* inside the family context' (Foulkes 1974: 276, italics added). Foulkes talks continually of the social permeating the deepest levels of the psyche 'the individual is pre-conditioned to the core by his community . . . and his personality and character are imprinted vitally by the group in which he is raised' (1966: 152).

But having got this far Foulkes does not take these insights further. He does not engage in the specifics of how the id is acculturated and what this might mean in practice. This gap will be filled in the next chapter with the help of Elias. In any case, the thing to be noted is that if the social permeates to the core, then no distinction can be made between a 'Freudian' unconscious and a social unconscious as they are both one and the same thing. If the analogy being used is that of container and contained, with nature providing the container and nurture the contained, then radical

Foulkes asserts that container cannot be distinguished from contained, and even if they could be differentiated, that the social permeates them both. To change the analogy, not only are the contents of the psyche permeated by the social, so is the structure of the psyche.

I will now attend to the subjects of race and racism from a Foulkesian perspective.

The notion of race

Orthodox Foulkes acquiesces with the view that there are such things as 'natural' groups to say 'there are fundamental social groups as the family, the clan, or even an entire nation.... These fundamental groups, *root groups* . . .' (Foulkes and Anthony 1957: 31). Although no mention is made of race, we may surmise from this statement that this Foulkes would think of 'race' as a natural grouping.

Meanwhile radical Foulkes challenges simplistic notions of identity in saying 'Human beings always live in groups. Groups in turn cannot be understood, *except in their relation to other groups* and in the context of the conditions in which they exist. We cannot isolate biological, social, cultural and economic factors, except by special abstraction' (Foulkes 1975: 252, italics added). This Foulkes makes relatedness central. Not only can things not exist by themselves, they can only be understood in relationship to other things around them. We may surmise from this that radical Foulkes would say that one can only ever understand the meaning of race by reference not only to other races, but also to the biological, social, cultural and economic factors in which they are formed.

Racism

A fundamental difficulty in trying to use Foulkes to think about racism, is that he never developed a theory of hate (Nitsun 1996). Both theories of Foulkes, the orthodox and the radical, concerned themselves with the social – albeit in different ways. Thus orthodox Foulkes concerns himself with the *penetration* of the individual by the social, whilst radical Foulkes focuses on the *construction* of the individual by the social. The difference between the two is important: the first implies that the individual exists prior to the social, and the second that the individual emerges from the social. But now, given that the social is riven with conflict, the absence of a theory of hate is at the very least a curiosity.[1] Perhaps this lack was an outcome of his desire to stress the therapeutic and nurturing aspects of groups, which he did by granting the need to belong a fundamental status.

As Foulkes makes no mention of racism I will approach the subject from the very few references that he makes to subjects that are in the *proximity* of racism.

The stranger

One avenue into the territory of racism, is through a discussion he conducts on strangers. Foulkes suggests that one is inevitably threatened by the presence of strangers. He puts forward two explanations.

The first is a recapitulationist theory – the contemporary individual repeating a pattern set down in prehistoric times.

> The 'passing stranger' in anthropological literature was often seized and sacrificed. . . . The stranger was, therefore, looked upon as a potential threat. So it was with the history of the race. With the history of the individual, there is something not wholly dissimilar.
>
> (Foulkes and Anthony 1957: 157)

Foulkes and Anthony are saying that we fear strangers in the here-and-now because the stranger was (allegedly) feared in primeval times by primitive man. The 'cause' of a contemporary fear of a stranger has been put in prehistory.

The second reason is culled from a particular developmental experience 'At a deeper level, the advent of the stranger into the group probably harks back to an earlier situation, when the new baby was first introduced into the family' (ibid. 157). This time the 'cause' of the fear of strangers in the here-and-now is put in an early personal experience. Both explanations imply that strangers will be inevitably feared and suffer from the same difficulties delineated in previous chapters, where we have also noted the problems with formulations of this kind.

The scapegoat

In a discussion on scapegoats, Foulkes and Anthony say that the 'scapegoat may be selected in the first place on the elemental basis of being different. He may be isolated because of differences in age, sex, religion, class, race, etc.' (1957: 156). This difference is said to be exploited by the group when there is an inner need in the victim to be punished, 'The [scapegoat] phenomenon is precipitated when the urgent need for the group to punish meets an urgent need in a particular member to be punished' (ibid. 157). In other words, they explain the expression of aggression in the here-and-now, as a manifestation of the transference from the internal worlds of victim and victimizers, the source of which is in the there-and-then.

The train

Foulkes and Anthony make a passing reference to skin colour in a discussion on communication we may sit opposite someone in the train who never speaks at all, and yet by his dress and posture, and by the colour of his skin, by his fidgeting, his tenseness . . . he may communicate much to us which we can . . . understand.

(Foulkes and Anthony 1957: 244)

Foulkes is conscious that things are not straightforward, and that there is a difference between what we think we see and actually see

one can be mistaken [in the belief that another is angry], but there will be special reasons why a mistake has been made, why we interpreted an expression . . . in a certain way. We can therefore never be completely mistaken – except in the 'location' of our experience. This is where observations such as 'projection', identification and projective identification come in.

(Foulkes 1974: 278–279)

The question now is this: is the skin colour communicating something to Foulkes, or is he projecting something into skin colour? As Foulkes is silent on the matter I will speculate about this. One possibility is that Foulkes thinks that skin colour is communicating something about belonging – something about where this person is 'from'. If the colour is 'white' then perhaps he might think that the person is from 'here' and is one of 'us'.

This line prompts several questions

1   what does 'from' mean?
2   what are the limits of 'here'?
3   what are the limits of the 'us'?

There have been black people living in Great Britain for many centuries (Fryer 1984), so it is not at all certain that a 'not-white' skin colour will necessarily be a signifier of a birth place outside Britain. What was true in Britain in 1957 is much more true now, there is an increasing number of not-white people born here. Yet somehow colour of skin retains its linkage with belongingness.

According to Foulkesian theory, the idea that skin colour is a signifier of belongingness, must of necessity be located in the social unconscious – which by definition, is *unconscious*. But now, which of the two versions of the social unconscious are we to use? The orthodox version, like aspects of the Freudian superego, consists of the internalized social. In which case what is taking place here is not so much a projection but rather the activation of an organizing principle as laid down in the superego. In effect the observer is in the grip of a transference from the unconscious regions of the superego.

The other speculative line is grounded in the idea of projection. This would say that skin colour is not communicating anything at all, but has become a container for the projection of instinctual elements from the id. As ever this begs another question: why should id elements be projected into non-white others rather than any other entities? This question cannot be answered without recourse to history.

When history has been introduced through the work of Norbert Elias, and also by tracking the evolving meanings of black and white, then we will be able to flesh out the radical version of the social unconscious. Anticipating the work that is to follow, it will be shown that Elias' civilizing process is nothing less than a description of the construction and evolution of the modern psyche as well as the construction of the social unconscious. This will allow us to go much further than the formulations from individual psychoanalytic theory allow. From an individualistic perspective all one could say is that instinctuality has been blackened and expelled from the conscious part of the psyche, or one could say that instinctuality has been projected *into* blackness. But the problem with this formulation is that it retains the instincts as something outside and prior to the social. It is said that the instincts exist first and *then* they are given particular expressions. With Elias, what a radical Foulkesian theory will suggest is not that one followed the other, but that from the first instinctuality and blackness have been used in the mutual construction of each other. This will then allow us to say that notions of blackness and whiteness, despite their historical contingency, are embedded deep in the contemporary psyche, indeed they are part and parcel of the very structure of the psyche.

Note

1 The fact that as a Jew he had to flee Germany with his family in 1933 must have made him extremely conscious of the hatred, fear and conflict in the social arena.

Chapter 7

Power: the generator of difference

Up to now I have been conversing with contributors immersed in the psychological domain. I am now going to introduce a sociologist – Norbert Elias. But why this change of territory and why Elias? First, Foulkes' ideas have been very influenced by Elias and so Elias already has a presence (albeit a hidden one) in group analytic theory and hence the developing argument. Elias' importance lies in the fact that his contributions overcome many of the difficulties in Foulkes' attempts at bringing a more holistic perspective to bear on the human condition. So although Foulkes made interconnectivity central, it was an interconnectivity that had been neutered of the social, thus rendering it apolitical. Foulkes managed this by leaving out the heart of Elias' theory which lay in his understanding of power relations. One of the tasks of this chapter then is to engage with the notion of power which in turn will have several critical repercussions on how the subjects of race and racism will come to be viewed.

An aspect of Elias' importance lies in the way he envisages the interrelationship of psyche and society, with each profoundly involved in the simultaneous and mutual construction of the other, and so he avoids giving a causative precedence to either individual or society.

The ultimate aims of the chapter are threefold. First, to show how 'us-es' and 'thems' are constructed and the means by which they are reinforced and represented in the mind. Second, to prepare the intellectual ground for the next chapter by cultivating the rationale for the type of treatment that the semantic history of black and white will be subjected to. Third, to subvert the idea put forward by the previous psychoanalytic theorizations of the linkage between faeces and revulsion as natural (and so universal and inevitable), by demonstrating its evolution in historical time.

These ideas are important to the themes that are being developed, which are that whilst the linkages between black negativity and white positivity are not natural, they are instated within the psyche none the less. Further, that their presence inevitably colours the emotional field and so contributes to how one experiences the world and oneself in it. Because of space, I will take up only the elements of Elias' work that have a very direct bearing on these matters, although his entire corpus could quite properly be said to be pertinent.

Power

Elias says that the debates about the primacy of individual or society are being conducted in an imaginary and impossible space, where it seems that individuals can exist outside societies and that societies are beyond individuals. It is then supposed that each of these – individual and society – is an autonomous system, each having nothing to do with the other. This eventually leads to the mistaken conclusion that the interests of the individual are of necessity in conflict with the interests of the social group. He says that it 'is of course possible that human culture runs counter to human nature . . . [but] far from being polar opposites, in the human case biological and social processes, in order to become effective must interlock' (Elias 1991: 6).

Elias' notion of *figuration* is a resolution of both Freud's error (which was to overemphasize the internal at the cost of the social) and Marx's error (which was the reverse).

> The concept of figuration . . . expresses what we call 'society' more clearly and unambiguously than the existing conceptual tools of sociology, as neither an abstraction of attributes of individuals existing without society, nor a 'system' or 'totality' beyond individuals, but the network of interdependencies formed by individuals.
>
> (Elias 1994: 214)

The paradox of social existence is this: that whilst individuals have will and intention which they assert in the service of conscious aims and goals, the possibilities available to them are constrained by 'society'.

The nature of relatedness and interdependence is such that it inevitably has power structured into it. Elias says that every social relation is a power relation. The key word here is 'relation'. Power is a relative category not an essentialist one 'Power is not an amulet possessed by one person and not by another; it is a structural characteristic of human relationships – of *all* human relationships' (Elias 1978: 74).

Thus one is inevitably constrained by the mere presence of others and one's relatedness to them. The notion of constraint can be taken to imply that there can be a state of no-constraint, of pure freedom. However, if one realizes that the thing that constrains is also the thing that gives form, then one can see that there is no possibility of existing outside constraint.

The consequences of these changes is that the focus of study is no longer individuals, nor is it individuals-in-relation-to-each-other, but the study of figurations of interdependence in relation to each other. Thus the study is one of the vicissitudes of power relations between these figurations, and the forms of psyche and society which they generate.

This point is important because if Foulkes and Elias are right and the social permeates the psyche at the deepest of levels, then this gives me grounds for suggesting that notions of blackness and whiteness – as critical aspects of the social – are similarly impregnated within the psyche. Where Elias uses as evidence the history of manners, I will use eventually the evolving history of the terms black and white.

The civilizing process

Elias' work draws together three disciplinary territories: the process of state formation in Europe through the power struggles between different constituencies (history), the changing structures of relatedness between people and groups of people (sociology), and the changing structure of the psyche (psychology). He underlines, time and time again, that the whole process is in fact seamless and all these elements are aspects of the same thing.

His window on to this complex space was a novel one, through a kind of social anthropology, which consisted of the analysis of the changing history of etiquette in western Europe over the last millennium. His 'data' consisted of books on etiquette, art, literature and accounts of daily life.

He perceives the standards of behaviour going through several phases, *courtoisie* during the Middle Ages, then *civilité* from around the sixteenth century. Then from about the first half of the eighteenth century, with the advent of nationalisms the idea of *civilité* begins to sink, and is slowly replaced by the term 'civilization'. Although Elias does not attend to it, we should add the reminder here that notions of race start gaining increasing significance in the latter stages in this sociogenetic process, and is an *aspect* of it.

Elias shows that *within* each of the phases (*courtois*, *civilité*, civilization), the changes in etiquette 'do not represent anything actually new. They . . . are variations on the same theme, differentiations within the same standard' (Elias 1994: 86). However, at the boundaries of the phases, that is when the social structures go through upheaval and transformation, there is a flurry of change to conventions of thought and behaviour which reflect the modifications in social structure and in turn affect psychological structures.

The socio-political imperative

The important thing about the forms of etiquette that we are going to examine in a moment is not only what they are, but more critically, the reason for their existence: to make a distinction between the haves and must-not-haves. Elias is stressing the function of the forms of behaviour rather than their content. In Fairbairnian language we can say that the type of behaviour is a technique that is designed to achieve particular types of object relations. The fact that Elias talks about court society in the singular and not court societies is significant, demonstrating that at that time the lines of differentiation between people were more 'horizontal' than 'vertical'. What 'slowly begins to form at the end of the Middle Ages is not just one courtly society here and another there. It is a courtly aristocracy embracing Western Europe with its centre in Paris' (Elias 1994: 267–268). Whilst the conventions of etiquette were not precisely synchronized between the courts and neither did they all move continuously in the same direction, an overall pattern is none the less discernible.

The reason for this level of identification between the courts was the logic of power. The immediate threat to each of the power bases was an internal one from *local* groupings, and in the task of minimizing these local threats they were of one mind and so they borrowed mechanisms and attitudes from each other.

> the absolutist-courtly aristocracy of other lands adopted from the richest, most powerful and most centralized country of the time the things which fitted their own social needs: *refined manners and a language which distinguished them from those of lower rank.*
>
> (ibid. 267, italics added)

Despite the enmity between the courts as they engaged in bloody conflicts over territories, they nevertheless saw each other as the same *type* of person; perhaps this is most evident when it came to marriage – they only ever considered marrying those said to be of 'royal' blood, never a local commoner. To a large extent this distinction is still maintained today.

However, as might be expected, those of lower rank continually emulated the habits and behaviours of those in the higher echelons of society, and in the process blurred the lines of distinction. This in turn set off a counter movement in the privileged circles – the progressive refinement in their manners to maintain their distance from the common folk. One of the key mechanisms utilized in the differentiation process is the use of so-called 'refinements' in the advancement of the threshold of embarrassment and shame (ibid. 82).

Elias says that the same kind of mechanisms that were employed to make social distinctions are later used to make distinctions between nations and, in a sense, create them. Importantly, at a later time these same mechanisms are also critical in the manufacture of races, which are born out of similar imperatives.

The sociological construction of the 'natural'

We have noted how and why the progressive refinement and elaboration of the standard of manners takes place. In addition to this, Elias describes two other interlinked movements: behaviours that are at one time acceptable in public becoming increasingly relocated in the personal and private, and external constraints replaced by internalized restraints. These are described below through the changes in eating habits.

In the Middle Ages people used their hands to take food from a common bowl and place it directly in their mouths. Each person dipped their bread into the common bowl repeatedly, picked out meats, put back partly chewed food, and so on. Progressively, plates are introduced, injunctions increasingly prohibit the use of hands to eat and serve, and instruments of eating and serving are made more complex. Eventually there are even rules about how the instruments are to be held, not 'with the whole hand, like a stick; you should always hold them with your fingers' (LaSalle 1729, cited by Elias 1994: 78).

Elias says that it is a mistake to explain this drift in eating habits through the notion of hygiene which is a modern rationale, and which coincidentally fitted with the already existing directional thrust. He demonstrates with much evidence that in the earlier instances the reasons given for the change in behaviours are not for cleanliness but so as not to cause offence to others. Offence however is not a natural phenomenon but an indicator of social standing, for example in this piece of advice 'If everyone is eating from the same dish, you should take care not to put your hand into it before those of higher rank have done so' (de Courtin 1672, cited by Elias 1994: 75). We can see then that repugnance is an aspect of social relatedness not nature, 'It is a far too dirty thing for a child to offer others something he has gnawed, or something he disdains to eat himself, *unless it be to his servant*' (Calviac 1560, cited by Elias 1994: 74, italics added). The rationale being utilized is not one of hygiene but of social standing.

Elias sums up 'There are people before whom one is ashamed, and others before whom one is not. The feeling of shame is clearly a social function moulded according to the social structure' (1994: 113).

Interesting as these changing eating habits are, their significance lies in the fact that they reflect the changing structures of society, and simultaneously make for changes in the psyche.

> People who ate together in the way customary in the Middle Ages, taking meat with their fingers from the same dish, wine from the same goblet . . . such people stood in a different relationship to one another than we do. And this involves not only the level of clear, rational consciousness; *their emotional life also had a different structure and character*. Their affects were conditioned to forms of relationship and conduct which, by today's standard of conditioning, are embarrassing or at least unattractive.
>
> (ibid. 55, italics added)

The changes in what is acceptable is witnessed in all walks of life from the expression of violence to rules about defecation. For example in the *courtois* period, it was a commonplace for people to defecate and urinate *shamelessly* in public wherever they happen to be. Elias cites the (to our ears) surprising caution from the fifteenth century 'Before you sit down, make sure your seat has not been fouled' (1994: 105). Eventually, this once commonplace spectacle takes place behind closed doors. As the *sight* of people relieving themselves becomes more infrequent, the focus moves to smell; for example the Duchess of Orleans complains in 1694 'The smell of urine is horrible' (ibid. 108).

The important thing to notice is that feelings of aversion have not always been associated with faeces, and so are not an inevitable part of the developmental process as the psychoanalytic theorizations have supposed. To be more precise, the degree and kind of aversion evoked by faeces is contingent on the norms embedded within the social unconscious. The treatises have 'precisely the function of *cultivating* feelings of shame' (Elias 1994: 110). There are a great many cultures that have very different relationships towards defecation. For example, anyone who has travelled by train through India will have witnessed entire villages squatting in rows, defecating in public, *shamelessly*. If one is not drawn by the idea of calling whole cultures pathological, then one is forced to concur that the advent of shame is not an unmediated organic process.

Over time we witness the progressive disappearance of some behaviours not only from the public domain, but also from the treatises on etiquette themselves. Through the ages, subjects that were allocated entire chapters to themselves become progressively shortened and eventually disappear altogether. The reason for this apparent evaporation is a shift in the location and method of social control – it has moved from the external world to the internal world, and the family has replaced wider society as the means of instilling the restraints. Elias based this idea on another piece of evidence, which was that the first books on etiquette were aimed at adults, and by the end of the Middle Ages they were aimed at children. Elias surmised from this that the expectation must have shifted – it was now expected that adults would already *know* how to behave. And if by now the adults 'know' how to behave, then this must mean that the injunctions have been internalized. This movement gathers momentum so that

> the social reference of shame and embarrassment recedes more and more from consciousness. Precisely because the social command not to show oneself exposed or performing natural functions now operates with regard to everyone and is imprinted in this form on the child, it seems to the adult a command of his own inner self and takes on the form of a more or less total and automatic self-restraint.
>
> (ibid. 114)

It is at this moment that the prohibitions take on the appearance of something natural and self-evident because they 'are associated with embarrassment, fear, shame, or guilt, *even when one is alone*' (ibid. 123, italics added). It now becomes a mark of moral fibre – allegedly a manifestation of one's nature – an *internal* quality.

In psychoanalytic language we have moved from shame to guilt. Here, Elias concurs with Freud (1915b: 280) to say that guilt (conscience) is nothing other than social anxiety *internalized*. The important distinction in Elias' theory is that the difference between shame and guilt is not one of *type*, but of *location*.

A partial summation

The critical points that have emerged from the preceding sections need to be drawn together. First, Elias' history of manners is more than an assemblage of the changing forms of behaviour; its significance lies in the use he puts it to in building arguments that describe how socio-political *necessities* precipitate changes in the structure of the psyche. Second, he describes the actual contents of the Freudian superego in terms of prevalent socio-political contingencies in historical time rather than as Freud does through prehistory. Third, he keeps in mind that whatever the psychological effects of certain prohibitions might be, their function is first and foremost that of differentiation of one grouping from another. Fourth, the types of aversion associated with faeces have been denaturalized and given socio-historic dimensions. Elias sums up the main points in this passage

> [behaviour which was initially discouraged] to spare others a distasteful spectacle and themselves the shame of being seen [doing something untoward] . . . later . . . becomes more and more an inner automatism, *the imprint of society on the inner self*, the superego, that forbids the individual to [behave in certain ways]. . . . The social standard to which the individual was first made to conform by external restraint is finally reproduced more or less smoothly within him, through a self-restraint which may operate even against his conscious wishes.
>
> (1994: 105, italics added)

Symbol theory: language, knowledge, mind

Having tracked some of the vicissitudes of social formation I will now attend to the mechanisms and manner in which they impact on the psyche.

Elias' symbol theory could be called his theory of mind; but it is more accurate to say that it is a level of description that shows how mind and society infuse, interpenetrate and construct each other. But even this description does not do justice to the radical nature of the concept because the structure of the English language compels me to reify the notions of mind and society as distinct entities which then interpenetrate each other. The problem is that the English language, and therefore our forms of thinking, are obliged to engage in what Elias calls *process reduction*.

Elias makes constant use of two ideas that are both aspects of process reduction a) that abstractions can have no life on their own outside the field, and b) abstractions are not only not antithetical to each other, but that these apparent opposites actually need each other to exist. A circle's 'inside' cannot exist without a simultaneous 'outside'.

This is the sort of thinking that Elias uses to argue that knowledge, language, consciousness and thought are all abstractions and aspects of the same thing – Symbol. Symbol is an additional fifth dimension that human beings reside in (the other four being the familiar four spatio-temporal dimensions). Each psychological breath is an endless mutual transformation process: we breathe symbol in, and it makes us what we are; we breathe out into it, and impact on it however minutely. We are made by history, and we make history, but because of the power differentials there is no symmetry or equivalence between the two directions.

Language

Elias gives language a critical role to play in all experience – internal and external. The question about whether humans make language or are made by language tends to be answered in one of two ways. The positivists lean towards the first and the structuralists the second. Elias, meantime, hangs on for dear life to both sides of the dichotomy. He says that it is futile to answer the question because in doing so one is perpetuating the other great fallacy – that of absolute beginnings. In fact it is the activity of locating an absolute beginning that throws up the conundrums that have the appearance of unstable chicken-and-egg paradoxes. By bringing into sharp focus the *interrelationship* between speaker and language, he makes a nonsense of the question saying 'both statements are valid: "every individual learns a pre-existing social language" and "social language requires individual speakers"' (Elias 1991: 99). The chicken-and-egg question is a cul de sac because neither chicken nor egg can exist without the other. Similarly 'the language one speaks, which forms an integral part of one's personality, is a social fact presupposing the existence of other human beings and preceding the existence of any particular individual' (ibid. 21).

The important thing about language is that it is a social phenomenon, and it is this which gives rise to the constraints it imposes on particular individuals.

> The compelling force which a language has in relation to its individual users is not the result of an extra-human, quasi-metaphysical existence

of language, but the fact that . . . [language] represents a unified canon of speaking which has to be observed by a whole group of people if it is to maintain its communicative function.

(ibid. 22)

Elias also argues that the thoughts in our minds are nothing but telescoped language, and hence although it appears to be personal and private, thinking is fundamentally a social activity, 'Thinking as well as speaking relies on socially standardised sound-symbols. Both are social activities' (ibid. 82).

Elias then asks how do words and concepts enter a language? Why is language made up the way it is? He answers that language emerges out of concrete necessity – out of our engagement with the world, *and remains connected to it*, 'Human beings have evolved *within* a world. Their cognitive functions evolved in continuous contact with objects to be recognised' (ibid. 98). In this way Elias is different to some discourse theorists for whom discourse sort of floats above the material world.

One is then compelled to face the fact that language is not just a passive tool used to represent the world, but that it also determines the kind of world that is experienced.

A people's language is itself a symbolic representation of the world as members of that society have learnt to experience it during the sequence of their changing fortunes. At the same time a people's language affects their perception and thus also their fortunes.

(ibid. 21)

Knowledge, world, mind

The use of the word 'learnt' in the quote above leads us towards another of Elias' ideas which is that language is the same as knowledge. But how can this be? For example a professor of history and I both speak the same language, English, yet she self-evidently has knowledge that I do not possess. This would suggest that language and knowledge are different things, or if not different, then certainly not identical. So clearly Elias is not speaking here at the level of particular individuals, but at the level of the language system, in which case his suggestion 'What cannot be represented by the web of symbols of a specific human group, is not known to its members' (1991: 57) makes sense.

We can shed further light on what Elias is trying to get at by noticing that the example of the history professor has implicitly drawn a third term into the discussion – mind. The example invites the analogy of a mind as a vessel that is initially empty, which then gets filled with knowledge, with this knowledge being held in the form of language (words and sentences). But Elias is insistent that this is not the case 'Language, reason, knowledge

... to speak, to think, to know ... all three activities are concerned with the handling of symbols' (ibid. 65). I read Elias as saying that the metaphor of mind-as-a-vessel is in itself an abstraction that can have no autonomous existence separated out from the other abstraction – its contents (thoughts and feelings) which are of necessity in language. I would add that if the metaphor of vessel is to be applied to mind, then it is a vessel with 'soft sides' whose shape is dictated by its contents.

But in fact Elias is saying something more than this. In using the word 'mind' we are reifying an activity. We impute a state where there is only process – our actual active thoughts. Our minds are constituted by our active thoughts and nothing else; both exist simultaneously and one cannot exist without the other. There is no container and contained, there is only process. When activity stops then both disappear. Here, Elias and radical Foulkes are in total agreement.

There is a further complication, which actually is a clarification, which is that minds do not exist in isolation, they exist with other minds in psycho-social contexts. Each of the elements, minds in the plural, psycho-social context and language, need the others to give it the possibility of existence. Thus, the 'structure of language reflects ... very clearly, not the nature of the human being, nor the individual person seen in isolation, but human beings in society' (Elias 1994: 68).

From this Elias infers that language holds within it the *type* of relationship that the language group has to the world and the others in it 'All symbols imply relationships. They indicate how the people who use a particular symbol layer connect the world and its various aspects and items with each other' (1991: 129).

And finally, the resonances that get embedded in language end up determining to some degree *how* they, the language group, will engage with the world and those in it

> languages which human beings speak have a fair share in fashioning their speakers' image of the world in which they live, including their image of themselves ... they have a determining influence on the outlook of small children who learn them as their mother tongue. They provide them with the means of orienting themselves far beyond the field of their personal experience.
>
> (ibid. 125)

Elias concludes 'No consciousness without knowledge, no knowledge without consciousness' (ibid. 120). Consciousness is 'another word for the condition in which stored sound symbols ... can be mobilised at will in the normal way' (ibid. 120), and the unconscious is the condition in which these stored experiences cannot be recalled at will and yet they act as effective determinants of action. This is one aspect of the unconscious – experiences that are 'forgotten' or, more dramatically, repressed. But there is another, more insidious aspect to what might be unconscious, and it is to this that I turn next.

The unconscious which is not repressed

We have reached the point where Elias has completed the circle. Let us reappraise the situation so far. The preceding argument has connected language to knowledge, and both of these to the world. Additionally, the structure of the mind, consisting as it does of thoughts (which are in language, language that is moulded by the world and reflects the relationships in it) reflects in some way the social structures of the world.

This is basic Eliasian substantiation for the idea put up at the start of this chapter, that the structures of society are reproduced in the structures of the psyche, with the result that 'a given language and particularly the mother-tongue, pre-empts an individual's thinking . . . it is not possible, within limits, to cut oneself loose from categories implicit in one's languages' (Elias 1991: 70).

So when one takes in a language, one takes in phrases and words which have 'a piece of the world . . . bound up in them . . . they include certain areas and exclude others as a matter of course, . . . [and within them there are] *hidden evaluations* which they implicitly bring with them' (Elias 1994: 4, italics added).

I would say that these '*hidden* evaluations which . . . [words] *implicitly* bring' are quite different from notions of the repressed and are critical in any rendition of the unconscious. I do not intend to deride the importance of events in the unconscious that 'cannot be recollected', because that would be to dismiss the psychoanalytic notion of repression. Things get repressed, and so cannot be recollected because there is something extremely painful, traumatic or problematic in them. In this process there is an *act of repression*, which is preceded by something traumatic. The traumatic thing might be 'just' a forbidden thought or wish, but it is traumatic none the less.

In contrast to the repressed, I think that what is so powerful and perhaps insidious about these '*hidden* evaluations' which are *implicit*, is that *they slide into the psyche with no resistance*. This idea is of profound importance to this argument because these hidden evaluations are nothing other than the social unconscious. As Harland says

> The individual absorbs language before he can think for himself: indeed the absorption of language is the very condition of being able to think for himself. . . . Words and meanings have been deposited in the individual's brain below the level of conscious ownership and mastery. *They lie within him like an undigested piece of society.*
> (Harland 1987: 12–13, italics added)

These undigested pieces of society contained in words and their associations are not representations of society *per se*, rather they are experiences and perceptions – and *collective* experiences and perceptions at that. And this is exactly the way that ideologies, held as they are in words and their sentiments, get transmitted over generations, 'The mode of intergenerational transmission of experience itself is no mystery. Ancestral experiences can be deposited in the concepts of a language . . . deposits of earlier experiences can be reinforced, blocked and . . . perhaps even extinguished by those of later generations' (Elias 1991: 16). These thoughts bring Elias together with Fanon.

All this while in this chapter I have been preparing the ground to bring black and white onto the stage. But before this can happen there needs to be an excursion into the subject of emotion.

Emotion – a difference with psychoanalysis

Let me begin by asking how do the previously mentioned 'hidden evaluations' get to be embedded in words? In fact Elias' notion of language is already a partial answer. He says that one of the functions of language is orientation. What he means by this is that words (which are experiences of bits of the world) and therefore the things that they allude to, have affects embedded in them. These affects, which are part and parcel of these 'undigested bits of society' literally orientate one to these things. If the affects evoked, however subliminally, are in the vicinity of pleasure then one is more drawn towards them, and if in the arena of fear or disgust then one moves away from them. '[Language] offers a separate name, a separate symbol for every experience within the reach of the group; it offers at the same time models of their relationship' (Elias 1991: 70). Anticipating the Barthesian schema of the next chapter, it could be said that the mythological is ever present in the linguistic level. So the evaluations are intrinsic to the words themselves. But we have yet to answer *why* does it happen in the way it does? And another question, *how* do these affects get to be there in the first place?

The clue to the 'why' question has already been given, and is found in the function that the affects serve – to orientate one in the direction of either towards or away. However, these associations are neither 'natural' nor arbitrary. They are *generated* by the vicissitudes of the power relations between competing figurations of interest groups. Elias is arguing that the emotions are evoked and utilized to fulfil functions of differentiation. This idea differentiates Elias from the forms of psychoanalysis which say that it is the vicissitudes of the instincts (and thus emotions) that drive the forms of society. Elias is stating the reverse – that the forms of society play a significant role in the moulding of the emotions. Elias is expressing a Fairbairnian sentiment in saying that the emotions are a *technique* that is exploited in the task of differentiation, and not the 'cause' of differentiation that they are mistakenly taken to be.

Let me now ask a deeper question: what is the function of emotion? Or to put it another way, why has evolution found it necessary to provide us with the capacity to emote? At their most basic emotions are a binary switch, the most elementary form of which must be something in the region of pleasure/unpleasure to signal the basic information safety/danger. This must be the most basic function served by the emotions, to orientate the subject to the world – external and internal. One could say that the emotions are a kind of compass produced by evolutionary mechanisms to facilitate survival in unknown territories.

It is uncontentious to assert that more biologically complex organisms have a greater range of emotional possibilities. In fact that statement is not sufficiently accurate. It is more true to say that the more complex the structures of (social) relations between the organisms, the more complex are the emotional possibilities. In fact, the causal direction is the reverse of the common sense one; it is not the case that complex organisms have a greater range of possibilities, but that the situation calls forth a greater complexity from the organism. These ideas are a commonplace to biologists (e.g. Plotkin 1997, Dunbar 1997).

Over time, evolutionary mechanisms have machined this binary possibility in humans to generate emotions that are increasingly differentiated and richly textured. This must have taken place to enable them to react to their peers and environs in ways that are more fine tuned and subtle.

Elias applies the same idea to human societies in historical time to say, that as societies get more complex they require more emotional complexity in individuals and this generates a new psychology. As we have seen, he says that feudal society was 'simpler' and cruder. He says that people were able to indulge their passions (positive and negative) more freely – the rule of the day being 'might is right'. Elias substantiates this thesis with a wide range of evidence: the *unashamed* pleasure taken in cruelty by the knights, the fact that the notion of privacy was very different from the one we know, the fact that people were prone to defecate, spit and so forth in a more uninhibited way, the fact that public nakedness was not uncommon, the fact that sexual matters were more open, and so on. *What this means is that the types of psychology that are generated in those that inhabit a social order, are not necessarily antithetical to that order, but are designed to sustain and enhance it.*

> natural and historical processes interact almost inseparably. The formation of feelings of shame and revulsion and advances in the threshold of delicacy are both at once natural and historical processes. These forms of feeling are manifestations of human nature under specific social conditions, and they react in their turn on the sociohistorical process as one of its elements.
>
> (Elias 1994: 131)

The emotions serve the function of guiding us (truly or falsely is another matter) towards or away from things. Feelings of aversion and repulsion work in the direction of increasing distance, and warmer feelings work in the direction of reducing distance. In saying this I am rehearsing the instinctual psychoanalytic thesis, but in the language of emotions. The difference is more than one of semantics. As I have already discussed variously, the solipsism inherent in instinctivism locates causality in the internal world relegating the external and the social to a secondary status. The notion of emotion is more helpful because it in itself it is a relational concept in that emotions are of necessity always *about* something. The psychoanalytic thesis is that things becomes infused with negativity or positivity through the process of projection, with the contents of the projection being material from the internal world. In contrast, Elias is proposing that the feelings of aversion and attraction that accrue to behaviours and the like, have been *socially* generated for socio-political reasons.

Of the two, what the more universalist psychoanalytic theories have to explain is how or why things which are emotionally neutral in one epoch become taboo in another.

Conclusion

By tracing the history of manners, Elias was able to make inferences about the changing structure of the psyche. He also showed that it was the more powerful that determined to a greater degree what was thought to be good and bad. He went on to show how these ways were taken up by all those who inhabited the social order, and instituted in their psyches.

His theory of minds is unusual in that it is not floating in a sociological vacuum. Minds always exist in the plural, and are always in a power relation with each other. The identity he draws between language, thought and knowledge, all as aspects of Symbol, is a powerful one because it says unequivocally that the structure of the social world is necessarily echoed in the structure of the psyche. The two sides of the coin are first, that language is knowledge and so Symbol has a foot in the external world, and second, language and knowledge *are* psyche – there is no container nor contained, only conversational activity – and so Symbol has a foot in the internal world.

It is this last point that is the launch pad for the next chapter. A preliminary rationale is as follows. If language and knowledge orientate the subject to the world, informing them somehow of what is good and bad, then what role do the words black and white play in this process? Where Elias has subjected the changes in etiquette to his analysis, I will subject the semantic history of black and white to the same process. Elias has shown that the process of state formation necessarily impacts on the structure of behaviours between people in their everyday lives as well as the structure of their psyches. I am going to consider the impact of the processes of imperialist expansion and the formation of Europe on the everyday lives of its inhabitants.

Elias was able to show that the linkage between faeces and aversion 'grew' in historical time, I will do the same for the negative and positive associations of the words black and white. Elias also demonstrated that the function of good 'manners' was primarily the differentiation of a more powerful 'us' from a 'them'. I will do the same for black and white, to show that the European 'us' is manufactured by a progressive whitening of European insides (emotions) and outsides (skins), with the simultaneous blackening of 'their' insides and outsides.

Chapter 8

Black and white

In Chapter 1 the idea of 'race' was discussed and related to notions of culture and ethnicity. One of the things that became clear very quickly was that whatever the problems with each of the concepts, the words black and white were invariably drawn into the naming of all three. The very fact that it seems possible to talk about the *black* races, or *black* cultures, or *black* ethnic groups, suggests a reversal: *that the critical terms here are not those of race, culture or ethnicity, but are those of black and white.*

So what I intend to do now is to subject the words black and white to a detailed historical and semantic analysis to see what this throws up. I should also make clear that in what follows I am limiting myself to the English language. Although comparative studies with other languages would be of great interest, my focus is on the British context, and the material discovered from the history of the English language will be sufficient for my purposes.

There are several things that I want to achieve through this investigation. First, to see what kinds of patterns are thrown up. Second, to test the veracity of the idea that the associations of black and white to negative and positive respectively are natural. Third, if they are not natural, then to inquire how and when these associations are acquired. Fourth, to contemplate what function these associations might serve.

Whilst engaging in this exploration, I have constantly in the back of my mind the Eliasian view that language is intimately bound up with experience: that language forms and constrains one's experience – not only of the external world, but also of the internal, psychological world. His view, and mine, is that by examining the structures of *language* and *society*, we discover something about the structures of the emotions and psyche. Thus, very broadly, the task of this chapter is to investigate the notions of black and white as aspects of *language*, and also to locate them in the *social* contexts in which the meanings are being formed. The next chapter takes this forward into the realm of the emotions and psyche.

I start with a naïve observation, but a surprising one none the less, that things ascribed blackness and whiteness do not usually correspond to the chromatic notions of black and white. It is clear that these terms refer to something more than colour – so what are they? Even a cursory inspection reveals two things. First, not only the ubiquity but also the variety of their uses – as nouns (the whites), as adjectives (white magic), and as verbs (to blacken); and second, that black is loaded with negative associations, and white with positive associations.

One of the first common-sense explanations that gets put forward for the negative associations to the word black, says that they arise because of the proximity of the word black to the word dark. The *speculation* links physical darkness with blackness by suggesting that primitive humans must have feared the dark of the night and looked forward to the light of day when they must have felt safer. The argument then proceeds by saying that the mapping of this fear of the dark onto anything black, including people, is unfortunate but inevitable. This is an explanation that naturalizes the associations and makes them ahistorical. The rest of this chapter can be thought of as an attempt to deconstruct this common-sense explanation.

To begin with the linkage between dark and black – is it inevitable? In a philological exploration of the word black James makes the following surprising observation 'Black . . . is not used as a synonym for *doerc* [Old English for dark] either with reference to night and the absence of light, or in figurative senses (other than "dark hair or complexion" . . .) until the 14th century' (1981: 20). Given that the common-sense explanation grounds the cause of the connection in nature and prehistory, why does the connection in English appear only recently – just 600 years ago? I will begin the answer by examining the linkage between black and dark, white and light through two disciplines, physics and semiotics.

The physics of 'seeing' black and white

The physicist represents light as a wave with two dimensions – height and length (Figure 8.1). The height of the wave affects the brightness of the light and the length of the wave determines the colour of the light. Each in turn is discussed in non-technical language.

The intensity of light

The taller the wave (amplitude) the brighter the light. Dark means an absence of light. For absolute darkness (zero amplitude) there would be no wave – just a flat line. Darkness is not a thing in itself, it is the *absence* of something – light. In this sense darkness does not exist, it is a reification. We are now faced with the peculiar realization that darkness cannot be seen. To see darkness would be to see no-thing, an emptiness, an absence, a void. One cannot visualize no-thing because it is not possible to positively register an absence. In sum, brightness and darkness are both to do with the *amount of light*.[1]

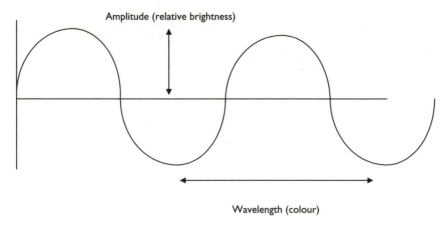

Figure 8.1 Light represented as a wave

The colour of light

Now to discuss colour. The longer the wavelength, the redder the colour. Colour is not only a wavelength, it is also a sensory experience. White and black are colours, in the sense that they can be seen; painters after all use pigments called white and black. However, they are rather peculiar colours in that they are different in kind to the others in the spectrum.

To the physicist black and white are technical terms with very precise meanings. The experience of seeing white occurs when all the visible colours of the spectrum are present at the same time. And black is an optical event when no light is present. So although optically black is an absence, the *Oxford English Dictionary* classes it amongst colours. This is because black in its literal sense cannot actually be seen because it is in itself total absence. So, in practice the word is used for objects that *approach* blackness without being literally black, for things that *can* be seen.

The point to be drawn from this is that black and dark are actually two very different *types* of things, the colour black is about the *kind* of light, whilst dark concerns the *amount* of light. Similarly, a triple conflation between bright, white and light has taken place. White is a colour, bright is its intensity, and light is the generic term that includes both colour and intensity.

Roland Barthes and semiotics

Having elaborated the distinctions between these categories through physics, I will now use Barthes' theory of semiotics to show the linguistic processes through which the slippages, dark to black and light to white, come about. Barthes (1984) breaks language down into two levels, the linguistic and the mythological.

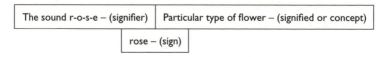

Figure 8.2 The linguistic level

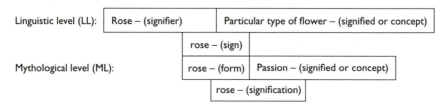

Figure 8.3 The mythological level

At the linguistic level an empty sound (the signifier) gets attached to a thing (the signified), and so becomes full of meaning (the sign). This is the language system we are born into, a world of words already full of meaning. The sound 'r-o-s-e' automatically conjures up a picture of the thing 'rose' *whether one wants to or not*, the two cannot be separated. One cannot go backwards, that is empty 'rose' of meaning and make it a non-sense sound again (Figure 8.2).

Whilst one cannot go backwards from the sign, one can go forwards into the next *mythological level*.[2] Here, the sign 'rose' is appropriated to point to something else, for example passion (Figure 8.3). This second use, Barthes says, is the process of mythification.

The importance of the second-order level is that we are born into this too and have little choice in the associations that are already injected into words. We are born into a language world where the word 'rose' *automatically* and apparently *naturally* not only makes us think of a particular sort of flower, but also conjures up an association with passion and romance.

Barthes defines the *function* of myth in the following way

> myth has the task of giving an historical intention a natural justification, and making contingency appear eternal. . . . A conjuring trick has taken place; it has turned reality inside out, it has emptied it of history and has filled it with nature . . . myth is depoliticized speech.
>
> (Barthes 1984: 142)

This conception of myth has many affinities with radical Foulkes' idea of the social unconscious, as well as Elias' ideas around language and Symbol. They are all descriptions of the transformation of history into nature. It is the fact that words exist on all these different levels simultaneously (sign, signified, form, etc.) that allows hidden meanings to be smuggled in clandestinely.

I would say that the process does not stop here at this double level, and that additional levels of myth (meta-myths) are part and parcel of the history of words. Each time, the signification of one myth is made empty to be exploited at the next level. For example, imagine a soldier strapping a rose on to a bomb before exploding it in enemy territory. The symbol of passion has been inverted into a symbol of passionate hate.

What is so valuable about this Barthesian analysis is that it shows up words for the powerful things that they are: possibly objective categories, but definitely complexities infused with history, affect and ideology. It shows how words connect the socio-historic world to the world of emotions, and it powerfully demonstrates how words will set off a chain of events in the mind *regardless of one's personal history*. As Foulkes and Anthony have said 'words are old and so carry layers of meaning' (1957: 245). I would say that each of these 'layers' referred to here are additional layers of meta-myths. This last point will become clearer as we use this methodology on the words black and white and their histories.

Semiotics: the darkness that is not 'black'

I will now use the Barthesian schema on the words black and white.

On the linguistic level, the *sound* b-l-a-c-k signifies the colour black, creating the *sign* black, which is now full of colour. Now the word black automatically conjures up a picture in the mind of the colour[3] black (Figure 8.4).

Similarly, the sound dark signifies the absence of light, and so the sign dark is now full of the meaning 'absence of light' (Figure 8.5).

But now there is a problem with the *sign* dark. Like a malfunctioning TV, there is a sound but no picture. As we have already seen, absolute

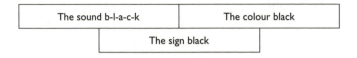

Figure 8.4 The structure of 'black' at the linguistic level

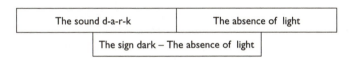

Figure 8.5 The structure of 'dark' at the linguistic level

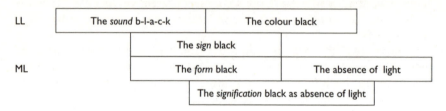

Figure 8.6 Transmuting darkness into blackness

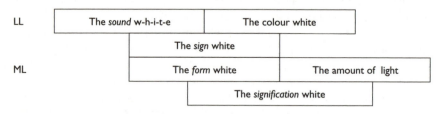

Figure 8.7 Transmuting white into light

darkness is *beyond imagination*, for how can one ever imagine an absence? Even as we try to imagine it, the associations of the word lead us to create something dark-like in our minds, that is something black. Blackness gets substituted for darkness. The picture black is clandestinely inserted in the place of dark. Barthes' diagram would now look like Figure 8.6.

So although blackness is used in the English language as a synonym for darkness, black is in fact a metaphor for darkness. *'Black' is the symbolic representation of darkness.*

Similar problems occur with the words bright and light. Brightness is a relative term, whilst light is a generic name, but both become held by the notion of white, with the result that white too comes to hold these two different meanings – for colour as well as for intensity (Figure 8.7).

Summing up, I have used physics to establish that each of the pairs black–dark and white–light are different kinds of thing, and used semiotics to show the mechanism of the slippages from one to the other.

The Holy Bible

The question that we are still faced with is how the associations of positives and negatives arose in the first place. James (1981) reminds us of the well-known fact that the terms darkness and light are widely used as spiritual metaphors for good and evil. Based on this, it is not unreasonable then to suggest that it is through this route that the associations are transported. In other words *notions of bad and good enter the words black and white via the words dark and light.*

In order to explore this suggestion I collected, amongst other things, every usage of black and white in the Authorised Version of the Holy Bible (1611). This task was made easier by the use of *Cruden's Complete Concordance* (Cruden 1769) which lists every occurrence of every word in the Bible. But why the Bible, and why this one? I will answer these questions in more detail as we go along but for the moment let me give some pointers. The Authorised Version of the Bible, the first *official* Bible translated into the English language, is important for several reasons.

First, it now allowed the 'ordinary' English-speaking person *direct* legitimate access to the Word of God, unmediated by priest. Second, the Bible was used as the ultimate handbook on how to recognize and discriminate good from evil in thought and deed. It was, and is, *the* moral and ethical template that continues to impress contemporary life in Britain. Third, it is well known that the structures and meanings of contemporary English have been significantly determined by the language of the Authorised Version. Fourth, the Bible, as the ultimate authority, was used to validate all sorts of political struggles, as well as intellectual and cultural endeavours from philosophy to geology and gardening. In brief, the metaphor and imagery in the Bible permeated all aspects of psyche and society. It established cultural norms which persevere even to this day.

On this basis I would argue that an investigation of the Authorised Version's use of particular words will grant us direct access to the aspects of shapes and structures within the British psyche, and specifically what might be called the superego.

I should stress that my concern is not with the Bible *per se*, but with this particular *version* of it in the English Language, as this was the text that made its impact on the ordinary English-speaking Briton and the English language. Thus, disputes about the accuracy of translation when compared to 'originals' in Hebrew, Greek or Latin are not relevant to the arguments being developed here. I am also not engaging in any way in a discussion about whether the content of the Bible is actually true or not; these issues are not relevant to the task at hand. What I am interested in is the use of particular words in the Bible and the impact these have had on the lives of men and women.

The use of 'light' and 'dark' in the Holy Bible

The term light in the Bible is intimately linked with goodness. It is the first thing created in the universe.

> 2. And the earth was without form . . . darkness was upon the face of the deep . . . 3. And God said, Let there be light . . . 4. And God saw the light, that it was good: and God divided the light from the darkness.
> (Genesis, 1)[4]

Darkness is initially used to mean the 'absence of light', however the fact that the light is good and is divided from darkness (verse 4), leads one to link the opposite of light (darkness) with the opposite of good (bad). The associations of light to good and dark to badness are everywhere in the Bible, and need no further verification. What I will turn to next are the uses of the words black and white. In what follows *every* occurrence of black and white in the Bible is taken up.

Black

There are some neutral uses of the word black, in St Matthew 5:36 and Leviticus 13:31. In Revelation 6:1–8 and Zechariah 6:2 black is the colour of a horse.

Blackness is used as a symbol for *spiritual* darkness, for example 'the blackness of darkness forever' (Jude, verse 13). In Job, 3:4–5, *darkness* is used to signify the absence of God and *blackness* is used to signify the terror that ensues from this.

Other passages use blackness to signify pain and suffering 'She is empty, and void, and waste: . . . much pain is in all loins, and the faces of them all gather blackness' (Nahum, 2:10); 'the people shall be much pained: all faces shall gather blackness' (Joel, 2:6). Further examples are found in Lamentations, 5:10 and Job, 30:26–30.

The basis for 'black skin' as a mark of suffering is found in the story of Noah. The ninth chapter of Genesis describes Noah drunk, naked and asleep. His son Ham sees Noah in this condition. For this 'crime' Noah curses Ham's *son* Canaan to be a servant to all and sundry. What is crucial to this story is the name Ham. Ham is a vulgarization of Cham. In Hebrew *ch'm* means black, hot, burnt, dark (James 1981: 26; Hill 1994: 398). This linkage allowed the story to be used as giving Biblical authority for nineteenth-century slavery: to be black is to be cursed to be a servant. It would appear that the *blackness* of the skin echoes the *darkness* of spirit. As we saw in Chapter 1, this story was also taken to be a description of how the earth came to be populated in the way it was with Ham (black), Shem (brown) and Japeth (white) populating Africa, Asia and Europe respectively.

Blackness is also utilized to signify the emotions of mourning, grief and depression, for example 'I clothe the heavens with blackness, and I make sackcloth their covering' (Isiah, 50:3); 'For this shall the earth mourn, and the heavens above be black' (Jeremiah, 5:28). Further examples are found in Jeremiah, 8:21 and 14:2.

In the following passage black is used as a counterpoint to beauty. The female lover in Song of Solomon says 'I am black but comely' (1:5). The pertinent word is 'but' as it undoes the word 'black'. In the Hebrew the passage actually reads 'I am black *and* lovely'. Presumably, by 1611 the negative associations with blackness were becoming so set that the translators found themselves changing this critical word. The allusion gathers greater force and significance when, at a later point, she describes her beloved thus 'My beloved is white and ruddy, the chiefest amongst ten thousand' (Song of Solomon, 5:10). His whiteness is a poetic counterpoint to her blackness.

Blackness is also linked to sin, for example in Lamentations, 4 the Jews are described in verse 7, before the exile, as pure and white, and in verse 8, having sinned, as become black '7. Her Nazerites were purer than snow, they were *whiter* than milk . . . 8. Their visage is *blacker* than a coal' (italics added).

In the next passage dark and black are used as theatrical devices to construct a sinful atmosphere '9. In the twilight, in the evening, in the dark and black night: 10. And behold, there met him a woman in the attire of a harlot' (Proverbs, 7).

White

I will now move on to collecting the usage of the word white and its variants.

On two occasions (Acts, 23:3 and St Matthew, 23:27) there are uses of white which are akin to a cover up or whitewash.

There are many general uses of white, every one of which signifies goodness of some description, for example *white* stone[5] (Revelation, 2:17) and *white* asses (Judges 5:10). According to Brown and colleagues (1990), the Judges passage is one of the most archaic parts of the bible where it is uncertain whether white means those who are actually pure, or those who pretend to be pure. In either case the linkage of white with purity is present.

Whiteness is also linked to Godliness 'behold a white cloud, and upon the cloud one sat like unto the Son of man' (Revelation, 14:14). Other examples are found in Revelation, 19:11–14 and 20:11.

In the following passages whiteness is linked to spiritual purity 'Wash me and I shall be whiter than snow' (Psalms, 51:7); 'Many shall be purified and made white' (Daniel, 12:10); In St John 4:35, the purity of those who are ready to be Christianized is signalled by their whiteness 'Lift up your eyes and look on the fields; for they are *white* already to harvest' (italics added).

There are a significant number of uses of white garments. The white garments on the outside echo the aura of holiness on the inside 'Thou hast a few names . . . which have not defiled their garments; and they shall walk with me in *white*: for they are worthy' (Revelation, 3:4). According to Brown and colleagues the defiled garments are a general symbol for sinfulness, whilst the white garments 'symbolise the glorified bodies which the faithful will receive following their deaths' (1990: 1003). Other examples are found in Revelation, 4:4 and 7:14; St Mark, 16:5; The Acts, 1:10; Esther, 8:15–16 and Ecclesiastes, 9:8.

To signal intense holiness white *becomes* light 'Jesus . . . was transfigured before them. And his rainment became *shining*, exceeding *white* as snow; so as no fuller on earth can *white* them' (St Mark, 9:2–3); 'And as he [Jesus] prayed, the fashion of his countenance was altered, and his rainment was *white* and *glistening*' (St Luke, 9:29). Other examples occur in St Matthew 17:2 and 28:3.

The Ethiopian

It will clearly be interesting to see how Ethiopians feature in the Bible, as they are people we would today call black. The Hebrew term for the Ethiopian is Cushite and the Authorised Version of the Bible uses both terms. Here is one example:

> 'And Miriam and Aron spake against Moses because of the Ethiopian woman he had married: for he had married an Ethiopian woman' (Numbers, 12:1).

There are several things of interest in this passage. The first is the obvious one that they are angry with Moses, not for marrying but for marrying an Ethiopian. Second, she is the only one that does not have a personal name, implying that the thing of significance is the *group* she belongs to. Third, the way that God decides to punish Miriam for rebelling against Moses is *by inflicting a skin disease* upon her, leprosy 'and, behold, Miriam became leperous' (12:10). It is difficult not to impute the intention of poetic justice; Miriam having attacked Moses' wife because of the colour of her skin, is visited herself with a blemish of the skin.[6] This is also the one place where becoming white is bad news 'behold, Miriam became leperous; white as snow'.

The first occurrence of Cush is in Genesis 10:6 in which the generations of Noah are listed. One of the sons of Ham is named Cush, which is Hebrew for Ethiopian, and this feeds the later rationalization for plantation slavery. There are numerous passing references to Ethiopians and Cushites, for example in II Chronicles, 14:9–15; Isiah, 11:11; Habakkuk, 3:7; Jeremiah, 36:14; Zephaniah, 1:1 and 2:12; Isiah 20:4–5 and Ezekeil 30:1–10.

In Jeremiah, 13:23 we find the saying 'Can the Ethiopian change his skin, or the leopard his spots? then may ye also do good that are accustomed to do evil'. Brown and colleagues say that God is saying to the occupants of Judah who have lived so long in sin, that it 'has now taken on a "natural" (sic) character' (1990: 279). The subliminal inferences that one might draw are 1) the Ethiopian's skin is become black because of long exposure to sin, and 2) there is little or no possibility of redemption.

The passage in Amos, 9:7 'Are ye not as children of the Ethiopians unto me, O children of Israel? sayeth the LORD' is taken by Brown and co-workers, to consist of God's warning to the children of Israel that 'Despite the fact that Yahweh has granted a special status to Israel, Israel is not the only people on earth that Yahweh cares for' (1990: 215). However, the poetic power of the passage is imparted through the subliminal assertion that even though the Ethiopian is the polar opposite of the Israelite, i.e. as far from God's chosen people as one is able to get, He still has their interests at heart. Ethiopians also feature in II Chronicles, 14:9–12 and Jeremiah, 38:7–9.

The findings

I will summarize the findings here.

1   What is striking about this collection, is the *consistency* of association whichever way the words are used, whether as nouns, verbs or adjectives, as symbols, metaphors, synonyms or concretely. It is as though white *cannot* be used even metaphorically for things evil, or even disagreeable and black cannot be used for anything good.
2   Perhaps the most surprising finding is that on the whole, white and black are *not used to describe a type of people*, they are used as signifiers of good and evil.
3   In the main, white on the outside (usually garments) is a reflection of the light within, and black on the outside (often skin) is a reflection of the dark within.
4   The word black is directly associated with spiritual darkness, pain and suffering, mourning, grief and depression. It is associated with sin, and it is used as the antithesis of beauty.
5   The references to black as a colour of skin, are not to do with skin colour *per se*. Skin becomes blackened as a *consequence* of suffering or sin or of being cursed.
6   The word white is used in the context of general goodness, Godliness, spiritual purity and light. There are many references to white garments, which 'symbolise the glorified bodies which the faithful will receive following their deaths' (Brown *et al.* 1990: 1003).

The Ethiopians and Cushites (people whom we would call black today) were marginal to the main thrust of the stories, and tend to signify a people 'not-of-God'. It is portentous that one of the sons of Ham is called Cush as it adds weight to the evidence that the tribe of Ham were made black, that blackness is a curse, and that it is almost irredeemable. 'Almost' that is, because in Acts 8 the possibility of redemption is held out through conversion. The only positive role allocated to an Ethiopian was to Ebed-melech, but having saved Jeremiah he disappears never to be heard of again.

We can see then, that the Bible does not tell its believers to hate and exploit black people *per se*, although many have been able to appropriate the text to grant divine blessing to the activities of hatred in general and the hatred of black people in particular. This feat has been possible through the exploitation of the linkages in the text between the *words* light/pure/white and dark/impure/black. I would argue that these ideas, associations and ways of thinking, were so powerfully driven into the psyche through sermon, prayer and liturgy, that they eventually became interchangeable terms. Moreover, one could say that *biblical language colour coded the notions of good and evil so effectively, that it taught the Christian to discriminate between good and evil by referring to the signifiers 'white' and 'black'.*

But what should be stressed is that in the Bible itself, whilst there are the linkages between black and bad, and between white and good, they are not directly applied to people as a type. What we can say instead is that Biblical text has prepared the ground for this to occur. This is particularly the case through a) the story of Noah and the fate of his grandson Canaan, b) the story of Moses marrying an Ethiopian, and c) the fact that through suffering or sin, one's skin is said to become black.

Apocalyptic prophesies and millennial anxieties

Having examined the text, I want now to think about the psychological space people were inhabiting during the Middle Ages to demonstrate why the language of the Bible was so highly cathected. It is hard in this day and age to comprehend just how central the Bible was to everyday life. People looked to the text for explanations and answers to the predicaments they found themselves in. The worlds of God and Mammon were completely intermingled. People saw divine intervention and retribution everywhere. The stories and prophecies in the Bible were 'live' texts that were experienced as pertaining to daily life situations. Satan and the Antichrist were seen everywhere.

Life at this time must have been a very anxious and charged experience. Precarious though existence was with death, disease and violence commonplace, people did not so much fear for their lives but for their *souls*. The issue was not just life or death, which is a one-off event, but *eternal* salvation or damnation. This would have resulted in existential anxieties being cranked up to terrifying proportions.

Judgement Day was expected to arrive imminently. In Revelation it says that God had bound Satan for a thousand years, but 'when the thousand years are expired, Satan shall be loosed out of his prison' (20:7). This was the millennium, a thousand years since Christ, the time was nigh. The world could end at any minute and those unprepared would be damned for eternity.

The power of the Bible resided in the fact that it was the source not only of these terrifying anxieties, but also of their resolution. These anxieties must be one of the main sources through which the words black and white come to be so cathected with fear and hope.

Anxieties were fanned not just by the Biblical prophecies in Revelation, but by other prophecies too – the most important of which were the Sibylline prophecies. People were constantly locating themselves in these stories, in attempts to understand the predicaments in which they found themselves. For hundreds of years before the translation of the Bible into English, its stories would have been familiar. Whatever the intentions of the authors of the Bible, what is of significance is what was read into the Bible. It was used to lend divine legitimacy to all sorts of political intrigues, by identifying whosoever the enemy happened to be with the Antichrist. This was true of external enemies like the Turks, and also of internal enemies including Kings and Popes. At the same time Kings and Popes – whether despots or not – used the Bible to lend themselves this same divine authority to justify their actions. Terrestrial battles were transmuted into cosmic battles.

In the next section I will describe the effects of the translation of the Bible on the internal politics of Britain, and in the section after that I will discuss its impact on the way external enemies were viewed.

The importance of the vernacular Bible

The bible is an ambiguous text in that it manages to be simultaneously historical and ahistorical. It is historical in the sense that it is obviously written by real people existing in particular moments of history. Yet, to the devout, the Bible is the immutable Word of God – spoken for all time, from outside time. This double vision allows that which is historical to be surreptitiously transmuted into something that is immutable, and makes the Bible mythological in the Barthesian sense.

The full significance of the translation of the Bible into English is understood when viewed within a larger context. The language of the courts in England during the Middle Ages was French and that of the church was Latin. The ordinary English-speaking person was excluded from both. Thus the translation of the Bible into English can be viewed as the expression of a new force in politics – the fledgling middle classes. This eventually formed the kernel around which national identities were formed. The historian Christopher Hill says 'The Bible played a large part in moulding English nationalism, in asserting the supremacy of the English language in a society which from the eleventh to the fourteenth century had been dominated by French-speaking Normans' (Hill 1994: 7).

Over time, English gradually began to creep into the language of church and state 'The first recorded use of English in a government proclamation occurred in 1258. . . . [By 1400] grammar schools were dropping French and teaching English' (ibid. 8).

John Wycliffe was the first to translate the complete Bible into vernacular English (1380). Previously the only available version was the Vulgate (AD 405) which was in Latin. Wycliffe's mission was the reformation of the established Church, and it was to this end that he contended 'that the church could be reformed only if everyone knew God's law, and this required that the Bible be translated into the language of the people' (Brachter 1993: 758).

Once 'common man' had access to the Word of God, they used what they found there as authority for many subversive political movements. One can see then that the language of English was literally a double-edged sword for the English authorities. On the one hand it was a sword that they used to cut ties above them (Rome), and at the same time it was being used by those below to challenge their authority.

The Wycliffe vernacular Bible was viewed as a seditious instrument although it was a faithful translation of the Vulgate: in 'the fifteenth century the mere fact of owning and reading the Bible in English was presumptive evidence of heresy' (Hill 1994: 10).

The vernacular Bible played a critical role in the transformation of culture. It stimulated literacy and was the book through which most people learnt to read, because often it was the *only* available book. This must have made a powerful, if not indelible impression on the mind.

> The availability of the Bible in English was a great stimulus to learning to read; and this in its turn assisted the development of cheap printing and the distribution of books. It was a cultural revolution of unprecedented proportions, whose consequences are difficult to over-estimate.
>
> (ibid. 11)

Other major translations followed (Tyndale 1526, Thomas Matthew 1537, the Geneva Bible 1560, amongst others), each had their own political agenda which they disseminated partly through 'spins' on the translation, and partly through marginal notes, 'helping' the reader to view passages in a particular light: inviting associations with contemporaneous issues. For this reason the marginal notes were particularly hated by the authorities. Three editions and some 18,000 copies of Tyndale's Bible are known to have been printed over a 10-year period. It cost a twentieth of the manuscript versions.

Secular and religious authorities sought to suppress printing itself to put a stop to 'unqualified people . . . [having] promiscuous license to read the Scriptures' (Marvell 1672, quoted by Hill 1994: 16). Unable to stem the tide, the authorities themselves made several 'authorized' translations, the last of which was the Authorised Version in 1611. The language in this version made it difficult to use as 'recruiting propaganda' and it contained *no marginal notes*. This translation was a political act, the intention of which was, paradoxically, to de-politicize the Bible.

The vernacular Bible was central to *all* aspects of life in the sixteenth and seventeenth centuries. Even Hobbes, accused of being an atheist, cited the Bible more than any other text in his works. Haklyut was brought to cosmology 'by reading the 107th Psalm', 'medicine sought Biblical authority', 'the Bible was a model for legal writers', 'writers on farming and gardening looked back to Adam' (Hill 1994: 20–42). And as we will see, it was also used to rationalize colonialism. But much before then it was helping organize emotions towards the Saracen and the Moor.

Norman Cohn describes the Sibylline prophecy written in the seventh century, called the Pseudo-Methodius, as

> composed . . . to bring consolation to Syrian Christians in their galling and still unfamiliar position as a minority under Moslem rule. . . . Under the guise of prophecy of things still to come it describes how the Ishmaelities . . . ravage the land. The Christians are punished for their sins by being subjected for a time by these hordes, who of course stand for the conquering armies of Islam.
>
> (1970: 32)

Cohn goes on to say

> In the ninth C . . . when . . . Christianity was gravely threatened by the victorious advance of Islam . . . a few clerics decided that Mohammed must have been the 'precursor' of a Saracen Antichrist and saw in Moslems in general the 'ministers' of Antichrist. . . . As Christendom launched its counteroffensive . . . popular epics portrayed Moslems as monsters with two sets of horns (front and back) and called them devils with no right to live.
>
> (ibid. 75)

The name of the enemy

Well before the advent of the Crusades, there was already a tradition of perceiving the Saracens as servants of Satan.[7]

> For medieval people the stupendous drama of the Last Days was not a phantasy about some remote and indefinite future but a prophecy which was infallible and which at almost any given moment was felt to be on the point of fulfilment . . . the threat of invasion by Huns, Magyars, Mongols, Saracens or Turks always stirred memories of those hordes of Antichrist, the peoples of Gog and Magog.
>
> (Cohn 1970: 35)

In the Dark Ages (as they are called) Jews were the ones who were more often than not elected as the terrestrial representatives of Satan and identified with the Antichrist. Increasingly, with the changing politics in the time of the Crusades, the Saracen and then the Negro came to share this role with the Jew.[8]

The colour of Satan at this time was not always black. He was often pale, but he always had some aspect of him coloured black: hair, clothing and so on. The monk Cesarius 1200–1250 says in *Dialogus Miraculorum* 'It is not uncommon for a demon to appear as a Moor' (quoted in Cohn 1993: 25). Satan was at times portrayed as a black cat. A chronicler from the eleventh century wrote 'the devil would appear to [the initiates] . . . sometimes as a Negro and sometimes as an angel of light' (quoted in Cohn 1993: 39).

So we can see that in and prior to the early Middle Ages, although blackness is playing a role in the naming of the enemy, it is not its defining term; the primary term for enemy at this time is Antichrist or Satan. The Crusades were going to change that.

The Crusades

The Crusades are central to the formation of a European and white identity. Out of the complex of reasons of why they came about, I will mention two. Elias argued that feudal rivalries in what was to become Europe, led eventually to local land becoming scarce which led to an impasse. This in turn primed the pump for a push outwards for new lands. Elias says that this social pressure was exploited by the Church and turned into a religious crusade.

As for the other reason, we have to look to the power struggles between the emperors of the eastern and western Roman Empire, the Catholic Church in Rome, and the kings and princes of various kingdoms who were all embroiled in a vast struggle for ultimate authority and power – both spiritual and terrestrial. The struggle between the papacy and the emperor of the western Roman Empire took on critical significance. The complexities of the battles and intrigues need not concern us here. In AD 1094 Pope Urban II emerged as victor having won Rome back from the hands of the emperor, but his power base was still extremely precarious.

When Alexius, Emperor of Byzantium (the eastern Roman Empire) asked Urban II for military help to drive back Turkish forces, Urban II used the opportunity to consolidate his position. On 27 November 1095 Pope Urban II proclaimed the first Crusade. By his appeal to a celestial authority he cut through, at a stroke, all terrestrial affiliations and bound them all to him under the banner of the Cross.

Urban exploited the terrifying millennial anxieties by making this a holy war. He announced that to take part in the Crusade was in effect to do a penance. Thus participation in the Crusades ensured one was made free of all sin and consequently guaranteed entry into the Kingdom of Heaven. Those who set out on the Crusades were setting out for the Kingdom of God, and if they were to die in the process then they would find themselves there anyway. Further, the Pope decreed that to kill the enemies of Christ was not a sin but a penance in itself. The holy war was a war of the forces of light against the forces of darkness. Inevitably Biblical imagery was used to equate the brown peoples of the Middle East with the Devil and his forces of evil. For example, the ' "King" of the Tafurs, a violent remnant of the first crusade, called the Moslems "the race of Cain" ' (Cohn 1970: 67); the Count of Toulouse lumps the Saracens together with the devil (Cantor 1963: 208) and so on.

But whatever the nature of the numerous labyrinthine intrigues of the instigators and participants, the process of the Crusades itself, resulted in Europe starting to define itself as Christian and white, by pitting itself against the brown Saracen, the Mohammedan. Thus the killing of browns by whites was seen not only as a moral duty, but also as a divine act sanctified by God.[9] These themes are crucial to the formation of a sense of European identity which was in the process of becoming Christian and white through contrasting itself with black pagans and idolaters. This then was one of the crucial historical moments that helped raise the significance and importance of the words black and white by reinforcing their associations to particular peoples through notions of evil and good.

The chosen people

From the sixteenth century Protestant England, isolated and surrounded by Catholic powers, came to think of itself as ' "God's chosen nation" against Antichrist' (Hill 1994: 266, quoting John Aylmer 1559, who also said in a margin 'God is English'). England and Scotland were identified with Israel and Judah. Various texts of the day used the Bible to argue that gentile Protestant English had succeeded the Jews as the Chosen People, because God's covenant with them in the Old Testament was negated by one in the New Testament. In 1643, this Covenant was actually instituted in the constitution of puritanism. This Covenant was a kind of legal contract – the English would do God's work on earth (expanding His Kingdom), and He in turn would look after them.

The Antichrist came in all sorts of guises, but for the Protestant he was primarily Catholic[10] 'In 1579 John Stubb . . . assumed that the English were a chosen people, and thought a marriage of Elizabeth to a popish prince would be like a Hebrew marrying a Canaanite' (Hill 1994: 266) (recall the earlier discussion regarding Moses' marriage).

The eschatology of the Prophecies had asserted that the Millennium would dawn once misbelief had been eliminated. During the time of the Crusades, the

> messianic hordes . . . saw no reason at all why that elimination could not equally well be achieved by the physical annihilation of the unconverted. . . . In the eyes of the crusading pauperes the smiting of the Moslems and the Jews was to be the first act in that final battle which . . . was to culminate in the smiting of the Prince of Evil himself.
> (Cohn 1970: 75–76)

With the dawning of the idea of the English as the Chosen People, these older prophecies and principles were resurrected. England *was* the New Jerusalem, and to hasten the coming of the Millennium it was the duty of the godly to enforce morality on the unbelieving masses if 'God was not to lose patience with England. . . . They had to be forced to be freely Puritan' (Hill 1994: 267). Cromwell's Puritans derived much of their fervour from the idea that the English revolution was furthering this same Cosmic battle against the Antichrist who was no other than Pope and King.[11]

These same ideas eventually energized colonialism and the drive to build Empires. The imperial project was justified and rationalized as a cosmic project – the conversion of all in order to hasten the second coming. Hill quotes T. Cooper from 1615 who bids his readers to do God's work 'in promoting his kingdom and demolishing daily the power of Satan' by colonizing Virginia and Ireland. Thus the expansion of the British Empire was thought to be 'contributing to the overthrow of the Antichrist and the establishment of Christ's kingdom on earth' (1994: 323). Killing was quicker than converting and achieved the same end – the reduction of unbelievers; this was one of the rationales that drove the genocides in Australia and the Americas.

As we have seen, the Bible was central not only to spiritual, intellectual and political life, but also to emotional life. Thus the imagery and the language of the bible (consisting of Judgement Day, the Antichrist, terror, good and evil, spiritual darkness and light, black and white, and so on) fuelled power politics and a burgeoning nationalism based on the Chosen; this in turn got enmeshed with colonialism as doing God's work and it infused all human relations and consequently was instituted deep within the psyche.

In conclusion, it is no coincidence that it is with the beginnings of European commercial and colonial adventures that the words black and white start *increasing* their respective associations with bad and good. The next section will take this up more closely.

A semantic history of 'black' and 'white'

The aim of this section is to look at the historical evolution of the accretions of meanings to the words black and white.

Much of what follows relies on the *Oxford English Dictionary* (OED) as it is widely accepted as *the* authority on the English language. In the section that follows, the known dates refer to the citation given in the OED for a particular term, as these are the earliest printed examples of the senses. Within definitions, the OED cites the first known written use of a meaning. In effect the OED provides a temporal map of the evolving meanings of words. It is true that the dates of printed examples of words do not occur simultaneously with the verbal usages of words, but the two must correlate closely with each other in time. The *Oxford Dictionary of English Etymology* (*ODEE*) was also utilized.

The *OED* (1989) lists 57 major definitions and uses of the word black when used on its own, and 66 definitions of white. Then there are literally hundreds of uses given for each word when combined in some way with another word. The *OED* says that there are an indefinite number of para-synthetic combinations many of which overlap and reappear in differing contexts in slightly modified forms. When one looks at the list of definitions and meanings, the organizing categories that immediately suggest themselves are negative, positive and neutral ideations.

The meanings of 'black'

Neutral

One of the earliest citations for the word 'black' from AD 890 is 'neutral' and to do with colour 'a quality practically classed amongst colours, but con-sisting optically in the total absence of colour'. There are many such uses from this time on, with the word on its own and in combination with other words as in coal-black, black bear, black bird, black board, black bass, black currants, etc. These combinations exist in such large numbers that the *OED* does not attempt to list them all saying 'their number may be increased indefinitely'. More recently the terms black and white goods have evolved to differentiate electronic goods (like stereos) from kitchen items (like fridges).

Positive

It is striking how few positive associations there are to the word black. Black belt emerges from the world of eastern martial arts and Black Stone is an Islamic sacred stone. Black Power as a positive assertion made its appearance in the twentieth century. Three other usages are black earth meaning fertile soil, black coated meaning of the professional classes, and finally the phrase 'in the black' meaning profit.

Negative

By far the greatest number of meanings associated with black occur in this section, and they are grouped under the categories dirt, emotion, death, evil and immoral.

DIRT

The earliest citation for black as a description of dirt is well into the Middle Ages in 1300, its meaning being 'Deeply stained with dirt; soiled, dirty, foul'. From 1753 there are citations meaning 'Deposit of dirt on the body, esp. under the finger nails', and from 1861 there is the word blacklet meaning 'a tiny speck of soot or dirt'.

EMOTION

Black is used figuratively to stand for two emotions: anger and sorrow, and usually for their intense versions: rage and misery. Its first association with sorrow occurs in 1659 to indicate 'clouded with sorrow or melancholy, dismal, gloomy, sad'. 'Black dog' comes to mean 'melancholy, depression of spirits, ill humour' in 1826.[12] In 1653 it is used to describe a countenance of despair or gloom. In 1590 is the first recorded use of black in the sense of a look of anger, for example to look black, black-browed, etc. Its use to mean 'clouded with anger, frowning, threatening, boding ill' occurs in 1709. By the eighteenth century the phrase 'black looks' is in common usage. These senses are derived from classical Greek through the word melancholy. James (1981) traces their evolution through associations with black foreboding thunderclouds.

DEATH

The first association of black with death in the English language is surprisingly late, in 1400 when it is cited as the colour of mourning. The habit of dressing in black for a funeral dates from this time. Black silk is not referred to until the nineteenth century. Black was a term used to describe a hired mourner at a funeral in 1619. The word is also used at about this time for black cloths hung in churches during funerals. The first reference to the black caps worn by judges whilst delivering a death sentence does not occur until 1838. In the mid-nineteenth century there is a new term 'black job' meaning a funeral, and at about the same time 'black work' was used as a synonym for undertaker's work; 'blackmaster' took on the meaning of undertaker in 1901, as did 'black man' in 1921 in Lancashire.

Instruments of death often end up having the word black attached to them. For example, a German gun in the 1914–18 war was called the Black Maria and in 1903 the black doctor was the name of a particularly nasty fishing hook.

EVIL

In 1581 was the first recorded use of black in the sense of 'foul, iniquitous, atrocious, horribly wicked', and in 1583 for 'having dark or deadly purposes, malignant'. In 1588 was the first reference to 'a blacke soule'. In 1591 'black man' stands for that of an evil spirit, and by 1658 it is synonymous at times with the devil. By 1893 the phrase 'black mass' has gained a new meaning in addition to that of 'mass for the dead', it now also means a satanic mass.

IMMORAL OR ILLEGAL

Once again it is the sixteenth century by the time there is a record of black being used in the sense of illicit as in the phrase 'black mail'. This was originally (1552) 'a tribute exacted from farmers . . . in the border counties of England and Scotland . . . in return for protection . . . from plunder'. From this it has come to mean any payment extorted by pressure. It had an additional meaning which was 'rent taken in the form of labour or produce as opposed to in money'. This is the root of the contemporary phrases 'black market', 'black money' and 'black economy' all meaning illicit trading of some description. Interestingly, during the fishing crisis of 1995 in the North Sea caused by over fishing, the fish caught and sold clandestinely were spontaneously called 'black fish' (BBC1, *9 O'Clock News*, 12 February 1995).

The meanings of 'white'

Neutral

The earliest meanings of white are the most straightforward ones to do with colour. In Old English white is used to indicate of the colour of snow or milk. In AD 888 it is also used to mean 'of no colour', i.e. clear, as in glass. In Middle English it comes to be used in additional ways to describe specific things, for example the white of an egg (*c.* AD 1000), the white part of the eyeball (*c.* AD 1400) and so forth. Through Middle English, white (like black) is increasingly combined with other words to name different sorts of substances and creatures because of their colour, for example white grouse, white perch, white poplar, white bread, white wine, whitebait, whiteboard. The verb 'to whiten' in its literal sense was being used from about AD 1000, as was the hyperbole – whiter than snow.

Positive

The positive connotations are grouped into the categories of cleanliness, things favoured, turning bad into good, and things legitimate.

CLEANLINESS AND PURITY

In its figurative usage the word white brings together themes of physical cleanliness and spiritual purity. The phrases 'stainless character' and 'white hearted' encapsulate these ideas succinctly. The earliest use in this sense is in

AD 971 to mean 'Morally or spiritually pure or stainless; spotless, unstained, innocent'. There are additional senses from 1394 to mean 'purity, stainless character or quality' and 'as a symbol of purity, goodness, truth, joy'.

During the twentieth century white starts being used in the sense of technologically sanitary: 'white room' means 'a clean and dust free room used for assembly . . . of delicate mechanisms'; 'white coal' and 'white fuel' are used to describe 'clean' non-polluting energy sources like water and wind power, and more recently also for lead-free petrol. The verb 'to whiten' meaning 'To free or clear from evil, guilt, or the like; also to cause to seem right, good, pure, etc. to give a specious appearance to' occurs from the fifteenth century.

FAVOURED, FAVOURABLE AND FAVOURITE

There are a whole set of phrases that use white to indicate something favoured. From the fourteenth century the word white is used 'as a vague term of endearment' and also as 'fair seeming, specious, plausible'. By the fifteenth century it has gathered more weight and is used in the sense of 'Highly prized, precious, dear, beloved, favourite, pet, darling'. By the sixteenth century the phrases 'white son' and 'white boy' occur meaning 'a beloved or favourite', and the phrase 'white hen's chick' signifies a fortunate person. In the early part of the twentieth century 'white haired boy' is used to signify a favourite.

TURNING BAD INTO GOOD

Then there are a group of words which, when white is placed in front of them, transforms their meaning from something bad into something good. As the *OED* says '[it frees it] from malignity or evil intent'. For example 'white witch' and 'white magic' in the seventeenth century, and the phrase 'white lie' in the eighteenth century. Similarly, in the twentieth century the phrase 'white propaganda' came to be used to indicate truthful propaganda, and the phrase 'white war' signified a war without bloodshed – economic warfare. The contemporary phrase 'white collar crime' derives from the idea of 'white collar workers', its definition by the *OED* as non-violent financial crime, implies that it is less harmful than other crime.

LEGITIMATE, HONEST

In the nineteenth century white used on its own means honourable, as in 'that's very white of you'. Also in this era 'White Father' was a term given to 'a white man regarded as protecting or controlling people of another race'. This gives rise to the phrase 'White man's burden' meaning the thankless task of looking after the peoples of the rest of the world. In the fifteenth century 'white rent' meant rent payable in silver, i.e. in the legitimate tender of the land.

From the twentieth century comes 'white market' which is defined as 'authorised dealing in things which are restricted', and in the jargon of the stock-market the phrase 'white knight' means 'a company that comes to the aid of one who is facing a take-over bid'.

GENERAL NEGATIVES

There are a few negative phrases. White elephant for uselessly splendid, and a nineteenth-century phrase 'white night' means a sleepless night. There are some new contemporary insults that are used by blacks about whites, for example white arsed, white trash, white meat and so on.

'Whitewash' first appears in the eighteenth century to mean concealing something problematic by covering it over with something white, i.e. pure. This same sense of using white to cover over something unsavoury occurs in several other contexts. In the same period 'white bonnet' described a fictitious bidder at auction. In the nineteenth century 'white cap' described 'a self-constituted body . . . who commit outrages upon persons under the pretence of regulating public morals'. Also in this period, members of some illegal or secret societies in Ireland and England were called Whitefoot and Whiteboys. The latter group were so called because they wore white shirts over their normal clothing.

Analysis: the evolution of black

On examining the data, three themes emerge. First, things that have no colour get named black. Second, things get made black retrospectively. And third, things that are already black, become increasingly negative over time. I will take each in turn.

Things named black

The words black and white begin their lives as descriptors of the material world, but from the Middle Ages on they start being used to describe things that evidently have no colour whatsoever – moods (black temper), behaviours (black looks) and events (death). James makes the point that things considered as dirt 'excrement, dust and mud . . . ashes – are by no means characteristically black in colour' (1981: 22), i.e. it is not 'natural' to call dirt black.

In the seventeenth century malice, slander and gossip get colour coded black through the phrases 'black babbling' (malicious gossip), 'black boding' (ill omen) and 'black mouth' (slanderer). During Queen Anne's reign the term for a bad shilling (one not made from silver but a base metal) was a 'black dog'. In the clubs and societies of eighteenth-century England, a black ball of wood was put into a ballot box to express an adverse vote, hence the term 'to blackball' (sometimes black beans were used). In this period poachers who poached with blackened faces were called 'blacks'.

From the sixteenth century criminal activity starts being blackened. 'Black Art' is sixteenth-century slang for lock picking. In 1877 Scotland Yard gathered together a collection of exhibits relating to crimes and called it the Black Museum. During this time 'black hole' meant prison as did 'black house'. Black house was additionally used to mean 'a place of business where working hours are long and wages are very small'. The figurative use of 'black mark' to mean censure is also noted for the first time in this century.

Through the trade-union movements in the nineteenth century the phrase 'black leg' was introduced, and so was the phrase 'to black', as in 'will not have anything to do with'. With the twentieth century came the phrases 'to put up a black' (meaning to make a serious mistake or blunder) as well as 'black propaganda' (falsified propaganda). The earliest citation given for black comedy in the *OED* is 1963. Black Monday was how the stock-market crash of 1987 was described.

Retrospective blackening

As the term black became increasingly established as an adjectival signifier of badness, not only did it begin to attach itself to new words and phrases, but also things that were not perceived as black at one time, became black at a later time. What psychoanalysis tells us is that shifts, slips and changes are not meaningless accidents but meaningful phenomena. The direction of the shift exposes something about the structures and colours of the social unconscious. What precisely this exposes will be taken up more fully later. Interestingly the phrase itself 'to blacken' meaning 'to stain, sully; to defame' emerges quite late, in 1625. Presumably, the phrase emerges at this time because it is required to describe the 'new' activity of blackening.

A good example of things being retrospectively blackened is that of the Black Death. It is usually supposed that this disease was so called because of its symptomatology. For example, the Chambers dictionary says that it is 'a deadly epidemic of bubonic plague . . . reaching England in 1348 (from the black spots that appeared on the skin)' (1982: 134). However, the *ODEE* says that it was a Mrs Markham who first used this phrase in 1823, and James (1981) says that it was a historian, Mrs Penrose, who coined the phrase in 1813. Whichever is true, it is clear that it was not called the Black Death until the nineteenth century. Before this time it is called variously the plague, the great plague and so on. Ziegler (1969: 17) discusses the various theories that have been put forward to explain why it is called the Black Death. These include the colour of the putrifying flesh, black spots, a black comet allegedly seen before the onset of the plague, the high number of people mourning and so dressed in black, and so on. Whilst he finds them all wanting for pertinent reasons, he offers no alternative explanation.

However, if one locates the change in name in history and views it as one amongst many instances of things getting blackened at this time, then it helps us make sense of it. The fact is that the naming of the plague a black one is nothing at all to do with the plague itself. The blackness has been read back into it from 500 years in the future. This feat is now possible because by the nineteenth century the word black has taken up sufficient associations with death, terror, illness and so on, for it to become natural to spontaneously name this horrific episode the Black Death.

Another instance of something becoming retrospectively black begins in antiquity with the Greek word *nekromanteia* which means divination by the dead. However, by the thirteenth century it was 'corrupted to nigromantia, black divination' (James 1981: 23). I would suggest that it is the historical fact of the crusades that encourages this slippage to take place. This gave rise to the contemporary phrases 'black art' and 'black magic'.

Another instance occurs with the son of Edward III, who lived in the fourteenth century. He was not called the Black Prince until the sixteenth century by Grafton in 1569 (*OED*: 251) as a way of signifying his malignancy. And by the seventeenth century the phrase Black Prince had become even more evil by becoming another name for the Devil.

In tracing the pictorial representation of the devil in west European art, James found that the devil was not regularly coloured black until the fourteenth century. Before then he is often painted red, but 'also green, blue, brown, and multi-coloured' (1981: 23).

Black becoming darker

A shift can be seen in the meanings attributed to words and phrases that already have black as part of their original structure: as the centuries pass they are seen to gain increasingly negative connotations. We have just seen that this is so of the phrase 'black prince'.

Blackbird meant originally and literally a black bird. By the 1880s it had gained a more sinister meaning, that of 'a captive negro or Polynesian on board a slave or pirate ship . . . hence Blackbirder, man or vessel engaged in slave traffic'.

In law in the seventeenth century the phrases 'Black Acre' and 'White Acre' were arbitrarily applied to two pieces of land to distinguish them from each other. But by the eighteenth century the first of these phrases had become an insidious verb meaning to litigate about landed property. The *OED* citation is from 1751 'She is now gone to town, black-acering, to her lawyers'. What is to be noted is that given that both phrases, black acre and white acre, had equal weight in their original usage, the new verb was not white acering.

Blackamoor was initially used without 'depreciatory force' (*OED*), it meant literally black Moor. But by 1663 it had become a synonym for devil. The citation in the *OED* is 'He is dead long since and gone to the blackamores below'.

According to the *ODEE* 'blackguard' in its original usage (sixteenth century) meant one of the kitchen menials in grand houses. It also meant literally 'a guard of attendants, black in person, dress' (*OED*). In the seventeenth century it comes to mean 'vagabond, loafing, or criminal class of a community' (*OED*), and by the eighteenth century it has increased its forcefulness to mean 'One of the idle criminal class; a rough; hence, a low worthless character addicted to or ready for crime; an poen scoundrel (A term of utmost opprobrium) . . . pertaining to the dregs of the community; of low, worthless character; brutally vicious or scurrilous' (*OED*).

In an interesting anomaly blackguard also comes to be the name for a kind of snuff. The *OED* explains 'when a shop-boy made a mistake in the preparation of some snuff, for which his master called him an "Irish Blackguard"; but the mistake turning out a fortunate one, the new preparation obtained the name given to its author'.

In the last part of the sixteenth century 'black letter' was a straightforward term for a particular type used by printers. By the eighteenth century the phrase 'black letter day' meaning a bad day, was in common usage. It derived this meaning from the custom of marking the saints' days in the calendar with red letters.

The transformation of the phrase 'black book' is a particularly clear one. Early usages are neutral and straightforward; particular books are called black books because they happen to be bound in black. Its first recorded usage is in 1175 with the Black Book of the Exchequer, containing accounts of royal revenues. Perhaps this is where the fiscal phrase 'in the black' draws its meaning from. During the time of Edward III (fourteenth century), the Black Book of the Admiralty set out rules for government of the Navy. There are other various references in the 1600s to particular official books bound in black. Then, in the time of Henry VIII, Cromwell's report of abuses perpetrated in monasteries was called a Black Book. This signals the beginning of the change of meaning. By the 1500s it comes to mean a book recording the names of those who have rendered themselves liable to censure (thus to be in someone's black books). In the nineteenth century black book was also taken to mean a book of black magic and so increased its proximity to evil and the devil.

There is an interesting intermeshing of two different discourses to do with the phrase 'Black Monday'. In the economic discourse, black is good and red is bad, in the sense of being in credit or overdrawn. So if one stays within economic discourse, the stock-market crash should have been called Red Monday. But at this critical moment, the force of black as a generic signifier of badness, overwhelmed red, the economic signifier of badness.

Analysis: the evolution of white

From looking at the evidence it would appear that there was not the explosion of associations with the word white as there was with black (reasons for this will be proposed in the last two chapters). The greater number of usages for white are most easily categorized under neutral than anything else. There is of course an increase in the positive associations with white as time goes on, but not anywhere near the extent as there was for black. So, for example, the phrase 'white book' did not become increasingly positive over time, whilst its counterpart 'black book' did gain in negativity.

However, there are growing instances of black things made white from the eighteenth century. The use of the word white drains the attached word of its negative connotations. Examples are white witch, white lie and so on. The uses of white in phrases meaning favourite does not start until the fourteenth century. The notion of white fuel for clean fuel is very modern. The colonial era gave rise to the type of phrase 'playing the white man', which equated moral honesty and whiteness. White, although it plays its role in some negative notions, does so in such a way that it manages not to sully itself in the process. The two main negative groups are that of 'cowardice' and that of 'cover up'. With cowardice, white signifies an absence of something, of blood, choler and so on. So white itself is not identified with cowardice. Similarly, with the cover up (as in whitewash), white covers up something bad, but is not bad in itself.

By locating the first appearances of the various uses of black and white over the ages, we will be in a better position to think about what has taken place (Figures 8.8 and 8.9).

Initial observations

The first and most surprising thing is to see just how recent the negative associations with black are – associations that one takes for granted, for example the association with dirt in 1300, death in 1400, evil in 1500, and so on. Although much less dramatic, the same is true of the word white. Of particular interest is the fact that the difficult emotions do not get coloured black until the seventeenth century.

But what can be made of the fact that the accumulation of meanings begins around the thirteenth and fourteenth centuries, and then accelerates away from about the sixteenth century? In order to answer this, we have to take another excursion into the domain of history.

From Christendom to Europe

The historian John Hale (1993: 3–7) suggests that before the idea of Europe had any currency, it was the notion of Christendom that held sway. However,

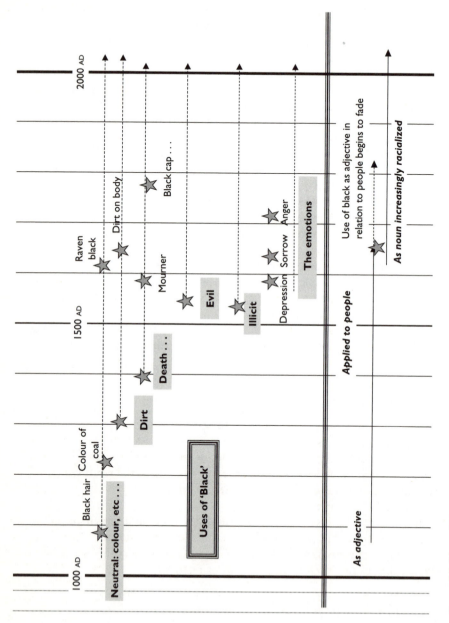

Figure 8.8 Map of black

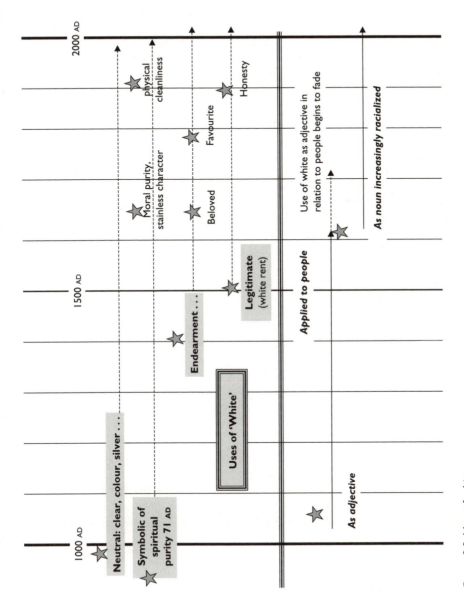

Figure 8.9 Map of white

during the Middle Ages the notion of a unified Christendom began to be fragmented from within into various orthodoxies, and eventually with the Reformation of 1529 all ideas of Christian unity were completely written off. Further, the conventional image of the Christian was also being eroded by the increasing numbers in Asia and America who were being converted.

The need for a new unifying principle was fulfilled by the secular idea of Europe; an idea that looked to Greek and Roman antiquity for its roots. It is at exactly this historical moment that the racializing mechanisms begin to be activated, although it is in fact during and after the Enlightenment that it comes into full flower as scientific racism. And as we have seen, as soon as race makes an entrance so do its handmaidens – the colours black and white. At about this time the story of Noah and his three sons was revived to enhance this process, after which it was not to fall out of favour for some hundreds of years. In fact in 1561 Guillaume Postel 'suggested that Europe should be renamed after Japeth, Japétie' (Hale 1993: 9).

In summary, there was a powerful confluence of movements which came together over this period: a) the replacement of Christendom with an idea of Europe; b) the racialization of peoples; c) the racialization of the concepts; d) the beginnings of colonialism and e) the beginnings of the Renaissance.

When all these are put together, then it is no coincidence that the notions of black and white as signifiers of difference are being stoked into a new and dangerous life as signifiers of the bad and the good in relation to people, things and the emotions.

I would say that the evidence delineates two historical periods of significance during which the words (and particularly black) start going through dramatic shifts in meaning. The fact that the word black starts gaining negative connotations during the Middle Ages, I would say is to do with the Crusades. The explosion of negative associations, which begin in the sixteenth century, I suggest is intimately tied up with the beginnings of the European adventures of imperialism and colonialism. The etymological evidence for this is first, that black and white start being used in increasingly racialized ways from this time, and second, it is in tandem with this that the words, now imbued with powerful associations, increasingly became dislocated from actual 'things' black and white. They became free-floating figurative adjectival prefixes and suffixes, attaching themselves to things of different hues in order to allocate them particular meanings and values.

People: from adjective to noun

This shift from Christendom to Europe can be mapped onto a shift in the uses of black and white. The first usages of black and white as applied to people, were as adjectives – referring to physical attributes. The *OED* says the words are applied to people who are 'Characterised in some way by this colour'. The earliest recorded usages of black in this sense are from the eleventh century for a person with black hair or black eyes. Similarly, white makes its appearance in 1200 in the phrase 'white haired'. People are also described as black or white because of their clothing, for example Black Monks in the thirteenth century because of the colour of their habits and in 1400 black knights because of the colour of their armour. Similarly, during this period are found the first mentions of White Sister, white monk, white friar, white nun, and so on. The first citation for the figurative use of white for skin complexion is 900, whilst the use of black in this sense occurs in the fourteenth century. What seems clear is that the words were used as more or less normal adjectives until the sixteenth and seventeenth centuries. It is important to note that up to this point the word black could be used for what is now called a white person (say black Tom) because of some attribute of theirs (e.g. black hair), and vice versa. The *OED* suggests that some of the surnames such as Black and Blackie derive from this usage.

Then, from the seventeenth century, the words start becoming racialized, that is they start being used as nouns – names for types of people. In becoming names they become essences. The noun white for the name of a people makes its first recorded appearance in 1604, and the noun black in 1625. From now on culture itself, with all its constituent discourses, starts being racialized with the words black and white getting increasingly fixed, glued as it were, to particular groups of people. Meanwhile their more flexible adjectival use, for aspects of people, starts to atrophy. This shift from *adjective* to *noun*, is *critical*. It embodies a shift from an attribute to an essence, from a variable to something immutable. This radical shift reflects the hardening attitudes from whites to blacks that come about as the European mercantile and colonial adventures gather momentum.

I would say that in the time of Christendom the notion of pagan sufficed as a means of distinguishing the relevant 'them'. But as this grouping began to be eroded from within through fragmentation, and from without through conversion, the secular idea of race was needed to redraw the boundaries between 'us' and the various 'thems'. By the time the words black and white start being used as nouns for people as a type, they have already been loaded up with many of the associations they are to bear (see Figures 8.8 and 8.9). To recall the broad history of the words as traced so far, they start out pointing to neutral material things, and then go on to colour a whole host of things that have no colour (moods, attitudes, etc.). The attitude towards things, either for or against them, are revealed by the colour allocated to them – white or black. So when the words get attached to types of people who do not actually correspond to those chromatic notions, it is part of the same continuum of events.

This suggests that from the beginning the words are not neutral descriptions of things seen but of things experienced. As soon as these words are used on people as type, they immediately tar the group with the brush

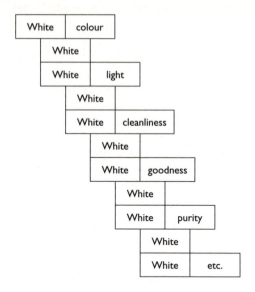

Figure 8.10 Levels of myth and meta-myth in 'white'

loaded with all its previous meanings. In Barthes' idiom, the phrases 'the white (person)', 'the black (person)', are myths. And myth, he says, is depoliticized speech. What this means in this context is that by pseudo-scientific subterfuge, political power relations have been transformed into natural relations.

Barthesian diagrams

We can use Barthes' diagrams (Figures 8.10 and 8.11) to represent the historical evolution of the words, the additional levels being meta-myths. When one looks at them in this way, we can see that the words are truly burdened.

Invisible signifiers

The last element to be drawn out from the evidence is that it appears that words have invisible signifiers in front of them. Take the two pairs of phrases, black economy and white economy, and black propaganda and white propaganda. In everyday usage one readily hears the phrase 'black economy' but its counterpart is hardly ever used. In a straw poll of some half a dozen colleagues not one (including me) had heard it. So in everyday usage it would appear that it is not necessary to place the word white in front of economy to mean the legitimate economy. Whilst this appears to

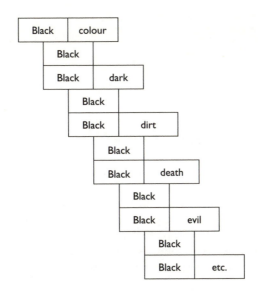

Figure 8.11 Levels of myth and meta-myth in 'black'

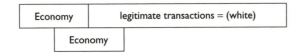

Figure 8.12 'White' as the invisible signifier

render the notion of the legitimate economy colourless, what has happened in fact is that the word white has become invisible; one might even say unconscious. It is because it is implicit that the legitimate economy *is* white, that the word black is needed to distinguish illegal economics. To use Barthes' terminology, the word economy has been made mythic. The colour of the legitimate economy is revealed to be white by the *necessary* presence of black to designate an illegitimate economy (Figure 8.12).

The reverse is true with the next phrase. In common parlance propaganda usually means lies. It is surprising (at least it was to me) to discover that there is a white propaganda which means true information, and that the correct phrase for what is commonly called propaganda is black propaganda which means falsified information (*OED*). In this instance it is the word black that is invisible. It is the fact that the word propaganda is already negative that makes the overt presence of the word black redundant. On the mythic level, the *form* propaganda points to black which then

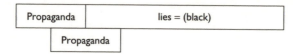

Figure 8.13 'Black' as the invisible signifier

becomes invisible in the *signification* propaganda. However, the twist in the story is that propaganda has *become* black (Figure 8.13).

Remember, Barthes says that on the level of experience the signifier and signified *cannot* be separated.[13] These ideas show how even though words might appear colourless, and therefore neutral and valueless, there is always, somewhere, the implication of colour invisible to the conscious mind. So, for example, the word lie has no obvious colour. But when it is juxtaposed with white in the phrase white lie, then one can see that lie has blackness implicit in it. Other examples of the same theme are black market, black money, white witch, white magic, and so on.

I am now in a position to assert that in broad terms, things that are valued, that are central and part of the establishment in this society are, either explicitly or *implicitly*, coded white. The obverse is true of things that are construed as less acceptable and marginal to the established norms, such things are explicitly or *implicitly* coded black.

It seems to me that there can be no neutral thing, there is always some emotional response to it. Even something as abstract as number, is to be *experienced*. Each person has their history with number, liking it or not at school, and so on. And affect is a basic part of each and every experience. Through the preceding chapters I have been developing the idea that there is no such thing as neutrality in the realm of human experience. There is always a position in relation to anything, a desire with a valence positive or negative, towards or away, and that the valences are internally coded black and white.

Conclusions

The work of this chapter can be described as an Eliasian analysis of the history of black and white in the English language and British context, and has resulted in the following clarifications.

First, the associations of positivity and negativity with whiteness and blackness are not natural in any sense, but develop within the context of a field of power relations. Second, the evidence has demonstrated that the terms black and white have become increasingly ubiquitous over the last thousand years, penetrating, organising and *structuring* all aspects of existence, both internal and external. The terms, for they are no longer just colours, tag all sorts of things, by colour coding them, and so locate them on a dual grid of morality and desire. Third, this has resulted in the English language itself becoming colour coded. Fourth, the fact that the emotions that are disapproved of start becoming coloured black at about the same time that the European imperialist adventure is taking place, is powerfully suggestive that in this process we are witnessing the mutation of aspects of the psyche in response to changing structures and the preoccupations of society. In other words, this is an echo of the Eliasian thesis: as society is becoming colour coded, so is the psyche. The final point is this: the notions of black and white, now powerfully cathected with negativity and positivity, have become signifiers of the valencies of desire, with the result that their primary function has become to signal the relative appeal of the things that they are attached to. There is a double movement here. On the one hand the attaching of black to a thing lends that thing a negative valency and so impels one to push it away, on the other hand things imbued with negativity are increasingly perceived as 'naturally' having something black about them. The reverse is true of white. The conclusion I draw is that blackness gets attached to a thing *in order* to cathect it with repellence, with the converse being true of whiteness. Thus white and black have been honed into powerful devices or instruments which are used to lever things into the territories designated as good and bad, in or out, us or them. These points will be further substantiated in the next chapter.

Let me end with an analogy for the use of the loaded words black and white – a shotgun blast. When the word is used all the compacted meanings, innocent and not innocent, are discharged. Some of the meanings hit and are registered consciously, but others that appear to miss are registered unconsciously. I would argue that once the associations are compacted into the words it is not possible to use them without activating in some way, *all* the associations. This is not so controversial a notion. Recall Foulkes and Anthony said 'words are old and so carry layers of meaning', and 100 years ago Freud based his technique of free association on exactly this kind of idea.

Notes

1 Absolute darkness is the absence of all light, zero amplitude. On the other hand, brightness (the counterpoint to darkness) can go on increasing indefinitely. This makes darkness–brightness an interesting scale. Although infinite, one pole of it is accessible. To elaborate on that: darkness is grounded in an absolute state, that of 'no light energy present', and therefore can be reached. On the other hand, there is no limit to the amount of brightness, it has no destination, it continues indefinitely to infinity. Darkness is an absolute term whilst brightness is a relative one (however, darker and lighter are both relative terms).

2 These are Barthes' own examples.

3 Remembering the caveats established earlier.

4 Citations from the Bible are denoted thus: (name of the book, chapter:verse); on the occasions that the verse numbers are included in the citation, then name

of the book and chapter are given. If the book consists of just one chapter, then (name of the book, verse).

5 'The white stone is an amulet [given by God], and the "new name" is a powerful magic formula' (Brown *et al.* 1990: 1002).

6 Professor Stanley Schneider (personal communication) says that according to rabbinical interpretation leprosy is not the real skin leprosy but rather is a rash of sorts. It is a mistranslation of an acronym in Hebrew which means 'for saying bad things about a person'.

7 The word Satan comes from Hebrew where it has associations with hatred, persecution and adversary.

8 Woman too had a role allocated to her in the demonization of the world. From the tenth century there was a common belief that the Antichrist would be born through a union between Satan and woman – a Jewish prostitute.

9 It is interesting to note two ironies. 1) The first people that were killed by the Crusaders were in Europe itself, local 'enemies of Christ', European Jews. In AD 1096 the Jews in Speir, Worms, Mainz, Cologne, Trier, Metz, Prague, Bavaria and many other places were slaughtered. These were the first pogroms to be repeated with each new crusade 'It was said that whoever killed a Jew who refused baptism had all his sins forgiven him; and there were those who felt unworthy to start on a crusade at all until they killed at least one such' (Cohn 1970: 70). 2) Once they crossed the Bosphorous in late AD 1096, the first people that the Crusaders killed with 'legendary nastiness' were Christians living on the outskirts of Nicaea. Speculating, this 'mistake' might have happened because, already, skin colour was beginning to be used to designate the enemy.

10 'William Erbery [1621] was prepared to extend toleration to Jews and Turks but not to papists' (Hill 1994: 296).

11 As political fortunes changed, Cromwell too came to be identified with the Antichrist.

12 Winston Churchill is said to have described his depression with this very phrase.

13 There is a parallel to this phenomenon in the world of arithmetic. It comes as a surprise to many to know that all the day-to-day numbers like 3, 17 and so on, should actually be written $^+3$, $^+17$. This is to be read as positive three, positive seventeen and so on. The positive is part of the *complete name* of the number, and is quite different from the operation +, meaning to add. Now, even though one might not 'know' that the sign is invisibly there all the time, one somehow acts as though it were. It is a convention that we are all part of, whether we know it or not, that the day-to-day numbers are positive numbers. Thus the absence of any sign means a positive number. The negative sign only becomes *necessary* when a negative number is being described.

Chapter 9

Categorization: the vicissitudes of difference

Given that racism operates on groups called races, and races as such do not exist, then we are left with the predicament of how racism generates its groupings. What we do know is that the groupings that racism relies on are those of 'us' and 'them'. We have also noted that because the notion of a group *per se* is not a straightforward one, there are always questions about which boundaries are utilized to manufacture the categories 'us' and 'them'. In order to engage with these issues one final element needs to be introduced, and this is the question of how categories come to be formed in the mind.

In sum, this chapter contains two themes. First, how the mechanisms of cognition are utilized in the construction of categories, and second, how power relations and the emotions are mobilized to sustain divisions between the categories.

Process reduction: habits of thought[1]

There are two prominent theories of thinking to be found in psychoanalysis, those of Bion and Matte-Blanco. It is to be granted that the work of Bion has much of value, however, it will not be utilized here for the following reasons. First, much of Bion's theory is grounded in the philosophical stream of idealism, and as such goes against the ethos being developed in this book. Elias' notion of process reduction which we have had occasion to evoke before, is a potent critique of the metapsychology behind Bion's theorizations.

For example, Bion's theory is built on the premise that thoughts, thinkers and the objects that the thoughts are about are three different things; this is the polar opposite of the arguments put up by Elias (1991) in which he demonstrates that the three cannot be separated, only abstracted. Elias continues by saying that there is a general misapprehension that tends to follow the process of abstraction, a misapprehension that began with Plato and has permeated much philosophy and psychoanalytic theory – including Bion.

The sequence is as follows: once something has been abstracted then, if one is not careful, it appears that the abstracted thing can have a life on its own – separate from the rest of the world. For example, take any number of circles of different sizes drawn on a piece of paper. Each of them has a particular area. It is possible to manipulate the notion of area in the mind by the process of abstracting it. So far so good. The error lies in the next step which is to imagine that there is such a thing as area *per se* which exists with no reference to any actual shapes at all. Further, because each particular circle has its own unique area, it could then appear that the particular area of each circle is but a manifestation of the general idea of area. This then leads to the next error of thinking that the general is prior to the particular, and the idea-of-a-thing is prior to the thing itself. Reality has been reversed by the device of forgetting that the generalized has been derived and abstracted from innumerable particulars, and by imagining that the abstracted can have a life separate from that from which it has been abstracted (area can only exist because of the presence of the circumference, and vice versa). It can be seen that Bion's notions of thoughts looking for thinkers and the contained looking for a container, poetic though they might be, are in fact expressions of these fallacies.

Further, because these generalizations are true for all historical circles – past, present and future – they have the appearance of existing outside time. This is the kind of thinking that must have led Plato to say that the idea-of-the-thing is immutable and eternal and has an existence before the actual. This is his philosophy of Ideal Types in which the material objects on earth are said to be poor facsimiles of the Ideal. In this way of thinking, purity can only be found in the idea rather than the actualization of the idea, and when the idea is made material, then it is thought to have been corrupted in some way. Bion expresses exactly this philosophy in suggesting that 'it is indispensable to have a thinker to produce a lie; whereas true thought does not require the prior existence of a thinker to think it' (Grinberg *et al.* 1985: 69).

It is also the case that Bion does not problematize categorization in the way that Matte-Blanco does, and so is less useful for the lines being pursued here. It is for these sorts of reasons that Bion is not given more of a presence.

From abstraction to antagonism

Another aspect of process reduction consists of the fact that our minds see 'states' when there are only processes. Although the processes of existence are infinite, our minds are such that they can only deal in finitudes. Consequently, our minds are obliged to break up infinite processes into bits and pieces (states). Bits and pieces have beginnings, middles and ends. It is often the case that we unthinkingly take these beginnings to be absolute, of having nothing to do with what has gone before, and of having an actual reality. Our thought processes are required to generate beginnings, because if we constantly kept in mind what has gone before, we would be embroiled in an infinite process, and our thought would never be uttered. So although all beginnings are in fact necessary but logical conveniences, we somehow experience some of them to be absolute. Thus the notion of an absolute beginning is akin to that of splitting.

Having abstracted states out of processes we are not only prone to the error previously discussed, of supposing that the abstracted elements can have an independent existence from each other, but also another error in which we perceive the abstracted states as being antagonistic to each other. For example, having abstracted an 'outside' and an 'inside' from a circle, one could say that the two are in direct conflict with each other – one gets bigger at the cost of the other getting smaller. However, in order to exist the thing called the inside needs its apparent opposite, the thing called the outside. Without one there cannot be the other. Whilst it is clearly non-sensical to talk about a circle's inside and outside being in conflict with each other, this is exactly the sort of thinking that leads one to imagine that biology and society are antithetical to each other and is also true of many of the great philosophical dichotomies: individual–society, body–mind, free will–determinism, death–life instincts, and so on.

We can see then that Elias' cautions encapsulated under the rubric process reduction constitute a theory of thinking in its own right, its very simplicity disguising its profundity.

Having said why I will not be using Bion, I need to say why I will be using Matte-Blanco. His relevance lies in the fact that at the centre of his theory of thinking is a description of the mind's struggle to manufacture the finite from the infinite and so is an elaboration of Elias' process reduction. As we will see, it is the vicissitudes of this process that make categorization such a problematic activity.

Matte-Blanco

Matte-Blanco's (1988) work augments and refines Elias' insights on process reduction to show how even notions of similarity and difference are abstractions that have the appearance of being antithetical to each other. This is, of course, critical to our concerns as notions of similarity and difference are deeply implicated in racialized structures. The precursors of Matte-Blanco's theory of thinking are found in Freud's distinction between primary and secondary processes. Matte-Blanco gives a quasi-mathematical description to each of these processes, he calls them symmetrical and asymmetrical logic.

The rules of asymmetrical logic are the ones we operate by in the day to day. It is called asymmetrical because if one statement is true, then its converse is not simultaneously true. For example if the boy is *on* the chair, then the converse (the chair is *on* the boy) cannot be true in the same moment of time; there is a spatial order here, one thing is above another. If Jack is following Jill, then Jill cannot be following Jack; there is a temporal order here, one thing comes after another. In the Eliasian language of processes and states we could say that this is the domain of abstracted states that are in some sort of relationship to each other. Asymmetrical logic is an either–or logic as well as an if–then logic, where things are very clear and distinct: boy and chair are clearly different things; there can be no mistaking Jack for Jill. This is the logic of the finite, of cause preceding consequence; because I missed my bus (cause), I am fed up and have to walk (consequence). A thing has a beginning and an end, it inhabits a particular space and time. Things are ordered and sensible – if this thing is a tree then it is not a house, and if that thing occurred at three in the afternoon then it did not occur at two in the morning. This is the logic of yes or no, and so is a binary logic of two states. It is a logic that relates particles to each other according to strict rules. I use the word particle to indicate that the objects of this logic have sharp edges, which locates them in particular bits of space and time: if I am in the kitchen then I am not in the dining room. This is the logic that Perry Mason uses when questioning the witness 'were you in the kitchen at three o'clock or not? Yes or no?'. There are no other alternatives here. The reason for this pedantry will become clear shortly.

Mathematicians formalize this logic into three rules that appear to be so self-evident that they hardly seem worth the bother of making them. But as we will see, their very obviousness will shortly be questioned. In any case, the first of these rules is called the *principle of identity*, which in ordinary language is as follows. A thing is itself, in other words the thing named X is different to something not-X. The second rule is the *law of the excluded middle*: a thing is either true or not true, it is either X or not-X. It cannot be both at the same time. The third rule concerns the rules of addition and subtraction; if something is removed then the original thing is smaller.[2] In a way this last rule is saying that there are always consequences and repercussions to actions.

Let me now turn to describe symmetrical logic. In this logic all the previous rules are broken. To our rational minds this is a mad logic where all sorts of contradiction are the norm. First let me give instances of symmetrical relations that do make sense to us. If Jack is *next* to Jill then the converse is also *simultaneously* true, Jill is *next* to Jack; ditto for 'Jane is the sister of Jill'; the sentences are symmetrical in the sense that if the terms are reversed, it still holds true. However, the statement 'John is the father of Jill' is asymmetrical in that Jill then cannot be the father of John. One could say that Jill is the consequence and John the cause.

But the rules of symmetrical logic say that even when the terms (John and Jill) are reversed, the statement remains true. It is called symmetrical because it remains the same (true) for both arrangements. In this crazy logic the order familiar to us collapses. Within the rules of this logic *both* statements are allowed and *simultaneously* true: John is the father of Jill and Jill is the father of John. Because of this, John is the logical equivalent of Jill – in other words, because they are interchangeable they are the same as each other. We can see what this means a bit more clearly by referring back to the three rules of asymmetrical logic. In this mad logic a thing can be itself and something else at the same time, it can be true and false at the same time, and actions do not necessarily have consequences – or certainly not the ones we might expect. The language of dreams utilizes this logic.

These peculiar things are possible because they are the outcome of the mathematics and logic of infinity. Thus asymmetric logic is the logic of the finite, and symmetric logic is the logic of infinity. Infinity being so big (infinitely big!), its properties are quite different from the properties of the finite. Whilst 700 plus 3 is 703, infinity plus 7 is still infinity. This is like saying one can do something and there will be no consequence – astonishingly the situation will be unchanged. Here all possibility and all impossibility exists simultaneously. In this symmetric logic before is the same as after (precisely because of symmetry), and so there is no time. Because place A is equivalent to place B, all of space is identical.

To sum up: *asymmetric logic* is a logic of the finite, of space and time, of either–or, of more than or less than. It is the logic of difference – indeed the basis of this logic is one where *difference matters*. In this logic things change because actions have consequences. *Symmetric logic* on the other hand is the converse. Things that were different to each other in the first logic are the same as each other here – they are *identical*. Peculiarly, there is no difference between tree and house. There is no time and there are no consequences. In this logic (infinity being so big) nothing changes. This is truly the domain of the eternal and immutable. Whilst symmetric logic homogenizes – makes things the same, asymmetric logic differentiates between things – (to put it rather clumsily) it heterogenizes. One is a logic of sameness and the other a logic of difference.

A semantic autopsy

The distinction between Matte-Blanco's model of thought process and those of Freud and Klein is important. The latter have an either–or model: Freud says that thinking takes place according to the rules of secondary process *or* primary process, whilst Kleinian thought processes take place according to a paranoid-schizoid *or* depressive mode of functioning. Each of these is an alternative to each other. Meanwhile Matte-Blanco says that all thought is in fact a *combination* of both logics. This totality he calls *bi-logic*. To illustrate the workings of bi-logic, it will be helpful to revisit the shoe shop first mentioned in *Taking the Group Seriously* (Dalal 1998: 165), and build on the discussion that was started there. The task before us is to examine the workings of a simple sentence by opening it up and conducting a kind of semantic autopsy on it. The shop keeper told us 'there are more brown shoes than red ones'.

Now, for this statement to be able to work, for it *to be able to say something* certain, things *need to be left unsaid* because if they were simultaneously said then distinction, and so meaning, would be destroyed.

The statement has created two categories – red and brown shoes. The first thing that has to be rendered invisible are the connections between these groups, for example the fact that they are all shoes. If this connection is remembered, then there is the danger that the groups would collapse into each other. In effect, the difference between the two groups is emphasized, and the similarities between them are rendered invisible – one could say made unconscious.

Now we can only ever meaningfully say a thing like 'the red shoes' by ignoring all the differences *within* the category red shoes – the fact that some are brogues, some are stilettos, and so on. It is clear then that in order to say 'the red shoes' what is being emphasized is their similarity, and what is made invisible are the differences within the category.

If we now step back from the whole thing we can see that at the level of the sentence the parts have been homogenized (made the same), whilst the space between the parts has been heterogenized. We could just say that asymmetric logic is being applied to the space between the categories, but actually something more active is taking place: asymmetric logic is being used to *create* the categories. However, this feat is only possible by the simultaneous application of symmetric logic within the categories. In effect we have temporarily introduced two absolutes – an absolute difference between the parts and an absolute similarity within the parts.

The use of diagrams will further elucidate the relationship between the two logics and the unconscious. When we make the statement 'more brown shoes than red shoes', we are *conscious* of the homogenized entities 'brown shoes' and 'red shoes', and that they are different to each other. Thus in the conscious domain, asymmetry is being applied to the space between the two entities, and symmetric logic to their insides. In a sense this results in the actual *creation* of these entities as well as the space between them (Figure 9.1).

But if we now looked to the unconscious realm (that which is hidden and rendered invisible), we would find the converse of each of the two logics (Figure 9.2).

If any of this unconscious level were made conscious, then it would literally destroy the previous image and replace it with another. Thus, shoes that find themselves to be in opposite camps to each other in one frame might in another frame find themselves together. In effect, we have X-rayed these apparently solid bodies and been able to look inside them and see that

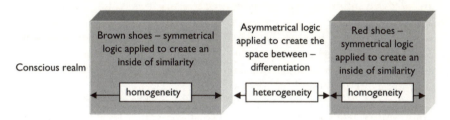

Figure 9.1 Relationship between red and brown shoes at the conscious level

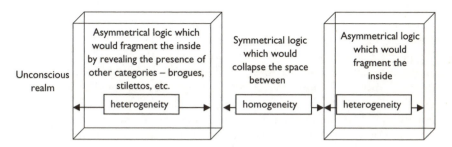

Figure 9.2 The hidden or unconscious level

their actual internal structure is the reverse of what appearances would have us believe.

We should not forget that the shopkeeper must have made the statement in which red and brown are the primary terms for some reason; the description is there to serve a purpose – perhaps to decide which shoes to order. In other words, we cannot leave *intention* out of the picture; this in turn is a reminder of the idea from Chapter 1 that the function and description cannot be separated. So, if one remembered the forgotten then we could also have another sort of statement (say more brogues than stilettos) which, although equally true, would not necessarily serve the original purpose, whatever it was.

Identity as an outcome of bi-logic

To begin with let me underline the points that have emerged from the preceding discussion.

The first thing that has been delineated are the details of the process of abstracting the elements red and brown shoes from a greater field called shoe shop. Second, we can see that as a description of the state of the shoe shop it is precarious, in that any number of alternative descriptions are ready to infiltrate and commandeer the conscious realm. Thus one has constantly to work in some way to keep them at bay; one way of doing this work is to render unconscious the additional information that is present. Third, the use of the term red or brown is nothing less than the allocation and construction of an *identity*. Fourth, this kind of process takes place continually in all thought processes.

We can see that the diagram of the sentence consists of two 'globules of homogeneity' with the space between them generated by a heterogeneity. The sentence could equally well be described as globules of *similarity* in a sea of *difference*. But most importantly not only can we describe the sentence as globules of consciousness in a sea of unconsciousness, but also as globules of unconsciousness in a sea of consciousness.

The idea that I would now like to suggest is this: *all identity formation is based on this sort of process*. What this means is that if one attempts to test the internal structure of an identity, say redness, then it will collapse into another, because behind the screen of homogeneity there lurks a multitude of other differences any one of which might get activated to take pole position. Even at the internal experiential level, the sense of self retains the impression of something solid by remaining at a sufficient psychological distance for us not to be able to know that at its centre there resides a symmetrized space – a homogenized heterogeneity.

The outcome of the preceding discussion can be encapsulated in two brief statements.

- The illusion of similarity is based on the repression of difference.
- The illusion of difference is based on the repression of similarity.

And instead of repression, one could equally say subjugation or repudiation.

Manufacturing the 'coloured' races

I have just given a description of the cognitive mechanisms that lie behind the post-modern problematization of identity as something essentially unstable. What I have also shown are the detailed workings behind the Eliasian idea of process reduction. When these two are brought together we can see that the idea of identity as a possession is an outcome of process reduction. What is being suggested is that rather than possession, identity is a name for a certain set of abstracted relationships embedded within other relationships. So all identities are continually menaced by the presence of other hidden relationships which threaten all the while to burst out and destroy them.

We are beginning to get a glimpse of how the coloured races get manufactured. The mechanisms will be attended to in more detail as we proceed, but we can already gather that the experience of perceiving dislocations on the spectrum (the spaces between the so-called races) are places where the continuum has been made unconscious. The work of the previous chapters also allows us to add that the places one is *compelled* to hallucinate the discontinuities between these so-called races are designated by the contents of the social unconscious, which in themselves are manufactured by the sociogenetic processes, in particular those of colonialism.

Imagine for a moment the hypothetical situation where the great and the good are designated by weight. In such a case our perceptual senses would organize the data in such a way that the differences in colour or gender would perhaps not even register on the conscious realm. What would register loudly would be weight, and as the social psychologists show (see p. 181) we would inevitably hallucinate dislocations on the weight spectrum too.

Reframing the instincts in the language of similarity and difference

It is possible to recast what Freud and Klein called the instincts of death and life in the language of similarity and difference by recalling Fairbairn's formulations. Remember how he described the tensions in any state of equilibrium in his model of social structures of family, clan, tribe and nation: he said that the continued existence of a structure (say clan) was threatened by libido which sought to join the clan with other clans, thus making them 'the same' at a higher level of synthesis, in the sense of belonging to the *same* tribe. At the same time the structure was threatened from within by aggression, which worked in the direction of fragmentation towards lower levels of organization where they would end up belonging to *different* families.

If we replaced the language of the instincts with notions of similarity and difference, then we would be able to say that these social structures are threatened from within by 'asymmetry and difference', and from without by 'symmetry and similarity'.

In actual fact this way of thinking also accords quite well with *elements* of Freud's theory of group formation. Recall that he had suggested that groups cohesed through individuals replacing their superegos with a leader or idea. Following this the individuals identified with each other, i.e. were the *same* as each other, and by this device incapacitated their self-preservative instincts (which under normal circumstances were said to attack anything *different* to the self). This sameness allowed them to bond with each other. If we strip his formulation of instinctivism, we can see that he too is describing a mechanism whereby difference within the designated group is incapacitated, thus leaving an *illusion of similarity* operating as the primary organizing principle. I will now bring some of Winnicott's work back into the discussion because of its pertinence to this very topic.

The Winnicottian schema

Winnicott (1980) had said that transitional spaces give an illusion of connection. They form the first bridge between the inside and the outside for the developing infant. The infant thinks that it magically creates something when it needs it (say the breast when hungry), but reality is more prosaic in that the mother is merely presenting the breast to the infant. Winnicott cautioned that this paradoxical space was a necessary developmental phase, and that it would be injurious to the infant if it were to be prematurely questioned and tested.

Winnicott also said that transitional phenomena were the basis of cultural life, and that they too took place in a paradoxical space that was actually illusory, i.e. a space that does not exist as a fact but does as an experience. It was this anomaly that made it paradoxical. Nevertheless, the work of this space is the same – to give the *illusion* of connection. He follows this to say that groups come together on the basis of this illusory experience

> We can share a respect for *illusory experience*, and if we wish we may collect together and form a group on the basis of the similarity of our illusory experiences. *This is a natural root of grouping among human beings.* Yet it is a hall mark of madness when an adult puts too powerful a claim on the credulity of others, forcing them to acknowledge a sharing of illusion that is not their own.
>
> (Winnicott 1951: 231, italics added)

I take the fact that group identity is based on an illusion to mean that the thing that holds a group together is nothing other than its name. In other words group identity is always an abstraction, a reification, its basis being the shared '*similarity* of illusory experiences'. And it is precisely because of its illusory nature that it needs to be defended so vigorously.

Once separation has occurred then there are two regions, it would appear that one region is within one's control (the me/us), and the other is not (the not-me/not-us). However, *within* each of these regions something peculiar is going on. Within the first region, the me/us, not only does the notion that all-is-me/us continue, but so does the notion *nothing-but-me/us*. And within the other region the reigning idea is that it has *nothing-whatsoever-to-do-with-me/us*. We are witnessing once more the operation of bi-logic. Red and only red versus brown and only brown – the dangerous knowledge of shoehood is annihilated.

But what has happened to the ambiguity? We find that we have been precipitated from a paradoxical space where both similarity and difference exist, to one where there is sharp-edged clarity: here *only* difference; there *only* similarity. This cognitive clarity is a defence against ambivalence and ambiguity, and it is here that one of the precursors of racism is to be found.

It could also be said that the region filled with phenomena designated as illusory by Winnicott, is in fact much closer to a description of the problematic of 'reality' than either of the states it is sandwiched between. It seems to me then that there are clear affinities between Winnicott's idea of the transitional space, Matte-Blanco's bi-logic and the post-modernist view of the world.

Let us also recall that Winnicott said that the first moment of existence, the I AM moment of individual or group, is a paranoid moment. This is because as the circle is closed, *things have to be excluded*; and the fear is that the excluded will resent and attack. In other words, it is the fact of existence that is said to inevitably precipitate anxiety.

This formulation is anti-essentialist as it allows anxiety and aggression into the existential frame without having to make recourse to instinctuality. Thus anxiety and aggression are reframed as aspects of *relational processes* rather than internal energies.

To summarize: the formation of a group precipitates an aggression to that which is thought of as outside it. Winnicott says that the kernel around which group identity forms is essentially illusory. Thus, the name of the grouping is in effect a reification. And precisely because it is a reification there is continual work to be done to distance the not-me from the me, the not-us from the us. We are now able to say with Winnicott, *that if the name of the grouping is a racial one, then this work of emotional distancing is nothing other than racism.* To be more specific: the activity of giving the group a racial name is nothing other than the process of racialization and this in turn is the same as racism.

These existential complexities are ever present and part and parcel of the human condition: they are an aspect of the deep topological structure of human existence itself. Racialized discourses rely on exploiting exactly these existential complexities. This in itself is not an explanation of racism, rather it is part of what makes it a possibility.

Kinship: social psychology, sociobiology and Freud

Experiments conducted by social psychologists suggest that our cognitive capacities are designed to help us 'see' and sustain the illusion of wholeness in ways that fit in perfectly with the ideas being developed in this section.

In 1959 Tajfel put up two hypotheses that were confirmed over the years in a great many experiments. He suggested that when a criterion was applied to some collection of things to generate groups, then one's perception worked in such a way that the difference between groupings appeared to be greater than it actually was, and the differences within groupings appeared to be less than they actually were. This finding applied as much to measuring sets of lines, as to groups of people. The psychologists refined their techniques until Tajfel and colleagues (1971) came up with the Minimal Group Paradigm. This was a situation where people who would never meet each other were allocated randomly to one of two groups, and separately each person was asked to engage in tasks. A consistent finding was that people tended to favour members of their own group, even though the group was a complete fiction, *it existed only in name!* Their unconscious strategy was always in the direction of maximizing the difference between the groups, *even when in absolute terms the us-group would be worse off.*

There are three things here.

1   Our cognitive mechanisms are such that we automatically reduce differences within perceived groupings, and increase the differences between them. These mechanisms are necessary to the process of generating groups out of a larger field.
2   One of the ways we unthinkingly increase the emotional distance between groupings is by favouring one over the other.
3   When the groupings consist of types of 'us' and 'them', then it is usually (but not always) the us-group that is favoured (the caveat occurs because as we will shortly see, the processes of identification are complicated by the vicissitudes of power relations).

These findings concur with the sociobiologist's contention that we are programmed to favour us-groups (see Chapter 1), but shows that they are wrong when they seek to explain the cause of it through the number of shared genes. What these experiments show is that once an us-group is constituted on whatever basis then, other things being equal, we will tend to favour it. If kinship groups happen to be the primary organizing principle in a particular context, then one will indeed favour kin; but if the primary organizing principle is say, political ideologies, then one will favour the grouping that one is part of rather than one's kinship group.

If we change the language a little and think of 'kin' as being of the same type rather than being biologically related, then we will see that Freud's thoughts on group formation are exactly in line with the findings of the social psychologists. Let us begin in this way: the imperatives of the socio-political context determine which grouping, which name, is the critical one at any particular time. Thus those that belong to that name could be said to be a kind of kin within that meaning system. Freud says that groups form by all their members being in thrall to a person or an idea, and on this basis experiencing themselves as of the same kind, as brothers and kin. Thus we can say that there are many different sorts of kinship, and the one that is critical at any one time will be contextually determined. We can also see that Freud, despite using the language of the instincts, was right after all, in that one experiences oneself as kin with others in the same grouping, regardless of its basis.

The formulations above work with 'other things being equal', however, the situation is such that things are not usually equal. One grouping is inevitably more powerful than the other, and this complicates the dynamics so that one will not always be prone to favouring the us-group but the more powerful group. This complication will be elaborated a little later, meanwhile two preliminary points can be made. First, if the names critical to a context are those of black and white, however they come to be there, then one will be impelled to experience those so designated as kin of a kind, regardless of the presence of other similarities and differences. The first impulse is to identify with the more powerful (and it is always possible to find attributes in the more powerful to make identifications with); thus the proclivities of the power-relational field determine to some extent which 'type' one experiences oneself to be. It is when this initial impulse is thwarted (also by the vicissitudes of the power-relational field) that other identifications and allegiances are either made or thrust upon one. Fanon's Tarzan story is an example of this. The experience of many migrants to Britain from the Commonwealth is also of this nature. They come expecting to be part of a similar strata of society (say professional classes) only to find that they are rebuffed as darkies. It is often only at this point that they make an identification with blackness and become politicized.

Having done this groundwork it is possible to see a little more clearly where we stand at present. We have three things before us: from Winnicott we have the powerful proposal that the only thing holding a group together is its name, from Elias we have the suggestion that the act of naming is predicated on the function that the name is to serve, and that these functions are intimately bound up with external socio-political processes, and from the psychologists we have two findings that we will tend to favour those who belong to the same name as us and that we hallucinate a reduction of differences within groupings and an exaggeration of those between them.

Thus names contain within them some reflection of the social relations from which they emerge, and those that are deemed to be part of this name are said to belong together.

The arguments are beginning to show that identity – the sense of who I am – is the same as that of where I belong. Belongingness is to do with a kind of sameness. But we have seen that the notion of sameness, can only be sustained by subjugating internal differences and external similarities. It is this fact that makes the act of naming so tendentious. In sum

- the act of naming elevates some differences and renders one blind to the presence of others
- the act of naming elevates some similarities and renders one blind to the presence of others.

In naming, this double movement is ever present.

The colour of denigration and idealization

The emotional counterpart to the cognitive mechanisms that facilitate the manufacture and maintenance of difference are those of denigration and idealization. These work in exactly the same way – eradicating differences within each grouping thus increasing the distance between them. Idealization is a notion of good and only good; a thing idealized can do no wrong. The reverse is true of denigration. This feat is only made possible by the application of symmetric logic to the internals of each grouping. One way of smearing goodness over the entirety of a grouping is to paint it white. Contrawise, the other grouping is painted black, thus denigrating it entirely, allowing one to say with some conviction 'no good will ever come of them'. The previous chapter has shown how the sociogenetic processes honed the notions of black and white to enable them to be used as powerful instruments of denigration and idealization.

The difference in emphasis with the traditional understanding of the mechanisms of denigration and idealization needs to be stressed. In the psychoanalytic literature denigration and idealization come about through the process of projection, the purpose of which is to evacuate one of the poles of ambivalence from the inside onto something on the outside, thus leaving one territory good and the other bad. In this model, the states of denigration and idealization are caused by the processes of managing internal difficulties and so the end result is, in a sense, an epiphenomenon. The argument of this book is continually progressing the quasi-Fairbairnian notion to say that the emotions are not causes *per se*, but that they are mobilized in order to organize the relations between objects in such a way that they reflect the power relations between them. Thus the emotions are used to enhance the perception of the distance between the 'us' and the 'them', in order that 'we' act towards 'them' in ways that accord with the well-being of the 'us'.

I do not wish to suggest that idealization and denigration do not occur by virtue of projection by individuals, rather, that at a societal level certain groupings are already cathected. Further, it will be argued that the projections of all individuals are patterned by the types of power relations that prevail, so that it is almost always the case that it is the more powerful that tend to be the idealized ones.

Foulkes: rethinking belonging

The fact that Foulkes gives the impulse to belong a critical motivational role in human relations makes his presence a pertinent one here.

There is a contradiction to be found in Foulkes which is helpful to us. Orthodox Foulkes follows Freud and others to say that there are such things as natural groups and he calls them fundamental groups (Foulkes and Anthony 1957). By calling them fundamental, he is saying that these groupings occur naturally, of their own accord. If they are natural then anything that diverges from this is, by definition, un-natural and so is experienced as an anomaly.

On the other hand radical Foulkes not only says that all groups are abstractions, but that the individual is also an abstraction. In this sense radical Foulkes is a post-modernist as he is undermining the notion of a 'whole' (Foulkes 1990).

The resolution that is emerging from the discussion is that although there are no such things as natural groupings, we find it necessary to keep inventing the fantasy of such groupings in order to give ourselves an illusion of stability. This idea will be further substantiated as the chapter progresses. But if one accepts this idea for the moment, that there is such a necessity, then the next question is what is the nature of this necessity? There are two components to the answer, one of which is psychological and the other socio-political. Whilst I have differentiated these two elements, I wish to stress that they are aspects of the same thing.

The psychological necessity is an emotional one. Foulkes says that in every human being there is a fundamental need to belong – to be part of something. Whilst I very much agree with this, there is a problem in the way it is phrased. It appears that first there are isolated individuals who then, secondarily, join in order to belong and become part of something bigger. The notion of 'joining' implies that previous to this joining there was separation.

But this is never the case, we were never separate. We are intricately joined and are part of the fabric of the universe from the first moment of existence. But because this vastness is too much to comprehend, we fragment and fracture, in order to abstract types of belonging that are comprehensible. Thus, it is more accurate to say that the psychological impulse to belong is not so much an impulse to join up with others, but of abstracting something partial out of the infinite, and then of giving it an appearance of a whole. This applies as much to the generation of groups as it does to the construction of narratives of history to be used as rationales of authenticity and purity – be they of the (white) Briton, (black) African or the (Hindu) Indian.

But the answer is not yet quite clear, so let me approach from another direction. To ask why do we need to belong, is to ask why do we have a need to be named? The brief but bizarre-sounding answer is that we have to be named in order to exist. Naming draws a boundary around a finite aspect of the infinite. Naming creates a necessary but ultimately illusory region of safety. This is Me, this is Not-Me. This is Us, this is Not-Us. This is the psychological part of the answer.

Multiple belongings

But where are we to make the cuts in the continuum of existence to construct the varieties of belonging? In order to answer this we have to bring in the socio-political which must have something to do with the outcome one desires. Desires require objects of desire. These desirous objects come in all sorts of varieties from status, to money, to love, to power. In brief, one desires resources and commodities, be they emotional, spiritual or material. We can now say that a function of power is to facilitate the fulfilment of desire.

As Elias showed, the more powerful put up barriers around resources by decreeing which differences are to be meaningful, for example the situation in which it is asserted that only men may become priests in some religions. Or consider the notion of 'a German people' alluded to earlier by Chasseguet-Smirgel (see p. 71). What attributes are utilized to include and exclude parts of the population from belonging to the name 'German'? Jew is not always the opposite of German. In each instance a set of similarities and differences are mobilized to make a division between those who will be allowed legitimate access to the resource and the rest. This is also the moment of the creation of a belonging group.

Let me change the language back to that of identity. It seems to me that to name a difference is not only to name an identity, but also to create an identity. So to say that we are connected and divided by an infinite set of similarities and differences, is also to say that we are subject to an infinite set of possible identities. Each identity is a name, like Indian or white or therapist. We can now reframe the issue in this way: given that we are subject to multiple identities simultaneously, then which ones get activated? The answers suggested are that it is not so much to do with an internal intrinsic sense of who I am, but to do with the outcome that the more powerful desire. To be sure this desire may well be profoundly unconscious, and so the process might well have the appearance of something 'natural' and internal – unmediated by the external world.

If one leaves power relations out of the picture then it makes the previous statements over-simplistic, because it makes it appear that individuals have a free choice as to what they may desire and so what identity they may 'choose' to fulfil that desire. Both Fanon and the notion of power relations remind us that whilst some are able to name, others get named. The ways in which this occurs and the consequences that follow are taken up in the next section. But first, it will be helpful to summarize what has gone before.

A partial summary

1   I have argued that identity is not a possession owned by a person, but the name of a relationship between people.

2   The name itself and the province that it delineates is predicated on the function it is to serve.

3   I have suggested that 'who I am' and 'what I am' is the same as 'where I belong'. This then leads to the assertion that there is an isomorphism between the sense of self and identity.

4   Because belongingness is always multiple, many of the varieties of belonging are conflictual, and this gives rise to an internal sense of feeling divided and at war with oneself.

5   Power has been defined as the capacity to sustain a version of reality in which certain identities and differences are made critical in the organization of the relationship between people and resources. Once this is established, then ideology does the work of sustaining these power relationships and of convincing all the participants that this is the natural order of the world.

6   Thus the threats to identity come from two directions. From the outside by other groupings seeking to undermine the status quo, and get for themselves a larger slice of the cake. And from the inside because, as I have already said, there are multiple claims on one's identity going on simultaneously. There is the constant danger that I/we will become something else, and because of this the act of being named triggers an existential anxiety.

7   These anxieties and threats to identity are combated by hanging on to particular names and essentializing them. When the essentializing tendency is too great, then it is known as fundamentalism.

8   Finally, when the name of the group is a 'racial' one, then this is racism.

Three modes of mental functioning

As we saw in Chapter 3, the psychoanalytic texts examined there tended to take the divisions of humanity either as self-evident facts, or as the outcome of splitting. In following this course a conflation between categorization and splitting has taken place.

It seems to me that although the notion of an us – the psychological experience of belonging – is designated as a categorization, its basis must always be splitting. In Dalal 1998 I conducted a prior discussion of the relationship between categorization and splitting, and so here I will state the conclusions that were formulated into a series of theorems (which will shortly be problematized).

1   Unsplit states must be ontologically prior to split states on an experiential level (otherwise the notion of split*ting* as an activity would make no sense).

2   Categorization is the act of dividing and naming the divides (the reverse is also simultaneously true, that categorization is the act of dividing

through the process of naming. In other words, naming and dividing are aspects of the same process).

3   Splitting consists of 'forgetting' that there ever was a connection between the divided.

Broadly, splitting is said to occur when the ambivalent nature of an object (internal or external) is unable to be endured. This is followed by the repression and projection of one of the split elements into some other space. According to the Kleinian account (Klein 1946), the mechanism of splitting is an aspect of paranoid-schizoid functioning. The post-Kleinians (Hinshelwood 1991) think of the paranoid-schizoid and depressive states of mind in two ways, as a progressive developmental move from the paranoid-schizoid to the depressive, and also as alternative ways of mental functioning that are ever present in the human mind, with a continual switching from one to the other.

Although this latter model is more open in that it is a description of an ongoing process, it is nevertheless a description of two alternative ways of experiencing – one primitive and one more evolved. However, what Matte-Blanco and the shoe shop have been demonstrating is that the two are not alternatives to each other, but that each is simultaneously part and parcel of the other at a structural level. Thus splitting is not a 'primitive' way of functioning, but a fundamental aspect of all thinking at all levels, and it is because of the power of splitting that we do not notice its continual presence. See below for an explanation.

One is only able to name the entity 'red shoes' by virtue of a temporary linguistic splitting between red and brown shoes: the connections between the two have to be severed for speech to be possible. If we are to describe this situation in Kleinian language, we could say that paranoid-schizoid functioning is a necessary state of mind for the generation of the space between two groupings. However, we cannot neatly say that the internals of the groups are the preserve of the depressive state of mind, because the depressive state of mind is one in which differences are accommodated. In contrast, within the shoe groups difference is not accommodated but annihilated.

This suggests that there must exist an additional state of mental functioning that is different to the paranoid-schizoid and depressive. Matte-Blanco (1988) has already named it: it is the symmetrized state of mind, wherein there is only homogeneity. For thought to be possible at all, all three states must be ever present.

I am suggesting (with the backing of Matte-Blanco), that theorems two and three do not have a linear relationship to each other – with splitting neatly following categorization. Instead, I suggest that the two theorems have a recursive relation to each other, with each feeding into the other. In other words splitting (theorem three) of some description is a prerequisite for the process of categorization (theorem two) as is the reverse.

Thus, the category red is predicated on its constituent elements being split off from consciousness, albeit temporarily. Something needs to be 'forgotten' for redness to come into being. Paradoxically, these forgotten elements threaten the veracity of the very vision of which they form a necessary constituent part. Further, whatever the 'level' that the thought processes are taking place at, from the minute to the gross, it will always be possible to break it down into these constituent elements. In other words the chosen perceptual depth of focus is a moveable point on an infinite spectrum. The structure of what is being described is not unlike Fairbairn's rendition of the levels of society. In any case, it should be stressed that these cognitive mechanisms are not pathological but inevitable and everyday. There is nothing untoward in the temporary splitting as long as one is able, in the next moment, to flip to the other perceptual state where one may see their similarity. The problem occurs when this flipping does not take place or, despite the flipping, information from one frame is not retained in the other. This lack cannot properly be called splitting at all, it is more like a disconnection.

We can now say that at a grosser level of experience, categorization is the naming and the creating of divides as in us/not-us. When the divide is turned into an absolute and the connection between the us and the them is rendered unconscious then this is splitting, and if the divides are given racial names through the processes of racialization, then it is racism. The potent fact about splitting is that one never has the conscious experience of having split something. From the inside the experience is of being completely identified with one part of the split as one is in a symmetrized state of mind which results in the conviction that the one has nothing whatsoever to do with the other part of the split. One can only ever know the split for what it is from the outside.

What the previous formulations have left out are the emotions. Splitting, in the conventional sense, gets its impulsion from a difficulty in the emotional field. Splitting and projection are used to redistribute the material in the emotional field. The question now is, is this second 'emotional' splitting different in kind from the 'cognitive' splitting of the previous discussions? I would say that the two are aspects of each other, and can never be discussed separately from each other, as there is no thought without emotion nor emotion without thought. Emotional splitting requires the prior existence of spaces designated as differentiated from each other; thus notions of category are drawn in from the first, and for categories to exist then the mechanisms of 'cognitive' splitting must be operational. Meanwhile, cognitive splitting requires a 'decision' as to where the divide is to be made in the continuum; this decision inevitably has emotional components to it, as well as the rational and socio-political components.

In conclusion it can be said that splitting is not at all a primitive mechanism as in 'first' (primo), but that much has already gone before it to make it possible. It is in fact quite sophisticated.

Sustaining the divide

The divide having been made between an us and a them, a number of mechanisms now come into play to bolster it, and these may broadly be put into two groups – the emotions and the workings of societies. Although here they are divided for the sake of explication, each is part of the other.

Border patrol: the preservation of power differentials

Elias and Scotson (1994) conducted a sociological study of a small town (pseudonym: Winston Parva) in the English Midlands in the 1960s, which they used to develop a general theory of power inequalities and detail the theory's workings. Their work focused on the interactions between two working-class groups: one that had been established for some generations who lived in the village, and the other consisting of recent arrivals (some 20 years previously) living on the estate. Although the division in the township was not along race lines, many of the attitudes and behaviours that one ascribes to racism were found alive and active in this setting.

The authors remark that there was hardly any difference between these two groups in ethnicity, colour, occupation, income, habits or education, save the fact that one of the groups had been established for a long time. This fact alone was sufficient to allow them to build a cohesive sense of 'we-ness', which they used (consciously and unconsciously) to exclude and subjugate the not-so-newcomers from access to any of the power resources in that community.

It is precisely the absence of the usual differences that allowed Elias and Scotson to clearly expose the workings of power figurations which they argue are universal and which are summarized as follows.

1   The established attributed to their own members superior human characteristics.
2   Unspoken social conventions somehow emerged which excluded all non-occupational social contact between two groups.
3   The taboo on contact was maintained by praise gossip on those who observed the conventions, and blame-gossip against suspected offenders.
4   The established accrued for themselves a charisma which was internalized by its members to become an integral part of individual identities; meantime the outsiders were 'painted' with stigma, which they too internalized and so tended to experience themselves through the eyes of the established 'where the power differential is very great, groups in an outsider position measure themselves with the yardstick of their oppressors' (Elias 1976: xxvi).

The empirical findings of Elias and Scotson illustrate and substantiate several of the ideas being put forward in this book. The most significant of these is that differences are not the cause of hatred, rather differences are fanned alive to organize hatreds in order to preserve power differentials. Their work also provides actual examples of symmetric logic being exploited in the service of the power differentials.

The questions that Elias and Scotson address themselves to are

> How do members of a group maintain among themselves the belief that they are not merely more powerful but also better human beings than those of another? What means do they use to impose the belief in their own human superiority upon those who are less powerful?
>
> (ibid. xvi)

These 'means' are nothing other than some of the practices of racism. The means of subjugation are not only socio-political but also psychological. In effect, what Elias and Scotson have exposed is the manufacture of a local ideology, that blooms into an entire discourse that penetrates and organizes psyches in ways that reinforce the socio-political status quo. And perhaps the most powerful thing about the whole process is the way the subjugation is sustained invisibly without recourse to explicit violence. There are two aspects to this, one being the actual practices of subjugation, and the other being their interiorization.

Asymmetrical we-images: a confluence of Matte-Blanco, Fanon, Foulkes and Elias[3]

By virtue of having been there longer and so more powerful, the established are able to evolve for themselves a global positive self-image (charisma), and impute to the outsiders a global negative image (stigma). These images are nothing other than the contents of the Foulkesian social unconscious, and so they go a considerable way in invisibly determining how one experiences the self, the world, and the relationships between them as natural. The established are able to act in this way because they have the upper hand in the power differentials, 'The ability of one group to pin a badge of human inferiority on another group and make it stick was a function of a specific [power] figuration which the two groups formed with each other' (Elias 1976: xx).

But as we saw earlier, the construction of an identity requires the homogenization of the internal space through the use of symmetrical logic to repress internal differences. This is the general cognitive mechanism. However, power imperatives ensure that this takes place in a very particular way in which it is the best that is used to symmetrize the more powerful, and the worst to homogenize the less powerful, 'The self-image of the established was modelled on the *minority of the best*, and inclined towards idealisation; whilst the image allocated to the outsiders was modelled on the *minority of the worst*, and inclined towards denigration' (Elias and Scotson 1994: 7, italics added). We can see that this description brings Elias and Matte-Blanco together. This is also an example of symmetric logic in action where the 'one' is equivalent to the 'all'.

Whatever the (mis)information gets called (mythology, ideology or discourse), Elias and Scotson describe its dissemination through gossip. The more cohesive a group, the more efficiently its communicational channels will work. Foulkes reverses the causality in this idea to say that communication is the glue that coheses the group, and so the more efficient the communication, the more cohesive the group. The importance of cohesion in this context is that whilst it is an outcome of having more power, it is also simultaneously a means of sustaining and appropriating more power 'one group has a higher cohesion rate than the other and this integration differential substantially contributes to the former's power surplus' (Elias 1976: xix).

Elias and Scotson describe the presence of 'gossip mills' in the village whose task it is to symmetrize information by straining out instances that confound the prevalent ideologies – we-bad, they-good; and by inflaming the instances that confirm them – we-good, they-bad.

The outsiders do not have this possibility because they have not as yet been able to dig their own network of gossip channels. In fact the situation actually militates against them coming together to form a more cohesive body in the following way.

Estate image

First of all we should remember the reason why all of this is happening: the construction of the we through 'the closing of ranks among the established . . . has the social function of preserving the group's power superiority' (Elias 1976: xxiv). Now, what is most lethal in this whole scenario, is that these ideologies enter the minds of those who inhabit this social space to become part of their psyches and emotions.

> Just as established groups, as a matter of course, regard their superior power as a sign of their higher human value, so outsider groups, as long as the power differential is great and <u>submission inescapable</u>, emotionally experience their *power* inferiority as a sign of *human* inferiority.
> (ibid. xxvi, italics original, underlining added)

And it is also the case that the differential appears to be a natural one 'power superiority is equated with human merit, human merit with grace of nature or gods' (ibid. xxiii). Thus the we-images reside in the minds of the inhabitants and are a fundamental part of the structure of their psyches.

This now generates a double movement, both parts of which promote fragmentation in the estate. First, the very fact that the image of others on the estate is cathected with negativity, will mean that one will not tend to be drawn to one's neighbours, rather the tendency will be one of trying to distance oneself from them, as consciously or not one will feel to some degree repelled by them. Second, the fact that the personal self-image is also a similarly negative one will mean that the impulse will be to hide the self rather than to share and risk exposing it to humiliation and ridicule.

The fact that try as one might one cannot get away either from a bad 'them' or the bad self, must in the end have a dire and debilitating effect on the psyche. This leads eventually to depression or expressions of anger and self-hate, which by the processes of symmetric logic can as easily be directed at others in the vicinity who are like me and therefore are the same as me. Elias is describing exactly the same mechanisms as Fanon and Friere – mechanisms that drive horizontal violence.

Village image

Whilst the effect of the estate's we-image is one of fragmentation, of turning everything against everything else, the effect of the we-image of the village works very differently. Because the village we-image is infused with positivity, it is attractive and so draws its inhabitants together. At the same time the villagers are impelled to pull away from those on the estate because they are impregnated with negativity. The end result is that the positive we-image of the village works in the direction of enhancing contacts between those in the village and entrenching the divide between the village and the estate.

We can see then that there is a profound asymmetry in the way that power relations impact on the psychological structures and intra-group dynamics of those on either side of the power divide, favouring one and not the other. There is no one causing this to occur, there is no conspiracy, rather it is the outcome of the workings of power. Further, these behaviours and dynamics are not the outcome of personal family histories and traumas, rather the social structures are patterning family dynamics which in turn modulate the developmental processes of the individuals born into them.

We might ask, why don't the outsiders reverse the situation by stigmatizing the established and manufacturing charisma for themselves? They can and do, but once again their possibilities are severely constrained by the power differentials. First, power is needed to manufacture and sustain mythologies, and second, if their self-image is a stigmatized one, then their attempts will not be very convincing. But as power figurations change and the outsiders gain more power, they are increasingly able to do so. These changes are part of a recursive process. As they feel better about themselves they inevitably gain in confidence and so do more, and this in turn sets aglow the charisma. We can observe these changes taking place over the last 50 or so years with the changes in attitude to blackness. Fanon's work is a description of the vicissitudes of these processes in the colonial context.

Asymmetrical projection: idealization and denigration

The psychoanalytic versions of charisma and stigma are idealization and denigration. We can see that Elias has described how the structure of the situation determines that the less powerful will tend to be the denigrated ones and the more powerful the idealized ones.

There is also a way in which individuals will tend to project in asymmetrical ways so that this division is reinforced. One of the reasons for splitting and projecting is to solve some internal conflictual situation by projecting one element outside the self to distance it from the other element which remains inside. These elements tend to be experienced as good and bad, and so the task becomes to protect the good from the bad. But now depending on whether the self-as-container is experienced as good or bad, different things are likely to happen.

If the we-image is an already idealized one, i.e. good, then one will be prone to projecting out the bad leaving the good behind. This works towards enhancing the good we-image. However, if the we-image is a denigrated one, then one is more likely to project out the good in order to protect it from the bad within. This time the projection works in the direction of enhancing the badness of the we-image. Thus even at the level of the individual, the structure of the situation will play a role in determining which of the good or bad elements individuals are likely to project out. The asymmetry between the groupings ends up working together to reinforce the already existing emotional auras of the more powerful and less powerful.

The colours of stigma and charisma: development and socialization

In this section I will attend in more detail to the psychological processes by which charisma and stigma come to constitute the self. The preceding discussion makes clear that one's feelings about oneself and towards others are critically informed by the milieu one grows up in. Psychoanalysis manages to render this milieu asocial by making a tacit distinction between psychological development and socialization.

This division is present in different ways and degrees in all the four psychoanalytic theories previously examined, but it is most clear in Freud where the pre-Oedipal phase is made out to be a pre-social one. What both Foulkes and Elias have done is to demonstrate unequivocally that this is a structural impossibility. They have shown us that because the developmental process takes place within a sociological milieu, the structures and preoccupations of this milieu are necessarily involved from the first. Further, as sociological processes are necessarily drawn into the developmental process, they must permeate the psychology of the individual at all levels. In Eliasian language, the actual abstraction of the developmental from socialization is an impossibility. To put it another way: in some way existing 'we's are necessarily part of the forming 'I's from the start of an infant's developmental process 'A person's we-image and we-ideal form as much part of a person's self-image and self-ideal as the image and ideal of him or herself as the unique person to which he or she refers as "I" ' (Elias, 1976: xliii).

For a sense of me/not-me to be able to develop, not only must there be a differentiation between the me and the not-me, there also has to be differentiations within the me to give rise to psychological structures. These differentiations – internal and external – do not happen on an *ad hoc* basis, but are intimately informed by the nurturing processes. Psychoanalysis has attended to these nurturing processes in great detail, although it has done so as though they took place in an asocial space.

Thus, what I am proposing is not a negation of the psychoanalytic endeavour, but an elaboration and extension of it. I am in complete agreement with the psychoanalytic idea that feelings of badness and danger are utilized in the differentiating and distancing process. This is both a logical and an emotional necessity because if the differentiated contained positives, then the emotional impulsion will be of necessity attraction and so an inclusive one.

Aversion: the invention of dirt

This point of agreement is also a point of differentiation from the psychoanalytic thesis, and is found in the question, from whence came these feelings of aversion, badness and danger? As we have seen, psychoanalysis has tended to answer that these feelings emanate from the inside and are projected onto the outside.

In fact this is not quite true. In one place Freud momentarily puts forward the modern notion that 'dirt is matter in the wrong place' (1908: 173). The fact that Freud placed the phrase in parentheses, in quotes, and in English in the midst of an essay written in German, leads one to suppose that he was quoting a previously existing English saying. In any case having cited this phrase, he does not come back to it and instead famously suggested that the character traits of being 'orderly, parsimonious and obstinate' were reaction formations designed to keep anal eroticism at bay. In effect, Freud's thesis is that the pull towards cleanliness is a defence thrown up by the developmental processes against sexuality, and specifically anal sexuality.

Whilst the genesis of this idea on dirt is often incorrectly attributed to the social anthropologist Mary Douglas, she was the person who developed the theme in her book written in 1966, *Purity and Danger*, in which she refers to 'the old definition' (1995: 36). She shows how notions of dirt and pollution are manufactured by all societies to define their boundaries and order their symbolic world, with the two interpenetrating each other, she says 'where there is no differentiation there is no defilement' (ibid. 161).

Her work is Eliasian to the core echoing his thesis that in the first instance, the unconscious function of generating differentials in behaviours were to mark and generate a distinction between varieties of us and them. Examples of the mobilization of disgust in order to construct and differentiate us-es from thems are found everywhere. Thus, once pork is cathected with disgust and impurity, then one will be driven away from it. The fact that symmetric logic is the primary organizing principle within each of the domains designated as us and them, will mean that anyone who engages with the tabooed substance will be immediately tarnished with the same associations. In India, for example, the Brahmin is repelled by the untouchable, because the untouchable touches substances designated as untouchable by the Brahmin.

What is so pernicious about the whole enterprise is the way that those subjugated by the power differentials come to believe the image that is given to them. The greater the power differential, the less able the subjugated are to defend themselves against taking this image in at a fundamental structural and emotional level. An extreme instance of this is the Japanese untouchable group, the Burakumin. There are no observable physical differences between this group and other Japanese. Yet when asked if they felt themselves to be the same as ordinary Japanese, one answered 'No, we kill animals. We are dirty, and some people think we are not human', and when asked if they thought of themselves as human the response was 'I don't know. . . . We are bad people and we are dirty' (Elias 1976: xxviii, quoting from Mark Frankland, 'Japan's Angry Untouchables', *Observer Magazine*, 2 November, 1975).

There are several things here.

1   difference is activated in order to differentiate
2   charisma and stigma are allocated one to each side of the divide which reinforces the division
3   the more powerful ensure that they are the beneficiaries of charisma
4   there are profound psychological consequences for both groups – charisma enhancing the self-image of the more powerful, and stigma debilitating the less powerful
5   the eventual outcome is that the situation comes to look like a 'natural' one.

As Elias pointedly says

> [in] discussing 'racial' problems one is apt to put the cart before the horse. It is argued, as a rule, that people perceive others as belonging to another group because the colour of their skin is different. It would be more to the point if one asked how it came to pass in this world that one has got into the habit of perceiving people with another skin colour as belonging to a different group.
>
> (Elias 1976: xlvii)

The conclusion one is led to is that some of the feelings of aversion attached to certain objects are not there because of projection, but because they have been generated by the workings of power differentials. These associations exist in the social order and are ingested by the developing infant. Foulkes would say that these pre-existing associations are contained in the social unconscious, and Elias would say that they are aspects of Symbol. In either case the incorporation of language is a fundamental part of this process. In the psychologist Jerome Bruner's pithy phrase, it is the 'entry into meaning', and pre-existing meaning at that

> When we enter human life, it is as if we walk on stage into a play whose enactment is already in progress – a play whose somewhat open plot determines what part we may play and toward what denouements we may be heading.
>
> (Bruner 1990: 34)

Some of these pre-existing meanings consist not only of what is we and not-we, but also *why* the two are necessarily differentiated. And by necessarily I mean that within the meaning system it appears to be a natural self-evident differentiation.[4]

Some conclusions

I am now in a position to be able to make a series of sequential assertions.

If it is true that the we is produced and sustained by the negation of the not-we, and it is also true that it is negativity that is used to distance and define the not-we, then the same *types* of negativity will be necessarily present in the 'I'. This must be so from two perspectives. First, the 'I' being part of the we must be made up of similar 'substances', and second, the same rules must be used to distance internal objects as external ones. It has been argued and demonstrated that two of the most potent instruments utilized increasingly over the centuries in the construction of these divisions are those of black and white. We have witnessed their use in the external socio-political world in which a white we is differentiated from a lesser black them, and we have observed that *at about the same time* the colour-less emotions also get blackened and whitened.

It is the confluence of these two streams that I find so persuasive in convincing me of the veracity of the assertion that the blackening and whitening of the emotions, the construction of the us and the they, and the precipitation of the 'I' from the we, are all emergent properties of the *same* psycho-socio-historical processes.

It is now possible to make sense of the earlier finding that the uses of black as a descriptor of negativity multiplied much more over the previous 400 years when compared to white for positivity. To my mind this consti-tutes evidence for the assertion that the activity critical to the construction of the senses of me and we is that of negation and exclusion rather than inclusion and assimilation. It is *because* exclusion is utilized more frequently, that black is found to be more predominant.

We are now at the hub of things. It follows from the above that if notions of black and white (with all the associations that have been delineated in Chapter 8) are deeply embedded in language and the struc-tures of society (which they are), then they and their associations will be deeply embedded in some way or other in the psyches of those born into these social systems. *All of this is to say, that the psyche has been racialized.*

Going further, by using the previous insights of Elias and Scotson it is possible to assert that in the contemporary era in the UK, the colour of charisma is white, and the colour of stigma is black. As we have seen, charisma and stigma are internalized aspects of the we-images and so are a part of I-images. From this it follows that of necessity, the psyche will be blackened and whitened. Finally, this process is identical to the previous one – the racialization of the psyche.

In sum, the work of this chapter is putting forward an extension and a challenge to the psychoanalytic one-way street in which the vicissitudes of internal psychological worlds drive forms of social relatedness. Whilst there is a truth to this at the level of the individual, what has been argued in this chapter is that the forms, shapes and possibilities of that individual's internal psychological world are severely constrained by the forms, shapes and preoccupations of the larger socio-historic milieu. Or more simply the vicissitudes of social relations drive what can take place in the internal world. The fact that both are true means that the relationship between them is a recursive one and so it is a two-way street. However, there is no power symmetry between the two because individual uniqueness is bound to be constructed out of material present *prior* to the birth of that par-ticular individual. Thus these larger socio-historic movements are not beyond the personal histories of individuals, but deeply embedded within them.

Notes

1 Some of material in this section was previously published in Dalal 1988 and 2001b.
2 Unless the thing removed is a negative.
3 Elements of the following discussion appeared in Dalal 2001b.
4 A Jain has a very different sense of 'me' and 'we' to the more atomized metropolitan one that feels so natural to me.

Chapter 10

Racism: the vicissitudes of racialized differences

This final chapter reflects on what occurs between people when the differences of importance between them are those of blackness and whiteness. This will be done by applying the general theory of difference and differentiation to the territories of race and racism.

The psyche, coloured and racialized

Many of the psychoanalytic disquisitions on racism examined in Chapter 3 proceeded on the assumption that only some people were racist. The previous chapters have demonstrated that racism is much more than this and none of us may escape so lightly, this includes myself and members of the so-called coloured races. It has been established that we are *all* racialized by the developmental process, and cannot *not* experience ourselves and the world to some degree in colour-coded ways.

It is possible to read even the instinctivist theorizations of Freud and Klein as substantiating this idea by the device of requiring the *explicit* location of the developmental process within the socio-political context. If this is done, then the logic of each of the theories leads to the same conclusion. So, in the Freudian schema, the superego as an instrument for distinguishing good from bad gets its guidance from that which is already established in society. If black and white divisions are utilized in the external world as differentiators of good and bad, then this same mechanism must be utilized in the ordering of the internal world, inevitably colour coding it. In the Kleinian scenario blackness and whiteness, attached as they are to objects and aspirations, are bound to become integral to the psyche through the series of introjections and projections that are the basis of the developmental process.

The Foulkesian schema is based on his belief that 'the so-called inner processes in the individual are internalizations of the forces operating in the group to which he belongs' (Foulkes 1971: 212). It follows that if racialized structures are part of these 'forces' operating in the social group, then these of necessity will become internalized and part of the psychological world of each and every individual within that group. As blackening and whitening are one aspect of these 'forces', then it must be the case that things in the mind – conscious and unconscious – will be whitened and blackened.

Elias' cogitations firm up this last proposition by locating it in a larger historical stream. Three distinct trajectories can be detected in the discourses generated by the Enlightenment. First, the repudiation of the passions through a process of relegating them to an animal domain; second, the relegation of coloured persons also to an animal domain; and third, the progressive generation of an idea of a European identity, a self-representation that is increasingly whitened (I have established that the function of the whitening process is *in order to differentiate* from the designated-as-coloured).

Now, psychoanalysis is unequivocal in stating that things repudiated are never annihilated, only relocated in the unconscious. We might put it like this – as the things blackened get pushed down into the unconscious, it results in the unconscious itself being blackened. Thus, as the passions are pushed outside the conscious image of the white European, they are at the same time delegated to the peoples outside Europe through the processes of splitting, repression and projection. Consequently the banishing of the designated-as-animal within and the distancing of the designated-as-animal without are part and parcel of the same 'civilizing' process, and it is the application of blackness that is the mechanism that drives both.

As we have already seen, the necessities of symmetric logic decree that all things cast out of the light of differentiation into the outer darkness of similarities, by the rules of symmetric logic are bound to coalesce and collapse one into the other – sex, death, violence, badness, blackness and 'them'.

The later Romantic project of rescuing the passions from the clutches of darkness did not simultaneously rescue the black person. Rousseau famously converted the primitive black into the Noble Savage. Whilst this noble figure was venerated as an idea and symbolically incorporated into the self-representation of the Eurpoean, it was done so in a particular and limited way. Thus whilst the Romantics strove to liberate the natural, noble affects within the breast of the European, their very naturalness meant that these affects continued to retain their associations with blackness, and in turn with black people *per se*.

I would argue that psychoanalysis, having been generated out of this very philosophical stream, is bound to have retained these unreflected associations and designations of blackness and whiteness. In other words the language of psychoanalysis must also inevitably be colour coded. A version of the shift we noticed from adjective to noun in the seventeenth century in relation to peoples, is found at times in psychoanalytic discourse too, but this time it is internal objects which are *named* 'black' and 'white'. Here is one example 'When the core identity initially forms, some unintegrated fragments of the self, both positive and negative, always remain unintegrated.

Because *these unintegrated black and white fragments* threaten ... [etc.]'
(Volkan 1997: 89, italics added).

Volkan is writing as though the good and bad unintegrated fragments *are*
white and black in themselves; he goes on to say that these black and white
fragments get externalized, thus implying that the world gets black*ened* and
whit*ened* because of the externalization of these internal fragments. Volkan
has got it back to front.

Retrieving uniqueness: three caveats

I need to make the point that the situation is not a situation *per se*, but a
moment in a process and so is not intractable. It is not the case that the
associations of blackness with badness are set in stone, nor that it is total,
nor that it has always been the case, nor that it will always be so, nor that
it is precisely the same everywhere. For example, it is clear that the socio-
political situation between black and white is not the same today as it was
50 years ago, nor is it the same everywhere in the world. We can even
see shifts that move blackness towards positivity occurring in the associations of black patients as described in the psychoanalytic papers cited in
Chapter 3.

What I do insist on however, is that in this day and age it is impossible
not to be structured in some way by the themes of black and white; no one
can escape from this because the only way one could is by the impossibility
of residing outside society.

The other caveats emerge from the tendency to globalize cultures and
make them mutually exclusive. This results in one imagining that *all* French
people have incorporated *the* French culture, and that French culture is
different in its entirety from say, *the* Ghanaian culture. But cultures do not
exist in vacuums, they overlap, interpenetrate and exist in relation to other
cultures. What we-are-not is the basis for the definition of the 'them'. In the
shoe shop, the red 'culture' has much in common with brown 'culture' –
but this similarity of shoe-hood has to be rendered unconscious to give the
appearance that they are two different things. The shape of the 'other'
culture is always impressed into the shape of 'our' culture – if only through
negation (but actually much more). Thus, when we take in 'our' culture we
also take in something of 'their' culture.

The final caveat pertains to the fact that when we look within any cultural system, we find not homogeneity, but systems of power relations
sustained by gossip and ideology. Thus, some groupings within that system
will be much better off than others. The Hindu system that is experienced
by the Harijan (untouchable) is very different from the one that is experienced
by the Brahmin (priestly caste), and so each will introject a very different culture, which in turn will inculcate very different senses of I-ness and we-ness;
this variation is also true (although in different ways and degrees) of two

people who are of the same caste. Thus, no two whites can imbibe exactly the same culture any more than two blacks can.

In sum, the focus on the larger socio-historical dimension does not necessitate a vision of people as clones. Diversity and individuality remain; the mistake is to presume that the individuality is asocial and has nothing to do with the preoccupations of the sociological milieu.

Elements of racism

I am now in a position to get to grips with racism itself. As we have seen, racism is an umbrella term that encompasses some very different types of things from habits of thought, to explicit expressions of hatred and violence, to conscious or unconscious feelings of aversion, to the invisible and impersonal racism structured into institutions. In what follows I will attend to each.

The structure of racialized thought

At its simplest, racialized thoughts are those that use the notion of race, or thoughts that are organized in some way by race. The previous arguments have demonstrated that the presence of notions of black and white also signal the presence of racialized thoughts. We may also say that racialized thought is the outcome of a particular arrangement of asymmetric and symmetric logic.

As race is so hard to pin down, let me start with something apparently more tangible – the idea of Britain. We may think of Britishness in two ways, as a cultural category and as a legal category. I will begin with the first of these.

Identity is predicated on homogenization and symmetric logic is utilized in this process. In saying 'I am British' I am saying that I belong to this category. This is fine so long as I do not look too closely *within* the category. As soon as I do I discover not one cultural group but a plethora of cultures, from London East End to rural aristocracy, many of which are antagonistic to each other. There are no meaningful sets of conditions that serve as a *necessary and sufficient* definition of British culture. In fact it would be true to say that the diversity is *infinitely* complex, and because of this one unthinkingly engages with the complexity British with the peculiar mathematics of infinity – symmetric logic. Any assertion that a belonging is based on a commonality – is being constantly threatened by the diversity within which constantly threatens to erupt and destroy the fantasy of homogeneity. The grouping called Christianity has elements as diverse as Ian Paisley, Father Ted, the Ku Klux Klan, the Seventh-Day Adventists, Protestants, Catholics, vegetarians, meat eaters, saints and sinners. In other words it contains diversities that emphatically deconstruct the claim to homogeneity.

The notion of something uniquely British is also undermined by the attributes shared with cultures designated as 'other'.

Now what of Britishness as a legal category? Here we have the idea of a nation, where the concrete marker for belonging is the possession of a passport. The next question is what is ownership of the passport based on? As we engage with this question we will discover that we are actually in the territory of race.

The first and most fundamental condition that gives one an automatic right to own a passport is of *lineage*. At its most simple the rule is that if one's parents are British then one is, *de facto*, British. This formula has the appearance of an explanation of what constitutes belongingness. But all it actually does is move the problem up one generational level, and simultaneously disguise the fact that the logic is based on the fantasy of blood and pedigree: we belong together because we share the same blood. With the appearance of the word same, we find ourselves once more in a symmetrized universe. 'We' belong because our ancestors belonged, therefore 'we' are somehow the *same* as our ancestors. The ancestral anchor is located so far in the past, that for all purposes it is as though the state of belonging were an eternal one. Because of this one may not ask questions about its beginnings, or at least if one does then the question is rendered meaningless by the notion of eternity which has no beginning and no end – all is symmetrical.

What we have here is an example of the error Elias cautioned against – that of looking for absolute beginnings. An absolute beginning can only be invented by the device of annihilating what has gone before, indeed, that is its purpose. Consequently, the place that this beginning is located in is not arbitrary but full of ideological intention which is to give the appearance of a *natural* belonging, from the beginnings of time.

The notion of blood is but one of the rationales of race. Banton (1987) has pointed out that race has two distinct schemas behind it – typology and lineage. Initially, discourses of race relied on the idea of lineage to promote and perpetuate their ideologies, where belonging proceeded along chains of procreation and sameness of blood. In what was to become Europe, this way of thinking emerged from the rationalizations used by the knightly classes to differentiate themselves in the early Middle Ages. Then, with the advent of scientific racism, the notion of type came to the fore and led to a taxonomy of humankind in which the notion of direct lineage was made less critical to the idea of belonging. People were now said to belong to certain *types*, and the differences between them were said to be measurable and so objective. Being objective these explanations too are made out to be universal.

These two versions of belonging are utilized alternately and clandestinely to manipulate the rules of national belonging to work against those designated as blacks in the following way. According to the rules of lineage, black people born in Britain should belong to the British 'us', but typology is used to decree that as they are of a different type, therefore they can never be one of us. Meanwhile lineage logic gets mobilized to say that as they are originally from somewhere else, then that too means they cannot *authentically* be one of us. Meanwhile, whites born in South Africa who should be excluded from belonging to an idea of Britain by the rules of lineage in historical time, are included by a lineage logic based on 'eternal time' to say that they originally came from here. Further, that they are said to be of the same type and so belong with the white 'us'. This is a use of symmetric logic on certain sections of the population and asymmetric logic on others. The notion of original flows into that of the eternal and unchanging, and leads to the idea that some people will always belong here, and others never. Flawed as this argument is, let us accept for the moment that, somehow, some people naturally belong to certain places, and see where it leads.

'They will never be one of us'

A material proof of natural belonging would be the fact that a passport is not needed. There are many people in Britain who have never owned a passport indicating their belongingness is (institutionally) unquestioned. But now we come across a difficulty which is the very existence of the label 'Black British'. Why has it come about? Its existence implies that there was a necessity for its invention. There are black people in Britain who, by the evidence of not needing a passport, would be deemed to belong 'naturally'.[1] But this clearly is not the case. A British Fascist says on television (13 June 1993, *Heart of the Matter*, BBC) that it does not matter how long 'they', the blacks, live here, they will never be one of us. And they cannot, because the us-ness is made identical to whiteness, and no matter how long they live here they will forever remain black. This argument has used the notion of *type* to subjugate the notion of *lineage*.

The hyphenated identity 'Black-British', valorized by many as a 'celebration of diversity', is first and foremost a marker of exclusion. The dilemma that it is born out of is this – how can they, the blacks, be allowed to belong together with the whites? The answer is that they are allowed to belong to an auxiliary space called Black-British, a distinction which retains the fantasy of the (pure white) Briton. To my mind, hyphenated identities are formed initially in reaction to the act of exclusion; it is Lal's ethnicity paradox in action (see p. 216) in which the marginalized take up the weapon that has been used against them and make it their own: blackness is made a celebratory emblem used in the transformation of black objects into subjects.

The myth that hyphenated identities are spontaneous natural categories 'just describing differences that exist' gets exploded by comments like this one made by a Frenchman, 'At the beginning of the century, Italian immigrants came here; now they've become French and you can't tell the difference. But the Algerians want to stay Arab' (*Guardian*, 24 May 1997, 'The Week', p. 5). The psychoanalyst Traub-Werner said exactly the same thing about Jews in Chapter 3.

There are several points to be made here. First, it is a moot point how much the Algerians actually want to stay Arab, and if they do whether *all* the Algerians want to stay Arab. It is also a moot point how much the Italians are allowed to become French, and how much the Algerians are not allowed to. There are two eternals here – an eternal 'us' and an eternal 'them'. In this universe neither shall be breached and never the twain shall meet. They are forever differentiated. This is indeed an example of splitting.

A colour-coded typology has been used to allow the Italians in and to keep the Algerians out. This is also where the symmetrized logic of infinities comes into its own. One of the outcomes of infinities and eternals is that change can occur with things remaining the same. What has happened here is that the eternal white French 'us' has accommodated the white Italian through the loophole of typology, and then by the logic of infinity has closed up as though nothing had ever happened; as the man said 'you can't tell the difference'. The eternal 'us' is unchanged; it is as it always was and so always will be.

We can see then what a powerful tool the alternate application of symmetric and asymmetric logic is. Symmetric logic and the use of type allows those who do not belong (by virtue of not having passports or citizenship) to be experienced as 'one of us' with no difficulty (say some white Rhodesians and South Africans in the 1960s); and the application of asymmetric logic renders those who *do* belong by virtue of lineage (blacks who have lived in Britain for many generations) to be experienced as 'not one of us', also with no difficulty.[2]

The additional twist is this: *having been excluded, the excluded are then accused of being stand-offish*. Phoenix quotes a young white man complaining 'They *can* call themselves English, but some of them choose to call themselves West Indian' (1995: 35).

'They are all the same'

This is symmetric logic at its most explicit in which the part is identical to the whole. One woman making a driving error equals all women are bad at driving. One criminal is a black man equals all black men are criminals. The symmetrization process is very powerful – seeing a person doing *one* thing untoward, leads into them being completely hateful. Implicit in this sort of thinking is a causal link between attribute and behaviour: he is a criminal *because* he is black, the blackness is made out to be the *cause* of criminality. Hence another black, if not actually a criminal, is certainly a potential one.

This slippage is so powerful and all consuming that at times it is defended against by an equally powerful inverse where it is not possible to allow for even one woman to be a bad driver, or even one black to be a criminal, because in symmetric logic 'the one' is the same as 'all'. Thus no woman is ever a bad driver, and no black is ever a criminal. This kind of defence is bound to fail because it, too, uses symmetric logic; it counters the charge 'all' with the insistence 'none'. Sometimes fighting fire with fire only further inflames the situation.

'We are being swamped by them'

It is often the case that when one or two black families move into a white area, the level of consternation is out of all proportion to the events. To paraphrase Winston Churchill, how is it that in the minds of the many, the few become so monstrously vast? The answer to this lies in part with the fantasy of purity and is linked to the following associated idea.

'We are pure, they are all dirty'

By definition, the notion of purity is that of an absolute; there can be no degrees of purity, it is an either–or state, a thing is *either* pure *or* not pure. Thus, purity is completely destroyed by presence of the tiniest speck of something considered contaminatory. Although there is no such thing as absolute purity in the real world, there is such a thing in the world of symmetric logic. To experience the 'us' as clean and pure requires the symmetrization and homogenization of the belonging group to an extraordinary degree. In this world a little is a lot. Thus, the presence of even one black person is experienced as too much – it is *all* spoilt. But what is spoilt is a fantasy, not a fact.

'I hate the blacks – but not you'

Many years ago, as a youth, I had the following experience. A class-mate complaining about the blacks being lazy, good-for-nothings, pauses and says in a conciliatory tone 'of course I don't mean you – you're different – you're more like one of us'. Some version of this interesting feat of mental gymnastics is fairly common. There are two levels here: the particular and the general. Although the particular is part of the general the linkage is somehow severed in order to preserve the symmetrical thought – I hate *all* blacks. We may surmise that the speaker was at first completely swept up by symmetrical logic, until my presence intruded. We may also surmise that my presence was 'felt' because its entry into the frame brought with it information that was discordant with what was already there. What takes place next in the speaker's mind is interesting; the discordant does not disrupt the ruling symmetrized ethos, instead the particular is treated as an anomaly. Because the symmetrical is an all-or-nothing space, the speaker cannot afford to take in this correction, because in this way of experiencing, if one thing is wrong then everything is wrong. The danger is that if the speaker discovers that he does not hate one particular black, then this is equivalent to not hating *any* blacks. Evidence is being read in ways that do not challenge the internalized status quo – the linkages black to bad, and white to good. Thus the black person, if good, must be made in some way not-black and (almost) one of us.

It is as though there were a horizontal split between two emotional zones, so that information from one cannot impact on the other. In one zone the *particular* individual is related to through asymmetric logic in which difference and discrimination is possible, whilst the generalized 'they' are related to through symmetric logic which is lumpen in its attitude. It is a real irony that the practices of prejudice and racism are called 'discriminatory' which are compensated for by legislation called the anti-discriminatory laws. Because as we can see, whilst prejudice and racism discriminate at a gross level of differentiation (say according to colour), in fact they rely on something that is the opposite of discriminating – a lumping activity wherein 'they are all the same'.

One for all and all for one

In the symmetric universe one difference, meaningful or not, equals *everything* is different. The difference of colour between self and other can spiral out of control to mean that everything between self and other is different. If I am good then the other, being different, must be bad. If I am clean then the other is dirty. If I am intelligent then the other is stupid, and so forth.

We are also bound to note here that in differing contexts, other differences become the organizing principles and precipitate the cascade of attributes. Sometimes gender has had this dubious privilege, other times religion, and so on. This is a reminder that I do not consider colour to be the *only* meaningful difference – but I do consider it to be one of the significant ones in the current context.

The evolution of institutional racism

Whatever the problems with Kovel's account, he is broadly correct in his delineation of the changing form of the *practices* of racism – from dominative, to aversive, to technocratic. The transformations in the forms of racism echo those of Elias' civilizing process, both beginning with crude violence and ending with something sanitized. In this section I will attend to an aspect of the last of these stages.

Once the structures of society take over and perpetuate the mechanisms of exclusion and subjugation, they become invisible amongst the day-to-day activities of living. It is at this moment that racism could be said to have become technocratic, or in modern parlance, institutionalized. In this phase the work of racism continues, it seems all by itself. What contribution do the notions of black and white make to this process?

Sanitizing violence

Let me begin at the point when the workings of power relations necessitated the transformation of relatively independent knights into a pacified upper class of courtiers (Elias, 1994: 269). The knights, unable to compete with the widening power differentials between themselves and the forming courts, were forced to abdicate their relative independence and join them. Now they were no longer able to live purely by the rule that might is right. Elias says 'When a monopoly of force is formed, pacified social spaces are created which are normally free from acts of violence' (1994: 449).

As overt violence became less possible *within* the pacified space of the court system,[3] intrigue came to replace it, resulting in the power struggles within the courts having the appearance of something more refined and proper. Meantime, the dirty work of appropriating resources was continued at a higher level of organization – the court itself. The system used its monopoly of violence to do the dirty work on behalf of the individuals that belonged to it, *and who continued to benefit from it.*

But this way of talking is beginning to undo the Eliasian schema. I have unwittingly anthropomorphized the system and so it seems as though the system is doing things *for* and *to* its members. The Eliasian term *figuration* is better because it keeps in sharp focus that the work of the system can only be done by the individuals who constitute it. Thus, strictly speaking, the individuals have not given up violence, they continue to use it but it is now in the service of a 'higher' cause – God, king or country. Socially sanctioned individual acts of violence are beginning to be sanitized; now, when one man murders another, it is no longer because of greed or lust, but for 'the greater good'. The fact that this man also happens to benefit from this greater good is rendered unconscious by making it incidental to the proceedings. Further, this man need feel no guilt whilst injuring another because it is in service of a higher noble purpose, and is more likely to experience a sense of grace. This was exactly the kind of mechanism that rationalized and sanitized the violence of the crusades and colonialism (it is also true of every self-righteous war).

When we add to this the fact that blackness was progressively gaining weight as a signifier of things 'beyond the pale', of things in the outer darkness where the normal rules of social functioning do not apply, then we can see that violence itself becomes colour coded. Now, when some violent act against the ethos of the system is committed, it is called a *black* deed.

I would suggest that something similar is taking place in contemporary Britain, where the state continues, in the name of duty, to do the dirty work for some of its citizens. This gives us a way of thinking about the *possibility* that the main institutions of society – health, education and law enforcement – work in ways that militate *against* the prospects of its citizens designated as black, and *for* its citizens designated as white. Because the work is conducted at this apparently abstract level, it makes it appear that the ordinary person has no part to play in this malign process. But as we have already noted, systems do no work, work is done by the individuals who constitute the system. The discussion in Chapter 2 on the pseudo-depressive position is also of relevance here.

Once the vicissitudes of the socio-developmental process instil the associations of blackness and whiteness in the psyche, then the work of sustaining the divide between the haves and must-not-haves is conducted automatically and unthinkingly by each individual to some degree. In what follows I will give a description of how this might come about. I will limit this discussion to the territory of the subtle and the unconscious, leaving the coarser expressions of racism out of the picture.

The gesture – return of the stranger on the train

Let me return to Foulkes' musings about the silent stranger on the train 'by his dress and posture . . . colour of his skin, by his fidgeting, his tenseness . . . he may communicate much to us which we can . . . understand' (Foulkes and Anthony 1957: 244). And let us assume this person's colour to be black.

It must be the case that the subliminal associations of blackness are such that mere visual contact will precipitate some gesture, some subtle adjustment of the white body in relation to the black other. The gesture will be something in the region of aversion or hostility or suspicion. At its most fundamental the adjustment will be one of exclusion. As this adjustment takes place on the subtlest of levels, it may be called an unconscious communication. The object receives this communication – again unconsciously – and must adjust his or her stance in turn. On the other hand, if the hostility has been sexualized then the gesture might be one of inclusion – but a problematic inclusion. Which one of these it is likely to be will be dependent on a mix of many psycho-social elements including class, gender, personal histories, and so forth.

The point about the associations embedded in the social unconscious is that all are impregnated with it – including the black passenger. Consequently, the black passenger is also a subject in his own right and not a mere object of the white, i.e. the black person is bound to feel and *act*, and not just *re-act*. However, there is no symmetry between the two protagonists

– power relations affect each of them quite differently. We have already seen some of the effects of this in Winston Parva (pp. 191–194).

The fact that white is cathected with charisma and black with stigma is likely to mean that the first gesture of the black-as-subject would be a gesture of inclusion towards a charismatic object. But the nature of the associations are such that this gesture is likely to be rebuffed by a gesture of exclusion from the white (the experience of many an immigrant from the Commonwealth attests to this).

This description as it stands is timeless, suggesting that the not-white is doomed to be rebuffed forever. This serves as a reminder that history needs to be incorporated into the analysis. History, an ongoing process, records amongst other things the vicissitudes of power relations. Thus the scenario is not fixed but made up of an endless series of gestures and responses to gestures. A series of rejections over a period of time will surely eventuate in calling forth from the rejected ones some combination of hostility or aggression or fear or depression, and so on. To put it straightforwardly once bitten, twice shy.

As a result of the accretion of experiences in the history of gesture and response, the black train passenger in 1957 is likely to be quite a different kind of person to one in 2000, as is the white. The evidence shows that many second, third and fourth generation blacks-as-subjects are not likely to open proceedings with a gesture of inclusion, but with a gesture of exclusion.

The gesture of exclusion from the black-as-subject confirms the associations in the minds of the whites-as-objects, that the blacks have a chip on their shoulder, or that they are inherently aggressive types, and so on. This kind of thought is possible by the device of erasing the accrued history of gestures, with the result that it seems that the black is *starting* the aggression. In other words an absolute beginning has been activated at exactly the point which makes it seem that the black is the *cause* of the trouble, because the provocations that have caused the black to cause trouble are nowhere to be seen – they are hidden behind the absolute beginning.

Putting it into Eliasian language we can say that the attribution of an *absolute beginning* at a particular point in the *process* of gesture and response, has resulted in changing the appearance of black anger from that of a gestural *response* to that of a more or less permanent psychological *state*. In this mechanism we are observing the workings of institutional racism.

Internalism in psychoanalysis

These ruminations suggest a possible reason why a psychoanalysis stripped of history is bound to read events in internalist ways. If history is removed, then one is forced to look for the causes of events in the here and now. And if the *only* things in the field of view are those of a black and his anger, then one is bound to look for the cause of the anger *in* the black, if only because there is nowhere else to look. Thus, internalism is a consequence of viewing individuals as closed, ahistorical systems.

This critique might be challenged on the basis that it misrepresents psychoanalysis, which *does* take account of the history of familial relations in the diagnostic process. Further, this internalized history is critical to the analysis of anger or any behaviour. Therefore, the individual is not thought of as a closed, ahistorical system, because although psychoanalysis does look inside, the elements of the inside that it is looking at, are in themselves patterns of history.

This is a fair challenge in as far as it goes. However, the difference in the two positions lies in the word history itself. As has been pointed out before, psychoanalysis takes account of a *developmental* history that is located in a socio-political vacuum. My contention is that one will not be able to comprehend the nature of the black's anger without incorporating socio-political history into the analysis. More, that the neglect of this frame will lead to a misunderstanding of what is actually happening. One of the ways in which this happens are found in a mechanism designated by the social psychologists as the 'attribution error' in which power relations pattern perceptual possibilities in such a way that one is prone to 'see' the causes of the same behaviours in black and white persons surprisingly differently.[4]

Attribution error

Duncan (1976) discovered that perceptions of the same video-taped act – *possibly* aggressive – varied according to the colour of the protagonists.

> In the versions of the Black perpetrator over 90 per cent of the [White] subjects judged the action to be 'violent' or 'aggressive' and tended to attribute it to some *internal cause*; in the White perpetrator versions less than 40 per cent coded it as violent . . . and were more inclined to believe in some situational cause for the action [i.e. an external cause].
> (Brown 1995: 100)

Taylor and Jaggi (1974) found that the perceptions of Hindus and Muslims in India were also skewed when presented with scenes in which a Hindu or a Muslim behaved in either a positive or negative way 'When Hindus were depicted in a positive light the behaviour was mainly attributed internally [by observing Hindus]; the same behaviour by Muslims was attributed externally. For negative behaviours the reverse occurred' (Brown 1995: 101).

However, it is not the case that this tendency of attributing to internal dispositional causes for good 'us' and bad 'them' behaviours universally takes place in all 'us' groupings. The status relations between the 'us' and the 'them' determines the direction of the attribution error. Brown (1995) cites important findings from Hewstone and Ward (1985) and Islam and Hewstone (1993) that indicate that this attribution error tends to be made primarily by members of dominant groupings. What this is saying is that the type and extent of the attribution error is determined by the emotional valencies of 'us' and 'them' images relative to each other. And as Elias has shown, these valencies are the product of the power relations between groupings.

The potency of the mechanism lies in the fact that it is entirely unconscious. It should also be noted that the propensity for perpetrating this error is not grounded in the developmental history or disposition of *particular* individuals, but is a general way of experiencing human relations. Further, it is the more powerful that are more susceptible to this mechanism. In sum, whilst the attribution error is a universal human phenomenon, the form it takes is determined by the patterns laid down by the power-relational field; and as this field is colour coded, we can say that the attribution error is also colour coded, with whites more prone to perceiving blacks in this light than the other way round.

It must also be the case that psychotherapists and psychoanalytic discourse itself cannot be immune to perpetuating the attribution error in its readings of societies and the actions of individuals. This in turn throws into question the validity of some propositions, for example that of eastern cultures as shame driven, and western cultures as guilt driven. This division replicates precisely the allocation of internal and external causes that are the basis of the attribution error.

Consequently, institutional racism is not necessarily a conscious conspiracy, but the activation of the set of racialized colour-coded conventions embedded within the psyches of individuals. Out of the many complexities and varieties of institutional racism, one trajectory is as follows. Other things being equal, the proclivities of the attribution error will impel white interviewers of job applicants to read interview-anxiety of blacks and whites in very different ways. The anxiety of the black interviewee is more likely to be read as a character defect (an internal cause and therefore fixed), whilst in the white interviewee it is more likely to be understood as due to the situation the interviewee finds themselves in (an external cause and so not a character trait). The statistical outcome of this emotionally loaded cognitive mechanism is bound to work in the direction of fewer black applicants succeeding in the job market.

We can now say that institutional racism is the outcome of the unconscious workings of colour-coded psyches, which in turn are the outcome of a socio-developmental process occurring in a colour-coded milieu.

We can also see how the attribution error will complicate the exchange of gestures on the train, reinforcing perceptions in one particular direction. Gestures of exclusion by blacks will be attributed to internal causes (aggressive natures), and gestures of friendship might be rebuffed with suspicion, what's he after? (situational cause). Both gestures are perceived as forms of pathology, and so are bound to set off the spiral of increasingly hostile counter-responses. Further, a white person is more likely to interpret his own feelings of hostility towards a black person as situational, by attributing the *cause* of the anger to the black person in some way, saying 'it is the thing that the black person is doing which is *making* me angry'.

Resistance: the return of the repressed

I will now return to a question that was voiced in Chapter 1: if racism is any use of race, then what is the difference between, say, the Ku Klux Klan and the Black Power movement. The working definition of racism from Chapter 1 compels one to say, contentiously, that both groups are racist. Clearly this lumping is unsatisfactory. This apparent equivalence between the two is also an outcome of *process reduction*.

Sections of the anti-racist movement have used the formula

$$racism = power + prejudice$$

to distinguish between the two saying that only whites can be racist and never blacks. This assertion relies on the idea that racism requires power to perpetuate it, and in this society it is the whites that are the more powerful. We can see that this formulation conceives of power as a possession belonging exclusively to whites. But by recalling Elias' injunction that power is an aspect of *relationship*, this dichotomy is falsified. Blacks can never be the complete victims of white subjects as they are never without *some* power and so, even according to the formula above, blacks have the capacity to be racist. And as Fanon has shown, indeed they can and are. The danger now is that a moral and logical equivalence is made between the two.

So how is one to differentiate between them? The anti-racist Wolfenstein's (1981, 1993) attempt to differentiate between the two ironically leads him to support the same distinction as the racist National Front (NF), a distinction between racism and racialism. The NF makes a 'careful distinction between "racialism" and "racism": racialism being the recognition of differences; and racism, being the propagation of hatred. The NF, say their publications, is only racialist, not racist' (Barker 1981: 26).

Because Wolfenstein recognizes that we cannot *not* think in racial terms, he makes a distinction between the use of the notion of race by the oppressors and the oppressed '[it is] important to differentiate between racism and racialism. Racialism is collective self assertion, as in Black Power and Black Pride. It does not entail claims of racial superiority. Racism, by contrast, is inherently supremacist' (Wolfenstein 1993: 333).

Whilst in considerable sympathy with the line being argued by Wolfenstein and the anti-racists, I would say that they are fudging the issue somewhat.

I would agree that Black Power is collective self-assertion, but would say that its claim is not just to pride, but also superiority. As the philosopher, Charles Taylor, cogently argues, the notion of 'different but equal' does not really hold water because 'difference so asserted becomes insignificant' (Taylor 1991: 38). Presumably the differences are being asserted by the varying groups because they have significance, and not just because they are straightforward descriptors of difference. These difficulties are an outcome of the attempt to distance the name of a difference from the use it is put to. Benedict (1983) reproduced this same error when she said that race was a neutral description of difference, and racism was the belief in the superiority of one race over another. These errors are the outcome of process reduction. The name, its use and the fact that it was evoked in the first place, are all parts of the same process. And when we recall that the difference that is being evoked, race, is a logical fiction then it shows up the whole process for what it is: a division into the haves and must-not-haves, a division that relies on the ephemeralness of colour. Some racisms are causal and others are consequential, some act and others are acted upon (of course this is never completely the case because of power being relative). The first of these is racist *per se* as it is racializing, whilst the second has been racialized. However, all are implicated in the generalized racialized dynamic. It would appear that all battles are fought within racialized terms. One can be for it or against it, one can love it or hate it, *but one cannot be outside it.*

Some are able to give themselves a name whilst others have a name thrust upon them. The 'black' was first named as such by the 'white'.

The situation is such that, in the first instance, one has no alternative but to use the name one has been given. If oppressions and atrocities are being perpetrated on those designated as blacks (or Jews, or Catholics, or gays, etc.) then it matters little in the moment that one or other of those so designated has no investment in that particular identity and another has more significance, say, being a psychoanalyst of the independent tradition. Initially, the oppressed are obliged to cohere around the very term they are oppressed by, and wield the language of oppression against their oppressors. The fact that the name of the oppressed has been cathected with revulsion and hate, means that when this very name is raised as the ensign of resistance it causes consternation in the more powerful.

> the liberal . . . points out that 'Black Power' itself is an offensive, sympathy losing phrase. 'Coloured Power' perhaps or 'Negro Power' would have been so much more palatable to the white power structure and less disturbing to the white psyche . . . [because] the connotations of 'Black' created by the white man himself are so frightening, so evil, so primordial that to associate it with power as well is to invoke the nightmare world of divine retribution, of Judgement day.
>
> (Sivanandan 1983: 66)

Miles says something similar

> those excluded by racism may use the idea of 'race' to define the
> focus and parameters of strategies of resistance to exclusion. Thus,
> these people having been excluded as an inferior 'race', the meanings
> are inverted in order to construct a positive identity and to define the
> population that becomes a political subject in the name of the idea of
> 'race', conceived as an imagined community of resistance.
>
> (1993: 57–58)

But what has to be remembered is that the use of the given name is a moment in an ongoing process, a process that will eventually dissolve the namer and the named into some other configuration. Lal (1986) calls this process the 'ethnicity paradox', in which the excluded group *reinforces* the very difference that was used to exclude it *as a strategic device in* order to mobilize and challenge the centre. Once successful it is not uncommon for the defining symbol to lose significance and for the movement to dissolve.

Thus, the Nation of Islam organizes its resistance along the same racial divisions that formed it. The Nation is not only a return of the oppressed, it is also a return of the repressed. When the Nation uses racialized language, then the white population are no longer *subjects*, but the *objects of racism* and so are disturbed. The bleaching out of history and process disguises the consequential nature of the Nation, making it appear that it is the Nation that is the *cause* of the problem by using divisive racial language, advocating separatism, and so on.

In this moment the white central body splits off and denies the existence of its own history of racialization, which it projects into this black object, resulting in experiencing itself as innocent and pure, aggressed from without. In a way they are right in that the white group are aggressed from without. However, a mistake has been made, which is that the analysis has begun in the middle of the story by the insertion of an absolute beginning. To use a medical metaphor, the black group is a symptom not the disease. *What is hard to accommodate is the fact that, inevitably, the symptom is made up of the same racialized constituents as the disease.* I do not wish to suggest that racism *is* a disease – this is only a metaphor.

Some implications for the clinical setting

To end I will make a brief excursion into the clinical setting in order to indicate some of the possible consequences that the theorizations of this thesis will have on the practices of psychotherapy. All the preceding arguments say that individuals are constituted by something more than the sum of their inherited biology and personal experiences, in the sense that the sources of aspects of the contents of the personal are to be found in the larger psycho-socio-historical frame; the personal is the social *personalized* and therefore individualized into a unique arrangement. This field applies to both patient and therapist, whatever their colours, and needs to be taken into account in the clinical setting.

There are several consequences of taking account of power on psycho-analytic theory and technique. The vicissitudes of power are integral to the sense of self, the experience of others and relationship to the world. An example being the attribution error which demonstrates how deeply our experience and therefore our psychology is patterned by the field of power relations. A psychological theory that takes no account of power is not only partial but also dangerously wrong. I say dangerous because *all* psycho-therapists (being human) must of necessity be subject to the attribution error, and so are likely to unthinkingly read clinical material in ways that differ according to how therapist and patient are positioned relative to each other in the field of power relations. In my opinion, the fact that so many black patients report profound feelings of being misunderstood and con-sequently drop out of therapy, must in part be because of the workings of this mechanism.

Transference, countertransference, guilt[5]

At its most fundamental the transference is precisely that – a transferring of material from one domain to another. In the main it is used in the sense of an expression of an internal cathected configuration that is played out (transferred) onto some external configuration (the analytic relationship). If the socio-historic is embedded at the deepest levels of the unconscious (as Foulkes asserts), then this material is bound to manifest in the transference and countertransference. This entails a broadening of the scope of the notion of transference to include socio-historical relationships between *groups of peoples*.

Take, for instance, the example of a black patient experiencing feelings of intimidation from his white therapist. Say the therapist takes up these feelings as a transference phenomenon to do with this patient's history with authority. As we saw in Chapter 3, the therapists tended to take up the personal component of the transference (instinctual constitution, rela-tionship to fathers, etc.) and appeared peculiarly blind to the socio-historic components. Why might this be? I will suggest that this occurs because the therapist is avoiding something that is painful and unresolved in them involving countertransference.

Racker (1985) distinguishes between two types of countertransference: concordant, when the feelings of the therapist echo those of the patient, and complementary, when they echo those of the object that the patient is projecting onto the therapist. In my view what is happening in the above scenario is that the white therapist is experiencing, to some extent, a complementary countertransference of a kind that echoes the feelings of the white overlord. The transference from the black patient might be positive – warm, benign and trusting feelings towards a benevolent despot, or negative feelings – anger, hate and envy. But whatever the case, does the therapist recognize and locate *parts* of the feelings correctly – in this instance in a historical relationship and not in a paternal relationship – indeed is he or she capable of recognizing it?

As Freud put it 'No analyst goes further than his own complexes and internal resistances permit' (1910b: 145). In other words the therapist can only interpret areas he or she has come to recognize through their own therapy and life experience. When material that has not been analysed in the therapist is evoked in the session, then it is the therapist's transference. In other words, it is the therapist repeating without remembering.

If the therapist consistently avoids the issue of the external reality, we have to ask why this is so: is it a resistance? And if so, what is the therapist avoiding remembering? One answer I would like to suggest is to do with the notion of guilt. By virtue of his colour the white, given other things as equal, does have it easier than the black in this society. To face this is to face guilt and the pain of that. If this area has not been addressed in the therapist's own therapy then it lies within – too hot to handle and so will be unconsciously avoided. The white therapist in this scenario is avoiding remembering that he or she does occupy a more privileged position than the black patient.

One consequence of being in the grip of this guilt is that the therapist is overwhelmed and incapacitated by it. The stance is that of being 'blinded by colour', and leads to a colluding with the victim position. What is said is 'poor you – isn't it awful'. Everything is outside the patient and he can only be commiserated with. An alternative possibility is that the therapist denies external reality and so avoids facing the guilt, thus banishing anxiety. The stance is 'colour blind' and is potentially victim blaming. What is said is 'we are all equal and if you end up there near the bottom of the pile, then it is you and your particular dynamic that have put you there'. In the first instance, the therapist is not remembering the patient's autonomy, the internal reality, whilst in the second instance the therapist is not remembering the external reality, but in both what is being repeated is the oppression.

Contextualization versus individualization

Whites and blacks will resonate differently to the same material by virtue of where they are positioned *as members of these groups* in the social context. This is not to deny variety within each grouping, but to say that the personal developmental history of each individual is deeply impregnated by the social. I will illustrate the argument through an anecdote.

I was speaking about the theme of colour when my clinical supervisor (white) said that he was not usually aware of the person's 'race' or colour in a session; it was not a significant issue for him. This surprised me as I am often conscious in groups, and in one to one situations, of my colour in relation to others.

Why might I be more sensitive than my supervisor on this matter? An internalist interpretation is bound to look for the cause inside me. Thus it might be suggested that I am overly sensitive or have a chip on my shoulder. In effect this is an interpretation of paranoia in which I am projecting some internal difficulty into the territory of black and white, which is now thought of as a vehicle for the expression of this latent difficulty. Another possibility is as follows. The white, by virtue of their colour, is in the mainstream and near the centre, whilst the black is marginalized and nearer to the edge. The closer one is to the edge, with the resultant danger of going over, the more one is aware of the circumstances that put one there – colour. Meanwhile, those at the centre have a vested interest (often unconscious) in maintaining the status quo by blanking out the colour dynamic altogether: if it does not exist in the first place then it cannot be changed. Thus, the difference between the feelings elicited in me and my supervisor are not just because of our asocial histories, but to do with where we are located in the field of power relations. Phoenix's empirical work supports this thesis, she found that 'colour was more important . . . to black young people's social identities than to white young people's' (1995: 40).

Context and resistance

If the black/white division is represented by patient and therapist, then this is likely to problematize the exchanges between them in additional ways. As we have seen, utterances are heard differently depending on whose mouth words come out of, and who is doing the listening. To take two external social facts: the patient arriving late because of a train delay, and being victimized for being black. What, if any, is the difference between them? They are similar in that they are both social facts, but different in that context allocates to them differing significances which call forth different types of affect. This difference in attached affect will determine how they will be handled.

To elaborate on this: the experience of some blacks living in Britain today (context) is that of somehow not quite making it, and when this is attributed to racism there is often a denial that racism exists 'You didn't get the job because the other person was better, it was nothing to do with colour'. The black's continual experience is of being caught in a powerful pincer movement, one prong of which is racism and the other the denial of racism. This, then, is the black context that informs how s/he *might* hear comments from a white therapist.

Now, the train delay as a social fact, exists to some extent outside the therapist and patient and as such is neutral. Thus, an interpretation from the therapist is more likely to be heard by the patient and worked with (of course the patient might for other reasons resist the interpretation of this fact too). The other social fact – social oppression – is different from the one above, in that both therapist and patient are implicated in actuality within it and, moreover, they are on opposite sides of the fence.

So, how might a black patient hear an interpretation from the white therapist, in this instance, the experience of social oppression, as a reflection of his or her inner dynamic? The black patient is quite likely to view such an interpretation with suspicion, in effect hearing the therapist saying 'you have a chip on your shoulder, and what you experience as the racist edifice does not exist'. In this sense the content of what the patient hears is transference material and the patient's reaction of suspicion can be thought of as a transference resistance; in particular a resistance to acknowledging a reality which contains within it, amongst other things, the patient's own contribution to the situation, both conscious and unconscious. An interpretation of the resistance at this point is no more likely to succeed than the original interpretation. The patient will entrench himself further, experiencing each new interpretation as further attack. The scenario is not an unusual one and leads to many black patients dropping out of therapy.

On technique

The alternative hypothesis I am putting forward is that *at times* it is more useful to begin by explicitly accepting this presented experience of social reality, which then allows the patient to begin working with the internal. To miss out the first step can block therapy. The model I am suggesting is one of moving from the outside in. In so doing the therapist gives the patient sufficient purchase on the outside world (trust), which will tend towards enabling the patient to temporarily 'let go' of the external and take the risk of looking not only at the internal aspects of the *same reality* but also of eventually re-appraising their experience of the external social. This suggestion flies in the face of the belief in certain schools of psychoanalysis, which is that all things have to be taken up in the transference and only the transference, and therefore all clinical events are to be understood as ultimately due to the externalization of material from the patient's psyche. The fact that each person's experience of the social is peculiarly subjective, is utilized defensively by some schools of therapy to stay away from the social altogether. In this way of thinking, any acknowledgement of the external social by the therapist is a capitulation of some sort, a seduction by the patient, and a defeat of the therapy.

There are two further dangers in reading all clinical material in pure internalist ways. First, at times it reproduces the double bind of the experience of racism and the denial of racism: the patient is told these experiences of yours are not real, not only are they distortions but more, you are setting up the situation in such a way that it is producing the very difficulty that you are complaining about. Second, the technique of the transference can be used by the therapist to remove themselves from the possibility that if the patient is experiencing something racialized taking place in the room, then the therapist is contributing to it. The transference is a very powerful instrument which can be misused to say to the patient, what you think is happening in the here-and-now between you and me, is in fact a reactivation of something from elsewhere. On the occasions when this version of events is fought against, then it is interpreted as resistance. It is a recipe for madness.

The unconscious

The model of the unconscious that was developed in the previous chapter problematizes the archaeological model of psychotherapy treatment. The fact that in the new model the conscious and unconscious have a recursive relationship with each other means that there is no 'bottom layer' to get back to. Whatever is made conscious, something else of necessity will be simultaneously rendered unconscious. And if that unconscious element were made conscious next, then something else *within it and beside it* will of necessity be rendered unconscious. In a sense the unconscious is constantly being created anew in relation to each element being made conscious.

It is possible to retain the analogy with archaeology by noticing that whenever something is revealed by removing the sand, the sand has to be put somewhere else, and so something else is necessarily covered. The complexity introduced by psychoanalysis is that the apparently inconsequential place one chooses to dump the sand, will not be inconsequential on all counts, rather it will always have some element of a cover up. This will be true of both analyst and patient with each trying to cover up different sorts of things. If the analysis is a true dialogue then the skirmishes within the analytic sandpit will inevitably be revelatory for both protagonists.

Thus, at whichever level one engages in the interlaced model of the conscious/unconscious, within a similarity there will always be difference, and within a difference there will always be a similarity. Every truth is based on the suppression of another truth. This process of deconstruction, or decompression, can be continued endlessly. There is an affinity here with the mathematical world of fractals, which gives us another way of thinking about the relation between the particular and the general – when one looks at the detail, as in a single psyche, we will find within it similar structures and relationships to those found at the more general social level and vice versa. This analogical linkage gives a neat way of modelling the relationship between the structures of psyches and the structures of societies, and why the colour-coded structures of one will of necessity be found reflected in the other.

White–white therapy

The preceding arguments suggest that issues of race and colour are ever present in the consulting room – even when the protagonists are both white and from the dominant culture, or both black. This is so for several reasons. First, notions of blackness and whiteness – cathected with their associations – are everywhere in the English language, and so ever present in the consulting room if only in the communications between analyst and patient. Second, the double nature of the notion of blackness is utilized continually to distance and displace things problematic. At one level blackness serves as a container, an auxiliary space into which untoward material is projected. At another level blackness is poured into material designated as repellent in some way in order to signify its repellence in order to repel it. The obverse is true of whiteness.

There is the additional fact that through the socio-developmental process all psyches have inevitably been racialized and colour coded, this must include the white analyst as much as the white patient. Consequently, both will organize clinical material into the approved and disapproved through the utilization of blackness and whiteness, sometimes explicitly sometimes implicitly. But because both utilize the same mechanisms, they are less likely to be noticed by either as they will appear natural and normal to both of them.

A final caveat: black and white internal objects

Despite the cautions voiced in the previous chapter that the associations of bad and black, and good and white are neither natural nor eternal, it is difficult not to feel defeated by the weight of history and accumulated evidence; and if this were indeed the case, then there would be no possibility of good psychic objects being colour-coded black, and the so-called black people would be doomed to hate and fear their own beings forever. However, the fact that the associations are an outcome of power relations, must mean that as these shift so must the associations. Further, Elias has said that power is always relative, and so no one is completely powerless. Thus hegemonies are continually being contested locally (say within family relationships) and globally through activism, albeit in ways that are constrained. The fact that the Black Power movement has thrown up many heroes and heroines, means that even in this very coarse sense we can see the generation and emergence of good objects that are black – black people to be admired and so able to be used as ego ideals by both black and white people. It must follow that through the introjections and projections of the

developmental process, these black objects become the signifiers and containers of goodness to some degree. But as the saying goes, one swallow
does not summer make; the relationship to good black objects remains
as yet complex and ambivalent. Of course, relationships to white objects
are also ambivalent, the question is one of degree rather than of clear-cut
distinction.

A more complicated instance of the confluence of good and black is
found in metropolitan youth culture in contemporary Britain, where the
black man has come to be viewed as super-masculine, and so something to
be emulated by white youth in dress, attitude and speech (Frosh *et al.*
2000). Here, too, the relationship is an ambivalent one – this black young
man, whilst admired, is also feared. Whilst the attractive attributes are
incorporated the black himself is kept at a distance. Additionally, the fact
that the vision of super-masculinity has, in part, been constructed by projection of repressed aspects of the 'civilized' psyche complicates the situation
even further.

The danger in talking about objects as black and white is that some
might take this to mean that these objects are the *property* of black and
white people, leading us back into the essentialist cul-de-sac. Here the claim
of white purity is countered with that of a black authenticity grounded in
blackness *per se*. This in turn would reduce the psychotherapy project into
an essentialist one, where black psyches were to be purged of alien white
objects and vice versa. Fortunately, reality is not so neat, or only appears so
in a symmetric universe.

Conclusions

Endings are as difficult as beginnings.

Elias has said that wherever one starts, something has gone before; but
wherever one decides to stop, something enticing is always visible just
beyond it. This sentiment is a reflection of one of the central ideas in this
work, that wholes are constructions that have a coherence enforced upon
them at the cost of neglecting many things of value scattered around them.

Let me, nevertheless, recapitulate the central points that emerged over
the preceding pages. As the central subject was racism, it seemed sensible to
begin by focusing on the territory 'before' it, the things called races that
were embroiled in racism. The project failed as racism kept rudely intrud-
ing into the discussions on race. This suggested that names were not necessarily straightforward descriptions of the world, but that the *uses* that a
name was to be put to were somehow involved from the first, even as the
name was being formed. This thought served as a prompt to constantly
keep in mind the territory 'before' the name – the conditions that make it
necessary for its invention. Similar difficulties were found with the notions
of culture and ethnicity. Next, the notion of race was tested and found to

be hollow, and this in turn threw up the conundrum that racism exists despite there being no such things as races. This led to the idea that more important than race or racism was the *activity of racialization*. It was also noted that despite the variations in the sorts of things considered to be races or cultures or ethnicities, the terms black and white were continually used to name all three. This prompted the thought that the notions of black and white were critical to the activity of racialization – the division of humanity into haves and must-not-haves.

This was followed by using psychoanalysis to think about racism. The models of human nature suggested by Freud, Klein, Fairbairn and Winnicott were used to infer theories of racism consistent to the world view of each. Broadly, three sorts of explanation emerged. The first consisted of explanations of why particular *individuals* might behave in hateful and racist ways; the cause being the externalization of some internal difficulty. As theories of individuals, some of these formulations were indeed convincing and sophisticated. The second theme concerned the individual *in* a group. Here it was proposed that when in groups, individuals regressed to a primitive state of mind and so behaved in primitive ways. The third theme consisted of a shift in focus from the insides of individuals to individuals in context. In particular, from Winnicott came the idea that existence precipitates anxiety and aggression. This fundamental anxiety was thought to be part of what made racism possible. The journal articles were disappointing in that they were extremely reductive with almost all social events understood as projections of internal difficulties.

Despite many points of dispute with the four theoreticians, each of them suggested interesting ways of thinking about the subject matter, but not in a straightforward way. For example, it requires the stripping of instinctivism from the Freudian corpus to reveal that the structure of his assertions are not dissimilar to the formulations developed in the later chapters. This is most clearly seen in the Freudian idea that the social has a presence in the psyche; the whole book could be thought of as an extension of this idea with the help of Foulkes and Elias.

Out of the four, Klein fitted in least well with the tenor of this thesis as her developmental metaphysic was the most internalist of them. Her proposal, in sum, was that the hatreds that manifest in the world were aspects of an endogenous death instinct that had escaped modification through the developmental process. Her thinking suggests that this pre-existing internal destructive principle is secondarily patterned by social exigencies. The argument I put up against this view is not its reverse, which would be to attempt to refute the idea that *every* human has the capacity to act in hateful and deadly ways to others – clearly every human has this capacity. The way through this difficulty was indicated by Fairbairn, which was a change in focus from instinct to object relation. The reversal implied by his work is that it is social exigencies that generate and elicit certain emotions for some object-related end. This recursive idea finds an echo in the earlier formulation, also recursive, that the desired end point (use of a name) is present in the start point (invention and evocation of the name).

Next, of the six additional psychoanalytic theories of racism that were briefly outlined, the work of Fanon was given prime importance. His thought, in particular his emphasis on the social and notions of black and white, opened up the possibility of viewing in a more comprehensive light the impact of race and racism on the construction of psyches.

Given that racism is a group phenomenon, the necessary group perspective was introduced via Foulkes. All of Foulkes' innovations were the fruit of just one simple idea: that human beings can never be thought of in isolation as they always exist in relation to each other. He developed a series of concepts that attended to the level of individuals-in-relation, such as the matrix and the social unconscious. Despite these innovations he did not take the final step, which was to consider individuals in power relations to each other, and this allowed him to retain the old nature–nurture divide within the psyche.

It required Elias to breach this final frontier of humans-in-*social* relations. Elias showed that hierarchical power relations between groups of people were intrinsic to the social and thus to the psyches of its inhabitants. He showed that society was driven by the vicissitudes not of the instincts but of power relations. He showed how differences were manufactured and sustained in the service of these power relations. Psychoanalytically speaking, perhaps one of the most critical things to emerge from Elias was that certain sorts of disagreeable associations were not always born of projection, but were generated by the processes of power relations in order to manufacture divisions into types of 'us' and 'them'. These associations exist in the social unconscious and as such are imbibed through the socio-developmental processes. One could say that as some names were taken in so were the antipathies embedded within them.

Next, all presumptions of the naturalness of the associations of negativity to blackness and positivity to whiteness were confounded by attending to the semantic history of the terms. It was argued that blackness and whiteness became the servants of racism, in that they were increasingly used as parts-of-names as a way of signalling the value and status of the named. From the 1600s, the confluence of an increasing sense of negativity with the notion of blackness, the naming of non-European 'them's as black, with the progressive labelling of emotions and behaviours designated as disagreeable as black, gave credence to the idea that societies and psyches were being organized in colour-coded ways.

These cogitations, when put together with Matte-Blanco's bi-logic, generate a general theory of difference to suggest that identity, the sense of self, was a description of a *relationship* of groups of individuals in social relationship to each other; and further, this sense of self was a fragile entity, ever ready to shape shift into something else. This model of identity had its basis in three territories, each of which worked to bolster the other two –

the mechanisms of cognition, power relations between groups of people, and the vicissitudes of the emotions. This way of thinking also gave up another model, once again recursive, of the relationship between the conscious and unconscious, with each embedded in the other. It was suggested that discourses of power informed to some degree where ruptures and divisions were hallucinated into the continuum of peoples; ruptures where the continuity and commonality between the groupings were rendered unconscious, to give the resultant groupings the appearance of difference of *type*. But because the boundaries between the named types (be they of race, culture or ethnicity) are difficult to delineate, the notions of black and white are elicited and applied to each of the *types* to aid the hallucination.

By continuing to use the word race we are perpetuating the fantasy that it exists. This is even more true of the fiction 'mixed-race', as it implies that those not so designated are of a pure race. It was because of the failure of all attempts at pinning down race on anything concrete, that racialized discourses were impelled into a slide towards relying on the labels 'black' and 'white': it is an attempt to fasten the chimera called race onto some aspect of tangible reality. But then we saw that the apparently solid notions of black and white also evaporated as one approached them. We can say then that the notion of race is a chimera that relies on a series of mirages to lend itself the appearance of something substantial, the so-called black and white races.

The fact that there is the constant danger of the imaginary 'us' dissolving into the 'them' resulting in another kind of 'us' and 'them', sets off two interlinked anxieties. The first is a profound existential anxiety that comes about as one starts to feel the sense of self dissolving, and so is resisted. The second anxiety is evoked by the potential loss, dilution or disruption of access to the vortices of power and status. I have argued that although elements of these anxieties are conscious and known, the greater part of these anxieties reside in what Foulkes has called the social unconscious, and it is the unreflected attempts at managing and defending against these anxieties that not only drives many of the relations between peoples designated as black and white, but also impels their designation as black and white.

The psychoanalytic perspective was retained but extended by insisting that psychological objects could not also be other than social objects. This is as true of objects like 'mother' as well as emotions, attitudes, behaviours and material things. Thus, the psychological developmental process should more properly be called a socio-developmental process. The internalized objects and object relations must bring with them all their aspects. It follows that as social objects are colour coded, so must be the psyche which is formed through their internalizations. And finally it is argued that the 'colour' attached to objects determines to some degree the affects that they stir, and this in turn determines to some extent the types of object relations that take place between them.

The model of human nature generated in this work is one where the forms of psyche are predicated on the forms of society, with the two in a recursive relationship to each other. Components of this model include an alternative model of the unconscious, and a problematizing of the notion of the whole. This last requires, at the very least, a rethinking of what we might mean when we say that the depressive position is predicated on 'whole body' relations. The scope of the notion of the transference has been extended to include new territories. A consequence of these modifications is that some of the conventional beliefs about how clinical material is to be read is put into question.

The resulting theory of racism is an integration of insights from three domains – the cognitive, the emotional and the sociological. Thus, racism can no longer thought of as primarily a result of splitting and projection, but as a complex psycho-social phenomenon that is driven by the pragmatics of the power relations in the world. Whilst psychological mechanisms play a critical role in this process, they are not elevated as *causal* agencies.

In the task of deconstructing some of the discourses of racism, the instruments provided by Matte-Blanco (bi-logic) and Elias (absolute beginnings and process reduction) were found to be invaluable. The work has also resulted in novel perspectives on the notions of black and white. First, it has exposed the historical nature of the associations that the words are cathected with. Second, and more critically, it has been demonstrated that they are not innocuous descriptors and names, but ways of organizing the field of power relations. It is the fact that the terms are powerfully cathected with positivity and negativity that allows them to be appropriated in the service of racialization. I have given the terms more weight than has previously been the case in the analytic world, consigning them critical roles as instruments in the organizing of society as well as psyche. In sum, I have shown that human relations, internal and external, are colour coded.

Notes

1 In immigration law the technical term for the bureaucratic procedure of becoming British, is to be 'naturalized'. 'Natural' has been made a verb. Presumably the recipient is then deemed in law to be equivalent to those who are 'naturally' British in the first place.

2 There is a parallel debate going on in the world of ecology, where there are questions of how it is that some species are thought to be 'native' and authentic and others 'alien' (Nicholson and Hare 1986, Agyeman and Hare 1988, Hare 1988).

3 There are two caveats. 1. This is more true of the courtiers than the monarch. The latter is less constrained than the others, but is never completely free. 2. The internal space is not completely pacified – overt acts of violence do indeed occur between rival groupings, but not in the same casual way as before.

4 Taylor and Jaggi (1974), Duncan (1976), Ross (1977), Pettigrew (1979), Hewstone (1989), Brown (1995).

5 Elements of this section were previously published in Dalal 1997b.

Afterword

The making of monsters: September 11th 2001

As this book was in the process of being completed, world events were calling forth a new opposition: Islam versus the West. The arguments and strategies developed through this book are of direct pertinence to this dichotomy in several ways.

1   Given more time and space it would be possible to show that this division too is colour coded.
2   The facts that much of the West is Islamic, and that neither polarity – the West or Islam – is a homogenous unity speaking with one voice, are all rendered invisible by the ministrations of symmetric logic.
3   It is also clear that the notion of an absolute beginning is being utilized by all protagonists to designate who are the evil ones; thus if the events of 11 September 2001 were monstrous, and surely they were, then one could say they were perpetrated by monsters. The question now is what part did the West play in the creation of these monsters? Those who blind themselves to this sort of question do so by making an absolute division between a good 'us' and an evil 'them'. Equally, those who seek to put the blame entirely on the West do so to obfuscate the contingencies of Middle Eastern politics that led to the 'creation of the Taliban in 1994 by Pakistani intelligence services working with Saudi funds' (Halliday 2002: 45).
4   Those who seek to explain this calamity as an outcome of a 'clash of cultures' or a confrontation of religious beliefs (on either side) are obfuscating the power struggles on global and local levels (within nations and within religious groupings) that are driving the complexities of the current situation. Once again, certain differences are being fanned alive and made absolute in order to service political ends. As Fred Halliday says 'culture and text, are contingent instruments, not causes' (2002: 46); readers will recognize something of Fairbairn in this.
5   Further, those who seek to explain the current situation through an allusion to ancient history do so in order to naturalize what is taking place, thus making it appear inevitable. Halliday echoes the arguments

developed in this book when he says 'The past provides a reserve of reference and symbol for the present; it does not explain it. The Ottoman siege of Vienna in 1683 or the Crusades do not explain current politics; *they are used by them*' (ibid. 125, italics added).

6 And finally, the internalist attempts to explain the events of September 11th wholly as a manifestation of the 'East's' envy of the 'West' are, (as I hope I have shown), not only facile and reductive but also dangerous in that it obfuscates the complexities of the situation.

Much more could, and should be said on these matters but not here, because although endings are in a sense arbitrary they are also, alas, necessary.

Bibliography

Ackerman, N.W. and Jahoda, M. (1948) 'The dynamic basis of anti-Semitic attitudes', *Psychoanalytic Quarterly* 17: 240–260.

Adler, A. (1933) *Social Interest*, London: Farer & Farer.

Adorno, T.W., Frenkel-Brunswick, E., Levinson, D.J. and Sanford, R.N. (1950) *The Authoritarian Personality*, New York: Harper.

Agyeman, J. and Hare, T. (1988) 'Towards a cultural ecology', *Urban Wildlife* 1: 3.

Axelrad, S. (1960) 'On some uses of psychoanalysis', *Journal of American Psychoanalytic Association* 8: 175–217.

Bailey, C. (1996) 'The health needs of children from ethnic minorities', in K.N. Dwivedi and V.P. Varma (eds) *Meeting the Needs of Ethnic Minority Children*, London: Jessica Kingsley, pp. 89–95.

Banton, M. (1987) *Racial Theories*, Cambridge: Cambridge University Press.

Barker, M. (1981) *The New Racism*, London: Junction Books.

Barthes, R. (1984) *Mythologies*, Great Britain: Paladin.

Basch-Kahre, E. (1984) 'On difficulties arising in transference and countertransference when analyst and analysand have different socio-cultural backgrounds', *International Review of Psychoanalysis* 11: 61–67.

Beisner, H.R. (1988) ' "I ain't nobody" – a study of black male identity formation', *The Psychoanalytic Study of the Child* 43: 307–318.

Benedict, R. (1983) *Race and Racism*, London: Routledge & Kegan Paul.

Bernard, V.W. (1953) 'Psychoanalysis and members of minority groups', *Journal of the American Psychoanalytic Association* 1: 256–267.

Bird (1957) 'A consideration of the etiology of prejudice', *Journal of the American Psychoanalytic Association* 5: 490–513.

Blum, H.P. (1994) 'Dora's conversion syndrome: a contribution to the prehistory of the holocaust', *Psychoanalytic Quarterly* 63: 518–535.

Boesky, D. (1974) 'Racism and psychiatry', *Psychoanalytic Quarterly* 43: 143–144.

Brachter, R.G. (1993) 'Translations – English Language', in B.M. Metzger and M.D. Coogan (eds) *The Oxford Companion to the Bible*, Oxford: Oxford University Press, pp. 758–763.

Brown, N.O. (1960) *Life Against Death*, New York: Vintage Books.

Brown, R. (1995) *Prejudice*, Oxford, UK: Blackwell.

Brown, R.E., Fitzmyer, J.A. and Murphy, R.E. (1990) *The New Jerome Biblical Commentary*, Avon, UK: The Bath Press.

Bruner, J. (1990) *Acts of Meaning*, London: Harvard University Press.

Butts, H.F. (1971) 'Psychoanalysis, the black community and mental health', *Contemporary Psychoanalysis* 7: 147–152.

Cantor, N.F. (1963) *The Medieval World 300–1300*, New York: Macmillan.

Carter, R.T. (1995) *The Influence of Race and Racial Identity in Psychotherapy*, New York: John Wiley & Sons.

Chambers Twentieth Century Dictionary (1972), Edinburgh: W&R Chambers, p. 134. Reprinted in 1987.

Chasseguet-Smirgel, J. (1990) 'Reflections of a psychoanalyst upon the Nazi biocracy and genocide', *International Review of Psychoanalysis* 17: 167–175.

Cohen, P. (1988) 'The perversions of inheritance: studies in the making of multi-racist Britain' in P. Cohen and H.S. Bains (eds) *Multi-Racist Britain*, London: Macmillan Education, pp. 9–120.

Cohn, N. (1970) *The Pursuit of the Millennium*, London: Palladin.

Cohn, N. (1993) *Europe's Inner Demons*, London: Pimlico.

Cruden, A. (1769) *Cruden's Complete Concordance to the New and Old Testament and the Apocrypha*, Frederick Warne: London.

Cushman, P. (1994) 'Confronting Sullivan's spider – hermeneutics and the politics of therapy', *Contemporary Psychoanalysis* 30: 800–844.

Da Conceição Dias, C.G. and De Lyra Chebabi, J.W. (1987) 'Psychoanalysis and the role of black life and culture in Brazil', *International Review of Psychoanalysis* 14: 185–206.

Dalal, F. (1988) 'The racism of Jung', *Race and Class* 19(3): 1–22; republished as 'Jung a racist', *British Journal of Psychotherapy* 1988, 4(3): 1–22.

Dalal, F. (1993) 'Race and racism – an attempt to organize difference', *Group Analysis* 26: 277–293.

Dalal, F. (1997a) 'The colour question in psychoanalysis', *Journal of Social Work Practice* 11: 103–114.

Dalal, F. (1997b) 'A transcultural perspective on psychodynamic psychotherapy', *Group Analysis* 30: 203–215.

Dalal, F. (1998) *Taking the Group Seriously – Towards a Post Foulkesian Group Analytic Theory*, London: Jessica Kingsley.

Dalal, F. (2001a) 'Insides and outsides: a review of psychoanalytic renderings of difference, racism and prejudice', *Psychoanalytic Studies* 3: 43–66.

Dalal, F. (2001b) 'The social unconscious: a post-Foulkesian perspective', *Group Analysis* 34: 539–555.

Davidson, L. (1987) 'The cross-cultural therapeutic dyad', *Contemporary Psychoanalysis* 23: 659–675.

de Zulueta, F. (1993) *From Pain to Violence – The Traumatic Roots of Destructiveness*, London: Whurr Publishers.

Devereaux, G. (1953) 'Cultural factors in psychoanalytic therapy', *Journal of the American Psychoanalytic Association* 1: 629–655.

Dollard, J., Doob, L.W., Miller, N.E., Mowrer, O.H. and Sears, R.R. (1939) *Frustration and Aggression*, New Haven: Yale University Press.

Douglas, M. (1995) *Purity and Danger – an Analysis of the Concepts of Pollution and Taboo*, London: Routledge.

Dunbar, R. (1997) *Grooming, Gossip and the Evolution of Language*, London: Faber & Faber.

Duncan, B.L. (1976) 'Differential social perception and attribution of intergroup violence: testing the lower limits of stereotyping blacks', *Journal of Personality and Social Psychology*, 34: 590–598.

Dwivedi, K.N. (1996) 'Introduction', in K.N. Dwivedi and V.P. Varma (eds) *Meeting the Needs of Ethnic Minority Children*, London: Jessica Kingsley, pp. 1–16.

Dwivedi, K.N. and Varma, V.P. (eds) (1996) *Meeting the Needs of Ethnic Minority Children*, London: Jessica Kingsley.

Elias, N. (1976) 'Introduction', in N. Elias and J. Scotson (1994) *The Established and the Outsiders*, London: Sage.

Elias, N. (1978) *What is Sociology?*, Columbia University Press: New York.

Elias, N. (1991) *The Symbol Theory*, London: Sage.

Elias, N. (1994) *The Civilizing Process*, Oxford: Blackwell.

Elias, N. and Scotson, J. (1994) *The Established and the Outsiders*, London: Sage.

Erikson, E. (1958) *Young Man Luther*, New York: W.W. Norton & Co.

Eze, E.C. (1997) *Race and the Enlightenment – A Reader*, London: Blackwell.

Fairbairn, R. (1935) 'The social significance of communism considered in the light of psychoanalysis', in R. Fairbairn (1994) *Psychoanalytic Studies of the Personality*, London: Routledge.

Fairbairn, R. (1943) 'The Repression and the Return of Bad Objects', in R. Fairbairn (1994).

Fanon, F. (1982) *Black Skin, White Masks*, New York: Grove Press.

Fanon, F. (1983) *The Wretched of the Earth*, Great Britain: Pelican.

Fernando, S. (1991) *Mental Health, Race and Culture*, London: Macmillan.

Fletchman Smith, B. (1993) 'Assessing the difficulties for British patients of Caribbean origin in being referred for psychoanalytical psychotherapy', *British Journal of Psychotherapy* 10(1): 50–61.

Foulkes, S.H. (1948) *Introduction to Group Analytic Psychotherapy*, William Heinemann Medical Books, reprinted in 1983, London: Karnac Books.

Foulkes, S.H. (1964) *Therapeutic Group Analysis*, London: George Allen & Unwin.

Foulkes, S.H. (1966) 'Some basic concepts in group psychotherapy', in S.H. Foulkes (1990) *Selected Papers*, London: Karnac Books.

Foulkes, S.H. (1971) 'Access to unconscious processes in the group-analytic group', in S.H. Foulkes (1990) *Selected Papers*, London: Karnac Books.

Foulkes, S.H. (1973a) 'The group as matrix of the individual's mental life', in S.H. Foulkes (1990) *Selected Papers*, London: Karnac Books.

Foulkes, S.H. (1973b) 'Oedipus conflict and regression', in S.H. Foulkes (1990) *Selected Papers*, London: Karnac Books.

Foulkes, S.H. (1974) 'My philosophy in psychotherapy', in S.H. Foulkes (1990) *Selected Papers*, London: Karnac Books.

Foulkes, S.H. (1975) 'Problems of the large group', in S.H. Foulkes (1990) *Selected Papers*, London: Karnac Books.

Foulkes, S.H. (1990) *Selected Papers*, London: Karnac Books.

Foulkes, S.H. and Anthony, E.J. (1957) *Group Psychotherapy – the Psychoanalytic Approach*, London: Karnac Books.

Freire, P. (1972) *Pedagogy of the Oppressed*, London: Penguin.

Freud, S. (1908) 'Character and anal eroticism', *Standard Edition IX*,[1] London: Hogarth Press, pp. 167–175.

Freud, S. (1910a) 'Five lectures on psychoanalysis', *Standard Edition XI*, London: Hogarth Press, pp. 3–58.

Freud, S. (1910b) 'The future prospects of psychoanalytic therapy', *Standard Edition XI*, London: Hogarth Press, pp. 139–151.

Freud, S. (1911) 'Formulations on the two principles of mental', *Standard Edition XII*, London: Hogarth Press, pp. 218–226.

Freud, S. (1915a) 'Instincts and their vicissitudes', *Standard Edition XIV*, London: Hogarth Press, pp. 117–140.

Freud, S. (1915b) 'Thoughts for the time on war and death', *Standard Edition XIV*, London: Hogarth Press, pp. 273–302.

Freud, S. (1920) 'Beyond the pleasure principle', *Standard Edition XVIII*, London: Hogarth Press, pp. 7–66.

Freud, S. (1921) 'Group psychology and the analysis of the ego', *Standard Edition XVIII*, London: Hogarth Press, pp. 69–144.

Freud, S. (1930) 'Civilization and its discontents', *Standard Edition XXI*, London: Hogarth Press, pp. 59–145.

Freud, S. (1933) 'New introductory lectures on psychoanalysis', *Standard Edition XXII*, London: Hogarth Press, pp. 5–182.

Fromm, E. (1982) *The Anatomy of Human Destructiveness*, London: Pelican.

Frosh, S., Phoenix, A. and Pattman, R. (2000) 'Cultural contestations in practice', in C. Squire (ed.) *Culture in Psychology*, London: Routledge, pp. 47–58.

Fryer, P. (1984) *Staying Power – The History of Black People in Britain*, London: Pluto Press.

Gerace, L., Aliprantis, A., Russell, M., Baumgartner, R.N., Wang, Z., Wang, J., Pierson, R.N. Jr. and Heymsfield, S.B. (1994) 'Skeletal differences between black-and-white men and their relevance to body-composition estimates', *American Journal of Human Biology* 6: 255–262.

Giddens, A. (1989) *Sociology*, Cambridge: Polity Press.

Gillborn, D. (1990) *Race, Ethnicity and Education*, London: Unwin.

Gilroy, P. (1987) *'There Ain't no Black in the Union Jack': The Cultural Politics of Race and Nation*, London: Hutchinson.

Gilroy, P. (1993) *Small Acts – Thoughts on the Politics of Black Cultures*, London: Serpent's Tail.

Goldberg, E.L., Myers, W.A. and Zeifman, I. (1974) 'Some observations of three interracial analyses', *Journal of the American Psychoanalytic Association, 55*: 495–500.

Goodman, M.E. (1964) *Race Awareness in Young Children*, New York: Collier Books.

Gordon, P. (1993) 'Keeping therapy white?: psychotherapy trainings and equal opportunities', *British Journal of Psychotherapy*, 10(1): 44–49.

Gould, S.J. (1984) *The Mismeasure of Man*, London: Pelican.

Greenberg, J.R. and Mitchell, S.A. (1983) *Object Relations in Psychoanalytic Theory*, Cambridge, MA and London: Harvard University Press.

Grinberg, L., Sor, D. and de Bianchedi, E.T. (1985) *Introduction to the Work of Bion*, London: Maresfield Library.

Groddeck, G. (1984) *Die Natur heilt*, Frankfurt-am-Main: Fischer Taschenbuch.

Gutin, J.A.C. (1994) 'End of the Rainbow', *Discover: The World of Science; Special Issue: The Science of Race*, 15(11): 71–75.

Hale, J. (1993) *The Civilization of Europe in the Renaissance*, London: Harper Collins.

Hall, S. (1980) 'Race, articulation and societies structured in dominance', in UNESCO, *Sociological Theories: Race and Colonialism*, Paris: UNESCO.

Halliday, F. (2002) *Two Hours that Shook the World – September 11, 2001: Causes and Consequences*, London: Saqi Books.

Hare, A. (1988) 'Woods ancient and modern', *Arboricultural Journal* 12: 177–180.

Harland, R. (1987) *Superstructuralism*, London: Methuen.

Hewstone, M. (1989) *Causal Attribution*, Oxford, UK: Blackwell.

Hewstone, M. and Ward, C. (1985) 'Ethnocentricism and causal attribution in Southeast Asia', *Journal of Personality and Social Psychology*, 48: 614–623.

Hill, C. (1994) *The English Bible and the Seventeenth Century Revolution*, London: Penguin.

Hinshelwood, R.D. (1991) *A Dictionary of Kleinian Thought*, London: Free Association Books.

Hirschfeld, L.A. (1998) *Race in the Making*, Cambridge, MA and London: MIT Press.

Holy Bible (1611) Authorised King James Version, London: Her Majesty's Printer, Eyre & Spottiswoode Ltd.

Husband, C. (ed.) (1982) 'Introduction: "Race" and the continuity of a concept', in C. Husband (ed.) *'Race' in Britain – Continuity and Change*, London: Hutchinson, pp. 11–23.

Islam, M.R. and Hewstone, M. (1993) 'Intergroup attributions and affective consequences in majority and minority groups', *Journal of Personality and Social Psychology* 64: 936–950.

James, A. (1981) ' "Black": an inquiry into the pejorative associations of an English word', *Community* 9: 19–30.

Jenkins, R. (1988) 'Social anthropological models of inter-ethnic relations', in J. Rex and D. Mason (eds) *Theories of Race and Ethnic Relations*, Cambridge: Cambridge University Press.

Jordan, W. (1977) *White over Black*, New York and London: Norton.

Klein, M. (1923) 'The role of school in the libidinal development of the child', in M. Klein (1988a) *Love, Guilt and Reparation and Other Works 1921–1945*, London: Virago Press.

Klein, M. (1928) 'Early stages of the Oedipus conflict', in M. Klein (1988a) *Love, Guilt and Reparation and Other Works 1921–1945*, London: Virago Press.

Klein, M. (1932) *The Psychoanalysis of Children*, London: Hogarth Press.

Klein, M. (1946) 'Notes on some schizoid mechanisms', in M. Klein (1988b) *Envy and Gratitude and Other Works 1946–1963*, London: Virago Press.

Klein, M. (1952) 'Some theoretical conclusions regarding the emotional life of the infant', in M. Klein (1988b) *Envy and Gratitude and Other Works 1946–1963*, London: Virago Press.

Klein, M. (1957) 'Envy and gratitude', in M. Klein (1988b) *Envy and Gratitude and Other Works 1946–1963*, London: Virago Press.

Klein, M. (1959) 'Our adult world and its roots in infancy', in M. Klein (1988b) *Envy and Gratitude and Other Works 1946–1963*, London: Virago Press.

Klein, M. (1988a) *Love, Guilt and Reparation and Other Works 1921–1945*, London: Virago Press.

Klein, M. (1988b) *Envy and Gratitude and Other Works 1946–1963*, London: Virago Press.

Kovel, J. (1988) *White Racism – a Psychohistory*, London: Free Association Books.

Lal, B.B. (1986) 'The "Chicago School" of American sociology, symbolic interactionism, and race relations theory', in J. Rex and D. Mason (eds) *Theories of Race and Ethnic Relations*, Cambridge, Cambridge University Press.

Lewontin, R.C. (1993) *The Doctrine of DNA – Biology as Ideology*, London: Penguin.

Littlewood, R. and Lipsedge, M. (1989) *Aliens and Alienists – Ethnic Minorities and Psychiatry*, London: Unwin Hyman.

Mannoni, O. (1964) *Prospero and Caliban: The Psychology of Colonization*, New York: Praeger.

Matte-Blanco, I. (1988) *Thinking, Feeling, and Being*, Routledge: London.

McDonald, M. (1974) 'Little Black Sambo', *The Psychoanalytic Study of the Child* 29: 511–528.

McGoldrick, M., Pearce, J.K. and Giardano, J. (eds) (1982) *Ethnicity and Family Therapy*, New York: Guilford Press.

Mead, G.H. (1913) 'The social self' in A.J. Reck (ed.) *Selected Writings: George Herbert Mead*, Chicago: Chicago University Press.

Meers, D.R. (1970) 'Contributions of a ghetto culture to symptom formation – psychoanalytic studies of ego anomalies in childhood', *The Psychoanalytic Study of the Child* 25: 209–229.

Meers, D.R. (1973) 'Psychoanalytic research and intellectual functioning of ghetto-reared black children', *The Psychoanalytic Study of the Child* 28: 395–417.

Mehra, H. (1996) 'Residential care for ethnic minority children', in K.N. Dwivedi and V.P. Varma (eds) *Meeting the Needs of Ethnic Minority Children*, London: Jessica Kingsley.

Miles, R. (1993) *Racism after Race Relations*, London and New York: Routledge.

Myers, W.A. (1977) 'The significance of the colors black and white in the dreams of black and white patients', *Journal of the American Psychoanalytic Association* 25: 163–181.

Nicholson, B. and Hare, T. (1986) 'The management of urban woodland', *ECOS* 7(1): 38–43.

Nitsun, M. (1996) *The Anti-Group*, London and New York: Routledge.

Nott, J.C. and Gliddon, G.R. (1857) *Indigenous Races, or New Chapters of Ethnological Enquiry*, London: Trubner.

Oxford English Dictionary (2nd edn) (1989) Oxford: Oxford University Press.

Pettigrew, T.F. (1979) 'The ultimate attribution error: extending Allport's cognitive analysis of prejudice', *Personality and Social Psychology Bulletin* 5: 461–476.

Phoenix, A. (1995) 'Young people: nationalism, racism and gender', in H. Lutz and A. Phoenix (eds) *Crossfires*, London: Pluto Press.

Plotkin, H. (1997) *Evolution in Mind*, London: Allen Lane, Penguin Press.

Polzer, A. (1991) 'Georg Groddeck's racism – a dismal discovery', *Journal of the American Psychoanalytic Association*, 39: 575–577.

Racker, H. (1985) *Transference and Countertransference*, London: Maresfield.

Rattansi, A. (1992) 'Changing the subject? – Racism, culture and education', in J. Donald and A. Rattansi *'Race, Culture and Difference'*, London: Sage, Open University Press.

Reich, W. (1970) *The Mass Psychology of Fascism*, London: Souvenir Press & Academic Ltd.

Robinson, C. J. (1983) *Black Marxism*, London: Zed Books.

Ross, L.D. (1977) 'The intuitive psychologist and his shortcomings: distortions in the attribution process', in L. Berkowitz (ed.) *Advances in Experimental Social Psychology* vol. 10, New York: Academic Press.

Rustin, M. (1991) *The Good Society and the Inner World*, London: Verso.

Schachter, J.S. and Butts H.F. (1994) 'Transference and countertransference in interracial analyses', *Journal of the American Psychoanalytic Association* 16: 792–808.

Sheperdson, C. (1998) 'Human diversity and the sexual relation' in C. Lane (ed.) *The Psychoanalysis of Race*, New York: Columbia University Press.

Sivanandan, A. (1983) *A Different Hunger: Writings on Black Resistance*, London: Pluto Press.

Smith, M.G. (1988) 'Pluralism, race and ethnicity in selected African countries', in J. Rex and D. Mason. (eds) *Theories of Race and Ethnic Relations*, Cambridge, Cambridge University Press.

Stein, H.F. (1984) 'The psychoanalysis of culture', *Psychoanalytic Quarterly* 53: 100–106.

Tajfel, H. (1981) 'Social stereotypes and social groups', in J.C. Turner and H. Giles (eds) *Intergroup Behaviour*, Oxford: Blackwell.

Tajfel, H., Flament, C., Billig, M.G. and Bundy, R.P. (1971) 'Social categorization and intergroup behaviour', *European Journal of Social Psychology* 1: 149–78.

Tan, R. (1993) 'Racism and similarity: paranoid-schizoid structures', *British Journal of Psychotherapy* 10(1): 33–43.

Taylor, C. (1991) *The Ethics of Authencity*, London: Harvard University Press.

Taylor, D.M. and Jaggi, V. (1974) 'Ethnocentricism and causal attribution in a South Indian context', *Journal of Cross-Cultural Psychology* 5: 162–171.

Thomas, M.D. and Sillen, S. (1979) *Racism and Psychiatry*, Secaucus, NJ: Citadel Press.

Timmi, S. (1996) 'Race and colour in internal and external reality', *British Journal of Psychotherapy* 13(2): 183–192.

Traub-Werner, D. (1984) 'Towards a theory of prejudice', *International Review of Psychoanalysis* 11: 407–412.

Van den Berghe, P.L. (1988) 'Ethnicity and the socio-biology debate in relations', in J. Rex, and D. Mason (eds) *Theories of Race and Ethnic Relations*, Cambridge, Cambridge University Press.

Volkan, V. (1997) *Blood Lines – From Ethnic Pride to Ethnic Terrorism*, New York: Farrar, Straus & Giroux.

Wallman, S. (1979) 'Introduction: the scope for ethnicity', in S. Wallman *Ethnicity at Work*, London: Macmillan.

Wallman, S. (1988) 'Ethnicity and the boundary process in context', in J. Rex, and D. Mason (eds) *Theories of Race and Ethnic Relations*, Cambridge: Cambridge University Press.

White, K.P. (1991) 'A home in the mind', *Contemporary Psychoanalysis* 27: 311–323.

Winnicott, D.W. (1950–1955) 'Aggression in relation to emotional development', in D.W. Winnicott (1987) *Through Paediatrics to Psychoanalysis*, London: Hogarth Press.

Winnicott, D.W. (1951) 'Transitional objects and transitional phenomena', in D.W. Winnicott (1987) *Through Paediatrics to Psychoanalysis*, London: Hogarth Press.

Winnicott, D.W. (1958) 'The sense of guilt', in D.W. Winnicott (1982) *The Maturational Process and the Facilitating Environment*, London: Hogarth Press.

Winnicott, D.W. (1963) 'Morals and education', in D.W. Winnicott (1982) *The Maturational Process and the Facilitating Environment*, London: Hogarth Press.

Winnicott, D.W. (1965) *The Family and Individual Development*, London: Tavistock Publications.

Winnicott, D.W. (1980) *Playing and Reality*, London: Penguin.

Winnicott, D.W. (1988) *Human Nature*, London: Free Association Press.

Wolfenstein, E.V. (1981) *The Victims of Democracy – Malcom X and the Black Revolution*, Berkeley, CA: University of California Press.

Wolfenstein, E.V. (1993) *Psychoanalytic Marxism – Groundwork*, London: Free Association Press.

Yinger, J.M. (1988) 'Intersecting strands in the theorisation of race and ethnic relations', in J. Rex, and D. Mason (eds) *Theories of Race and Ethnic Relations*, Cambridge: Cambridge University Press.

Zaphiropoulos, M.L. (1987) 'Ethnocentricity in psychoanalysis – blind spots and blind alleys', *Contemporary Psychoanalysis* 23: 446–462.

Ziegler, P. (1969) *The Black Death*, Collins: London.

Zilboorg, G. (1947) 'Psychopathology of social prejudice', *Psychoanalytic Quarterly* 16: 303–324.

Note

1 All Freud citations are from the Standard Edition of the Complete Psychological Works of Sigmund Freud (SE).

Index

Note: page numbers in *italics* refer to diagrams